WORLD WAR I
AN ILLUSTRATED HISTORY

WORLD WAR I
AN ILLUSTRATED HISTORY

AN AUTHORITATIVE ACCOUNT OF THE COURSE OF THE GREAT WAR, WITH ANALYSIS OF DECISIVE ENCOUNTERS AND 500 PHOTOGRAPHS

IAN WESTWELL

HH

Contents

Introduction

World War I was the first truly total global conflict, a titanic struggle between the then leading world powers for not only the domination of Europe but also the large areas of the entire planet that they had colonized in the 19th century. Even with such high stakes, the outbreak of the conflict was greeted with considerable popular enthusiasm in many – if not all – quarters. After years of sabre-rattling and accelerating arms races as well as intensifying economic and geopolitical rivalries, it was thought, not just by militarists, that a short, sharp war would bring a new stability to world affairs.

Like most wars, World War I turned out in ways that the participants did not anticipate at the outset. Almost everyone thought that the war would be short, a matter of months at the most. Economic and industrial developments were believed to have made it impossible for fighting to continue for long. In fact the reverse was true. Industrialization and mass production meant that armies of previously unequalled size could be supplied and kept fighting – leading to a casualty toll never before seen.

Military leaders struggled to cope with the consequences of the scale of the fighting and the new technologies involved – it was the first major war of aircraft, tanks, submarines, quick-firing artillery, poison gas and much more. It is hardly surprising that generals sometimes failed to make best use of these novel resources, but few were the stupid and unfeeling blunderers of popular belief.

When the Great War ended after more than four years of bitter combat in which the outcome was in doubt until the final stages of campaigning, few were really able

Below: People everywhere welcomed the outbreak of the war. These young Berliners have been called up to serve in the German Army, 1 August 1914.

Right: Belgian infantry manning trenches near Uskub (now usually called Skopje) in 1915. Britain, France and other Allies deployed large forces to the Balkan Front around Salonika from 1915 but they achieved little until the final months of the war.

to comprehend the sheer scale of the destructive events they had witnessed. Empires had toppled, new countries had emerged and the United States had been transformed into an international colossus. Despite the heavy loss of life, the victors could at least console themselves with the thought that they had won "the war to end all wars" – the popular rendering of the title of H. G. Wells's overly optimistic 1914 book entitled *The War That Will End War*. Yet the peace they had secured at such immense cost was transitory and was destined to last just two decades.

How This Book is Organized

This work has five main chapters, one on each of the five war years, plus an introductory chapter on the causes of the war and a concluding chapter on its aftermath and long-term legacy. Each chapter is split into separate two-page sections that cover the war's battles and campaigns or the weapons that were used. In addition there are feature boxes on a variety of subjects including key personalities and points of special interest. Together, all these elements provide a detailed, highly illustrated history of World War I that not only explains what happened but also how the war was fought.

Below: British troops blinded by poison gas wait for medical attention. Every major army was using gas by 1918, though this form of warfare would have been considered barbarous only a few years before.

Timeline

Although many accounts of World War I are centred on the war's principal theatre, the Western Front, the actual chronology of events makes it abundantly clear how closely related the developments there were to victories and defeats elsewhere around the world.

1914

INTERNATIONAL EVENTS
Assassination at Sarajevo (28 June); Austria-Hungary declares war on Serbia (28 July); Germany declares war on Russia (1 Aug); Germany declares war on France (3 Aug); Britain declares war on Germany (4 Aug); Austria-Hungary declares war on Russia (5 Aug); Serbia declares war on Germany (6 Aug); France declares war on Austria-Hungary (10 Aug); Britain declares war on Austria-Hungary (12 Aug); Turkey declares war on Allies (1 Nov); Russia and Serbia declare war on Turkey (2 Nov); Britain and France declare war on Turkey (5 Nov)

WESTERN FRONT
Main German invasion of Belgium begins (4 Aug); Battles of the Frontiers (14–25 Aug); Battle of the Marne (5–10 Sept); Race to the Sea (15 Sept–24 Nov); First Battle of Ypres (19 Oct–22 Nov); Battles of Flanders (11 Oct–30 Nov); First Battle of Champagne (20 Dec–30 Mar 1915)

EASTERN FRONT
Russian invasion of East Prussia (15–23 Aug); Battle of Tannenburg (26–30 Aug); First Battle of the Masurian Lakes (7–14 Sept)

BALKAN FRONT First Austro-Hungarian Invasion of Serbia (14–21 Aug); Second invasion of Serbia (6–17 Sept); Third invasion of Serbia (5 Nov–15 Dec)

MESOPOTAMIAN FRONT
British land in Mesopotamia (7 Nov)

WAR AT SEA Battle of Heligoland Bight (28 Aug); Battle of the Falklands (8 Dec)

1915

INTERNATIONAL EVENTS
Italy declares war on Austria-Hungary (23 May); Bulgaria and Serbia declare war on each other (14 Oct)

WESTERN FRONT Second Battle of Ypres (22 April–25 May); Second Battle of Artois (9 May–18 June); Second Battle of Champagne (25 Sept–6 Nov); Battle of Loos (25 Sept–16 Oct)

EASTERN FRONT
Gorlice–Tarnów Offensive (2 May–27 June); Capture of Warsaw (5 Aug)

BALKAN FRONT Austro-German invasion of Serbia (6 Oct)

ITALIAN FRONT First four Battles of the Isonzo (23 June–7 July)

MESOPOTAMIAN FRONT Battle of Nasiriya (24 July); Battle of Ctesiphon (22–26 Nov)

GALLIPOLI CAMPAIGN Allied naval attack on Dardanelles (18 Mar); First Allied landings at Gallipoli (25 April); British evacuate Gallipoli (10 Dec–9 Jan 1916)

1916

INTERNATIONAL EVENTS
Germany declares war on Romania (28 Aug); Italy declares war on Germany (28 Aug)

WESTERN FRONT Battle of Verdun (21 Feb–18 Dec); Battle of the Somme (1 July–18 Nov)

EASTERN FRONT Brusilov Offensive (4 June–20 Sept);

CAUCASUS FRONT Battle of Koprukoy (18 Jan); Battle of Erzerum (13–16 Feb)

ITALIAN FRONT Trentino Offensive (15 May–17 June); Battles of the Isonzo (Fifth 11–29 Mar; Sixth 6–28 Aug; Seventh 14–26 Sept; Eighth 10–12 Oct; Ninth 1–14 Nov)

MESOPOTAMIAN FRONT
Fall of Kut (29 April)

WAR AT SEA Battle of Jutland (31 May–1 June)

1917

INTERNATIONAL EVENTS United States declares war on Germany (6 April); Greece declares war on Central Powers (2 July); China declares war on Austria-Hungary and Germany (14 Aug); Brazil declares war on Germany (26 Oct); United States declares war on Austria-Hungary (7 Dec); Russia agrees to an armistice (15 Dec)
WESTERN FRONT Battle of Arras (9 April–15 May); Nivelle Offensive (16 April–9 May); Battle of Messines (7–14 June); Passchendaele/Third Battle of Ypres (31 July–10 Nov); Battle of Cambrai (20 Nov–7 Dec)
EASTERN FRONT Russian Revolution begins (11 Mar); Russian Kerensky Offensive (1–19 July); German Riga Offensive begins (1 Sept); Bolshevik Revolution begins (7 Nov)
BALKAN FRONT Battle of Lake Prespa/Doiran (11–17 Mar); Battle of the Vardar (5–19 May)
ITALIAN FRONT Tenth Battle of the Isonzo (12 May–8 June); Eleventh Battle of the Isonzo (18 Aug–15 Sept); Battle of Caporetto (24 Oct–12 Nov)
PALESTINE FRONT Battle of Magruntein (8 Jan); First Battle of Gaza (26 Mar); Second Battle of Gaza (17–19 April); Battle of Beersheba (31 Oct); Battle of Junction Station (13–14 Nov); Capture of Jerusalem (9 Dec)
MESOPOTAMIAN FRONT Second Battle of Kut (22–23 Feb); Fall of Baghdad (11 Mar); Battle of Ramadi (27–28 Sept)
CAMPAIGNS IN AFRICA German forces leave German East Africa (25 Nov)
WAR AT SEA Germany announces reintroduction of unrestricted submarine warfare (31 Jan)

1918

INTERNATIONAL EVENTS Russia signs Treaty of Brest-Litovsk (3 Mar); Romania and Central Powers agree peace (8 May); Armistice with Bulgaria (30 Sept); Armistice with Turkey (30 Oct); Armistice with Austria-Hungary (4 Nov); Romania declares war for the second time (10 Nov); Armistice with Germany (11 Nov)
WESTERN FRONT Operation Michael (21 Mar–5 April); Lys Offensive (9–29 April); Aisne Offensive (27 May–17 June); Second Battle of the Marne (15 July–4 Aug); Amiens Offensive (8 Aug–4 Sept); Assault on the Hindenburg Line (26 Aug–12 Oct); Battle of St. Mihiel (12–16 Sept); Meuse–Argonne Offensive (26 Sept–11 Nov); Flanders Offensive (28 Sept–11 Nov); Picardy Offensive (17 Oct–11 Nov)
EASTERN FRONT Germany launches Operation Faustschlag (17 Feb)
BALKAN FRONT Battle of the Vardar (15–25 Sept); Recapture of Belgrade (1 Nov)
CAUCASUS FRONT British enter Baku (24 Aug); Turks recapture Baku (26 Aug–14 Sept)
ITALIAN FRONT Battle of the Piave (15–23 June); Battle of Vittorio Veneto (24 Oct–4 Nov)
PALESTINE FRONT Battle of Megiddo (19–21 Sept); Anglo-Arab capture of Damascus (30 Sept–1 Oct)
MESOPOTAMIAN FRONT Tigris Offensive begins (23 Oct); British enter Mosul (14 Nov)
CAMPAIGNS IN AFRICA German forces from East Africa surrender in Rhodesia (25 Nov)
WAR AT SEA Austro-Hungarian naval mutiny at Cattaro (1 Feb); British raid on Zeebrugge and Ostend (22–23 April); Ostend raid (10 May); German naval mutiny begins (3 Nov); German Navy is interned (21 Nov)

Allied War Plans Volunteers for Britain's "New Army" begin their military drill without uniforms.

July 1914 – The Road to War German troops on the way to take part in the attack on France.

Assassination at Sarajevo Gavrilo Princip is arrested shortly after making his attack.

ORIGINS OF THE WAR

The assassination of Archduke Franz Ferdinand, heir to the Austro-Hungarian throne, by a Bosnian Serb nationalist on 28 June 1914, caused barely a ripple of public interest across most of Europe when it was first reported. Yet what at first appeared to be no more than the most recent incident in a long-standing but localized squabble over power and influence within the Balkans had much wider repercussions. The assassination on that summer Sunday was not the cause of World War I but it was the catalyst that dragged all of Europe's great powers into a conflict of global proportions in not much more than one month.

World War I was the product of many deep-seated issues dividing the various great European powers – economic, political and territorial, for example – that were exacerbated by the fact that those involved were bound together by secret treaties which placed them in mutually antagonistic camps, commonly referred to as the Central Powers and the Triple Entente. Some key figures also failed, deliberately or otherwise, to do very much to halt the slide to hostilities in July 1914. They were psychologically prepared to go to war to put right their grievances, and it was their sense of the inevitability of war as much as any other factor that made it more than likely that armed conflict would break out sooner or later. Few, however, appreciated that the war would be prolonged, worldwide and destructive on a hitherto unseen scale.

July 1914 – The Road to War Rejoicing crowds in Berlin greet the outbreak of war.

Allied War Plans Men of the 11th Hussars, among the first British troops to fight, crossing to France.

Austro-Hungarian and German War Plans A band plays for soldiers leaving for the war.

Assassination at Sarajevo

The Balkans had been torn apart by international rivalries and local wars before World War I but the assassination of the little-known heir to the throne of the Austro-Hungarian Empire in June 1914 sparked a conflict on a truly global scale.

In the years before the outbreak of World War I, Europe's great powers had divided into two mutually antagonistic political blocs, largely because each country had reason to believe it might be threatened by a neighbour. Austria-Hungary and Russia feared that they might clash over their ongoing rivalries in the Balkans, where Serbia, which had close ties with Russia, was seen as a danger to Austria-Hungary. Germany feared that France would at some stage try to regain the provinces of Alsace and Lorraine that it had been forced to cede to Germany after the Franco-Prussian War (1870–71). Germany tried to maintain good relations with Britain but matters began souring when Kaiser (Emperor) Wilhelm II came to the throne in 1888 and embarked on a vast warship-building programme to challenge Britain's traditional naval supremacy. Britain also grew alarmed at Germany's rapid industrialization and its search for overseas colonies.

KEY FACTS

Date: 28 June 1914

Place: Sarajevo, in the Austro-Hungarian province of Bosnia

Outcome: The assassination of Austria-Hungary's Archduke Franz Ferdinand and his wife sparked a Europe-wide crisis.

Above: This satirical map indicates how Germany saw itself surrounded by enemies before World War I.

Competing Alliances

Germany had joined with the Austro-Hungarian Empire to form the Dual Alliance in 1879 and then the Triple Alliance emerged when Italy joined the original pair three years later. Germany and Austria-Hungary agreed to aid Italy if the latter were attacked by France, while Italy agreed to stay neutral if Russia attacked Austria-Hungary. France and Russia entered into an alliance in 1894 and the Anglo-French *Entente Cordiale* was formed in 1904. Kaiser Wilhelm's support for Austria-Hungary in the Balkans angered Russia and this led to an Anglo-Russian alliance, ending long-standing disputes in Central Asia. Britain, France and Russia formed the Triple Entente in 1907.

With such a degree of mutual suspicion in Europe, in an age of rampant nationalism, it was perhaps hardly surprising that militarism took hold, especially in Germany, and that most of the rival nations began to plan for war on the basis that it was better to mobilize first in the

Left: Franz Ferdinand and his wife Sophie are greeted on their arrival at Sarajevo on 28 June 1914.

Above: A photograph purportedly showing the arrest of Gavrilo Princip moments after the assassination.

event of a crisis and strike against an enemy before he could take the initiative. Germany faced a potential war on two fronts and perceived a need to attack before France and Russia could bring their numerically superior armies into the field. In the years immediately before World War I, there was even a feeling among generals, and indeed large numbers of ordinary people, that war was probably inevitable, but none expected it to be sparked by the death of a seemingly obscure Austro-Hungarian archduke, Franz Ferdinand, and his wife in the Balkans on 28 June 1914.

Serbia and Bosnia

Ferdinand was heir to the Austro-Hungarian crown and was paying an official visit to Sarajevo, the capital of Bosnia. The former Turkish-controlled province had been incorporated into the Austro-Hungarian Empire in 1906 but the annexation was unpopular both with the Serbian majority living in Bosnia and within neighbouring Serbia itself. A small group of ardent Serbian nationalists led by Gavrilo Princip carried out the assassination and, if the gang had been acting alone, then the matter might have ended with their swift capture. However, it soon emerged that they had planned their mission in Serbia and that certain elements within the Serbian secret service had helped them. Austria-Hungary saw Serbia's complicity in Ferdinand's death as clear evidence of the latter's hostility and as part of its plan to incorporate Bosnia into a greater Serbia. This enlarged and more powerful state would challenge the weakening empire's own position in the Balkans and Serbia was likely to sponsor further unrest among Austria-Hungary's Slavic minority for its own geopolitical ends.

THE BLACK HAND

A Serbian secret society formed in 1911, the Black Hand was officially known as "Unity or Death". Its mission was nothing less than the political integration into Serbia of various Slav minorities in both Austria-Hungary and Turkey. Many of its members were serving Serbian officers, including a colonel by the name of Dragutin Dimitrievic, who helped the assassins involved in the death of Archduke Franz Ferdinand in June 1914. The Black Hand organization was quashed by the exiled Serbian government during 1915–16 and Dimitrievic was executed.

Left: The trial of the Sarajevo assassins. All were found guilty and those of age were sentenced to death. Younger conspirators, including Princip, were imprisoned.

July 1914 – The Road to War

The assassination at Sarajevo initially looked like a localized squabble between Austria-Hungary and Serbia but the crisis soon spread, dragging in all of Europe's great powers in just four weeks.

News of the assassination of Austria-Hungary's Archduke Franz Ferdinand in late June 1914 did not arouse much interest in most of the European press but it did spark a stark diplomatic response from his country's government. Some senior figures, notably the Foreign Minister, Leopold von Berchtold, and the Army's Chief of Staff, Field Marshal Franz Conrad von Hötzendorf, saw the assassination in Sarajevo as a golden opportunity to teach Serbia a lesson, but only if Germany would guarantee to support their actions by preventing Russia from coming to Serbia's aid. Emperor Wilhelm II gave Germany's backing to the Austro-Hungarian ambassador on 5 July, told his ministers of his decision and then left for a cruise.

Above: Theobald von Bethmann-Hollweg, German Chancellor 1909–17, believed that a short, successful war would heal his country's deep political divisions.

Austria Fights Serbia

An ultimatum stating the reparations required because of the assassination was presented to the Serbian government on the evening of the 23rd but the terms were so humiliating that Austria-Hungary did not expect that Serbia would agree to them. Russia now intervened, telling the Serbs to accept the greater part of the ultimatum, but the Russian government also warned Austria-Hungary that it would not allow further action against Serbia. However, Berchtold and Conrad had no intention of accepting Serbia's largely conciliatory reply when it arrived on the 25th – the army had already begun mobilizing the same day – and Berchtold convinced Emperor Franz Joseph to sign a war declaration on the 26th.

Below: German troops expected a quick victory and the graffiti show that Paris was their objective.

Wilhelm II returned from his holiday the same day but was not told of Austria-Hungary's ultimatum until the morning of the 28th, the same time that Berchtold was informing the Serbian ambassador to Vienna that a state of war existed between their two countries. Russia began a partial mobilization of its forces two days later and Wilhelm and his confidants saw the emerging crisis as an opportunity to extend their own country's power and influence. Germany began a general mobilization and on the 31st sent a message to the Russians stating they must cease their now-general mobilization. The Russians refused and Germany declared war that afternoon.

EMPEROR WILHELM II

Wilhelm II (1859–1941) came to the German throne in 1888 as a firm believer in autocracy. He wished to make his realm stronger both economically and militarily and make it a colonial power. He was largely successful in the first two aims but Germany was never more than a second-rate colonizer. Wilhelm, however, was no diplomat and was increasingly seen as an overbearing militarist, one who saw war as a means of uniting his politically polarized country. His character flaws are regarded as being a major factor in bringing about the outbreak of the war.

Above: Emperor Wilhelm II was invariably seen dressed in military costume and was especially fond of his various awards and medals.

DECLARATIONS OF WAR

Now the various alliances came into play. France's Prime Minister stated that his country "would act according to its interests", a form of diplomatic speak that Germany took to mean that France would honour its alliance with Russia. Germany declared war against France on 3 August and its troops immediately invaded Belgium and Luxembourg in accordance with a long-standing war plan. Britain was a guarantor of Belgian neutrality and issued a stern warning to Germany on the morning of the 4th. The German Chancellor, Theobald von Bethmann-Hollweg, failed to persuade the British Foreign Secretary, Edward Grey, to renege on his country's treaty obligations and Britain declared war on Germany at midnight. Only Italy stood back from the brink. Its government argued that Austria-Hungary's mobilization against Serbia was outside the defensive provisions of the Triple Alliance accords.

Large crowds appeared in the streets of the combatant nations' capitals in those early days of August. Most were gripped by patriotic war fever and the outbreak of hostilities was greeted with something approaching wild enthusiasm. Most of the people, like the generals and politicians, expected a campaign that would end with the victorious troops being home by Christmas.

Right: Huge crowds gather in the centre of Berlin to celebrate the outbreak of the war in August 1914.

Allied War Plans

The large armies of France and Russia went to war with the intention of attacking their most powerful opponent, Germany, simultaneously from both east and west, while Britain's powerful navy was poised to impose an economic blockade.

France's war-fighting strategy arose out of the loss of the provinces of Alsace and Lorraine in the aftermath of its humiliating defeat during the Franco-Prussian War. Plan XVII was devised by the French Commander-in-Chief, Marshal Joseph Joffre, during 1911–14 and called for the various French armies to muster along a line adjacent to the two provinces, between the Belgian and the Swiss borders, once mobilization had been ordered. They would then drive forward with the utmost aggression into both Alsace and Lorraine. Joffre did realize that his plan left the Franco-Belgian border undefended but he was of the opinion that the Germans would not be able to advance west of the River Meuse without leaving themselves dangerously over-extended.

Above: Russia's Tsar Nicholas II inspects his troops as they prepare to go to war, August 1914.

Below: Britain was gripped by war fever in late summer 1914 and volunteers like these "New Army" recruits flocked to the colours.

Russian Plans

Russia actually had two war plans depending on whether Germany advanced into Russia or France first. In the former case the Russian Army would fight a defensive war, while the French pushed into Alsace and Lorraine. However, it was generally thought that Germany would attack France first and in that case Russia would follow Plan 19. This was originally conceived in 1910 by General Yuri Danilov with the backing of the then Minister for War, General Vladimir Sukhomlinov, and it called for an immediate invasion of the neighbouring German province of East Prussia. Danilov ignored those who thought Austria-Hungary was an equal if not greater threat, those who proposed an advance into central Germany through Silesia, and those who objected to his plan to do away with Russia's frontier fortresses and use their guns elsewhere.

Danilov and Sukhomlinov had powerful rivals, not least the head of the Army, Grand Duke Nicholas, and these gained strength in the years before the war. The idea of making an attack into the Austro-Hungarian province of Galicia became more credible and Plan 19 was modified in May 1912. The attack into East Prussia was kept, although the number of armies earmarked for the operation was reduced from four to two, the frontier fortresses were not downgraded, and three armies were mustered along the border with Austria-Hungary. Another was in reserve to be sent to either East Prussia or Galicia as required.

Above: Mobilization begins in the Russian capital, St Petersburg, as reservists head for their depots.

BELGIUM AND SERBIA

Both Belgium's and Serbia's war plans were dictated by geography and the relatively small size of their armed forces. Both intended to defend their frontiers for as long as possible and then fall back into fortified cities, in Belgium's case, or the rugged interior, in Serbia's case. They both hoped that either events elsewhere would see their more powerful opponents divert forces away from them or that their allies, principally France and Russia, would come to their aid.

BRITISH INTENTIONS

Britain's war plan was largely dictated by the small size of its army compared with those on the continent and the larger size of its navy in comparison to that of Germany. The small British Expeditionary Force (BEF) was to be transported to France as quickly as possible and fall in on the left flank of the French forces in the north, largely to protect the key Channel ports where the BEF disembarked. The Royal Navy, Britain's greatest military asset, was to blockade Germany. It was to Britain's good fortune that the greater part of its fleet was in home waters for a review during 18–20 July, so that the order for it to disperse was rescinded and its warships were sent to their war stations on the 28th.

Right: Elements of the small British Expeditionary Force sail for France in the first weeks of the war.

Austro-Hungarian and German War Plans

Both Germany and Austria-Hungary had developed intricate war plans before 1914 and these relied on rapid mobilization, using their railway systems, so that they would avoid having to fight on two fronts at the same time.

France and Russia signed what was effectively an anti-German alliance in 1894 and the German Army Chief of Staff, Count Alfred von Schlieffen, recognized that Germany might face an unwinnable war on two fronts at some date in the future. He therefore devised a war-fighting strategy, the Schlieffen Plan, to prevent such an outcome. His aim was to defeat France quickly before Russia could mobilize its huge reserves of manpower.

Above: Count Alfred von Schlieffen was the architect of his country's bold war strategy.

The Schlieffen Plan

Schlieffen realized that any advance from Alsace and Lorraine into eastern France would be slow and costly. This was largely because of the various fortress complexes that the French had built along their mutual frontier since their defeat and the loss of the two provinces in the Franco-Prussian War. A push through the Swiss Alps would also be too ponderous because of the mountainous terrain. Schlieffen therefore decided to send a huge enveloping force through the southern Netherlands and Belgium because their borders were less well defended and the French would be unprepared for such a move.

A holding force would be positioned in Alsace and Lorraine between Metz and the Swiss border and Schlieffen expected that a combination of these troops, the difficult local terrain and Germany's own frontier fortresses would delay the expected French attack there. Schlieffen positioned his main strike force to the north of Metz so that it would swing west and then south to trap the French pushing into Alsace and Lorraine. Once France had been defeated, the bulk of the German Army was to be rapidly transferred east by rail to link up with a small force that had been left to guard East Prussia and then crush Russia with Germany's full strength.

THE SCHLIEFFEN PLAN
The ambitious scope of the original version of the plan.

Above: Germany's efficient rail system was the cornerstone of its plan to defeat France and then turn on Russia. Here, a military brass band serenades the departure of a troop train as loved ones make their goodbyes.

Schlieffen retired in 1906 and was replaced by General Helmuth von Moltke. Moltke felt it necessary to modify the original scheme because Russia was now expected to mobilize faster than his predecessor had envisaged. Nor was he willing to give up any German territory. Thus he strengthened the forces lying between Metz and the Swiss border and those in East Prussia. The former rose from 5 per cent of total mobilized strength to 25 per cent and the latter from 10 to 15 per cent. Thus only 60 rather than 90 per cent of the Germany Army would be committed north of Metz. Moltke also dropped the idea of attacking through the Netherlands in the mistaken belief that Britain might not go to war if only Belgium's neutrality was violated. This modification meant that his forces would have to advance on a narrow front and would face the fortress complex of Liège.

War by Timetable

The Schlieffen Plan relied on timing above all else. No one doubted that Germany's efficient rail system and mobilization programme would be up to the job of getting the troops to the border, but it was an enormous gamble to believe that troops, some marching many miles a day as they moved into enemy territory, would keep to the strict timetable devised by the German General Staff. The plan also made enormous assumptions about how the French and Russians would react once war had broken out.

Austria-Hungary

The Austro-Hungarians had two war plans. One was based on a localized war in the Balkans against Serbia, while the other, more likely, scenario was a war on two fronts against Serbia and its great ally, Russia. In the latter case Austro-Hungarian units would fight alongside German troops and it had been agreed that they would advance into Russian Poland to take the pressure off the German troops in East Prussia.

Above: Field Marshal Helmuth von Moltke was Schlieffen's successor and watered down his war strategy with disastrous consequences.

Field Artillery Russian artillery in action at the start of the war on the Eastern Front.

Frontier Fortresses Storeroom inside Verdun's Fort Douaumont during the great battle in 1916.

Germany's West African Colonies British West African troops training in marksmanship.

1914 – EUROPE GOES TO WAR

Even as war was being declared, the clauses in the secret treaties, which bound the Central Powers and Triple Entente together and guaranteed that the various signatories would offer each other military support, came into effect. The mobilization of each country's armed forces mostly went smoothly, largely due to years of planning down to the tiniest detail. Germany and Austria-Hungary mobilized around 6.5 million men in a few days in late July and early August 1914, while the various Allies put about 9 million men into the field. Yet neither side was able to deliver the knock-out blow that the generals and their political masters – and the various general publics – expected.

The fighting in 1914 was concentrated on the Western Front. There were only two major battles in the east and campaigns elsewhere were small. The fighting began with a series of sweeping movements across Belgium and north-east France. However, German plans for a swift victory were thwarted near Paris in early September and, over the next two months, the trench lines began to appear. Just five months of fighting in the west cost the Allies 1.2 million casualties and the Germans at least 680,000. Hopes of swift victory had been dashed but the enthusiasm for war remained largely undimmed.

The Invasions of Serbia 1914–15
Worn out Serbian troops during their retreat from their homeland in 1915.

Coronel and the Falklands
An outgunned British cruiser falls victim to German fire at Coronel.

Operations in Poland and Galicia
Russian besiegers around the Austrian fortress of Przemyśl.

The German Invasion of Belgium

The Schlieffen Plan called for four German armies, consisting of around 940,000 men and 2,900 artillery pieces, to march rapidly through Belgium, a small country defended by fewer than 120,000 troops and 320 guns.

By early August 1914 Germany had two armies positioned in Alsace and Lorraine along its border with France, two more facing Luxembourg and three close to the narrow border with Belgium. The latter five armies were the key components of the Schlieffen Plan and were set to launch a great arcing offensive that would first take them west through Belgium into north-eastern France where they would swing due south. The greatest effort would be made by the northernmost two armies – the First of General Alexander von Kluck and General Karl von Bülow's Second, around 580,000 men and 1,700 guns in all.

KEY FACTS

Date: 4 – 25 August 1914

Place: Belgium

Outcome: The advancing Germans pushed rapidly through the country while local and Anglo-French forces were forced to retreat.

Below: German mounted troops in the largely deserted streets of a Belgian city in the first weeks of war.

Fall of Liège

As speed was crucial to the success of the Schlieffen Plan, Belgium's frontier fortresses were to be neutralized as soon as possible, so on 3 August a specially trained 30,000-strong detachment from Bülow's command, under General Otto von Emmerich, crossed the frontier and made for the fortress city of Liège. Attacking under cover of darkness on the 5th/6th, Emmerich's troops tried to drive through the gaps between the city's outer ring of 12 steel-and-concrete forts but were mostly repulsed due to the determination of the commander of the Belgian 3rd Division, General Gerard Leman. German troops under General Erich Ludendorff actually broke into the city a few days later but the forts fought on. Bülow brought up his heavy siege artillery, including a handful of huge 30.5cm (12in) and 42cm (16.5in) howitzers. Despite Liège's supposed invulnerability, the big guns made short work of its forts between the 12th and 16th and the city surrendered.

Kluck's and Bülow's armies could now renew their advance through Belgium. Kluck's troops beat off a small Belgian counter-attack near Tirlemont on 18–19 August and occupied Brussels, the capital, the next day, while Bülow advanced along the east–west line of the rivers Meuse and Sambre. King Albert, the Belgian Commander-in-Chief, had by now wisely recognized that his army, which was outnumbered four-to-one and far from well-equipped, had

absolutely no means of halting the German steamroller. He therefore sent one of his divisions to garrison Namur, which stood in Bülow's path, while he and the remainder of his force occupied Antwerp. Both cities were protected by rings of fortresses. Kluck detached a corps to blockade Antwerp and prevent any Belgian sorties against his right flank but the bulk of his First Army and Bülow's Second Army still continued westward.

Above: General Alexander von Kluck (fifth from left), commander of the German First Army, poses for a photograph with his staff.

Belgium Conquered

Bülow crossed the Sambre on the 22nd. Namur, which was now behind his lines, had come under attack on the 20th and the siege proper began the next day. The fighting followed the same pattern as at Liège. Heavy howitzers destroyed the outer nine forts in quick succession and the city surrendered on the 25th, although much of the garrison escaped. By the end of the third week of August, virtually all of Belgium had been overrun and, thanks to the heavy howitzers, its fortresses had not unduly upset the Schlieffen Plan's exacting timetable. Nevertheless, both Kluck and Bülow still had a very long way to go to complete their orders and, thanks to a combination of frequent combat and long daily marches under an unusually warm late summer sun, their troops were becoming increasingly fatigued.

Below: Stunned Belgian civilians look on as German troops march through Brussels on 20 August.

THE GERMAN OCCUPATION OF BELGIUM

Virtually the whole of Belgium was occupied by the Germans from 1914 until late 1918 and its citizens suffered greatly. The people lived under strict martial law; any resistance was met by hostage-taking, imprisonment and executions. Some 20,000 Belgians were forcibly transported to Germany for war work in 1916 and 1917. Belgian industry was given over to war production for the Germans and they also stripped the country of rolling stock, food and raw materials.

Right: German troops guard Belgian civilians accused of resisting the occupation.

Frontier Fortresses

Several European countries built elaborate frontier fortresses along their vulnerable borders, supposedly to protect them from invasion, but they proved to be white elephants and many were utterly shattered by heavy artillery.

The idea of building fortresses at vulnerable points along a country's border with a potential enemy was nothing new, though there was something of a mania for constructing or renovating them in the latter part of the 19th century. Many European nations built frontier fortresses but the greatest concentration was to be found along the much-contested border between France and Germany.

Above: The heavily damaged interior of one of Namur's nine main forts gives a good indication as to why the city surrendered after a siege of less than a week (18–23 August 1914).

Below: The centre of the Belgian Fort de Loncin at Liège was smashed by a single German howitzer shell.

Fortress Designs

Although there was no set design for frontier fortresses, they did have several features in common. More often than not they were built around a strategically important town or city, often on a river, and the urban area was then ringed by a string of forts that were built roughly equidistant from each other and several miles from the centre. The space between them might be covered by smaller forts or the gap might be plugged by trench lines dug if war seemed likely. Generally, they had only small garrisons – approximately 1,000 men in a bigger fortress – but these could be rapidly reinforced from a central reserve.

One of the most important figures in fortress construction was Belgian Henri Brialmont, who was responsible for the most modern defences of Antwerp, Liège and Namur and whose radical ideas were taken up by other nations. His forts were either triangular or pentagonal in plan according to the terrain. They were based on an underground central section constructed from reinforced concrete, which was topped by armoured cupolas. The concrete was some 2.5m (8ft) thick and overlain with 3m (10ft) of earth. There was a parapet around the central section from where infantry could command the interior of the fort and could fire down on any attackers. The central section was further protected by a deep, wide dry ditch with sloping sides, and various other cupolas for artillery and machine-guns were positioned between the parapet and ditch. Barbed-wire entanglements filled the base of the ditch and an "unclimbable" iron fence ran around the outer edge of the fort.

In Brialmont's designs the only visible parts of the fortress were the upper surfaces of the central section and the individual gun cupolas. Some military commentators believed that the cupolas were very vulnerable to artillery fire and came up with designs that could be retracted when the gun was not in action or being reloaded. Two large engineering companies were especially involved in developing such retractable cupolas, France's Saint-Chamond and Germany's Gruson, and their designs were fitted to numerous fortresses across Europe. Among these were Verdun and Belfort in France and Brest-Litovsk in Russia.

Above: The Germans captured this munitions store in Fort Douaumont, Verdun, in February 1916. It was retaken by the French in October.

Fortresses in Action

The much-vaunted fortresses proved to be of considerably less value during World War I than their most vocal advocates believed. Some, like Liège and Namur, rapidly succumbed to bombardment from heavy artillery; others were simply bypassed and left to "wither on the vine" as the fighting rapidly moved elsewhere, while others were downgraded and had their artillery weapons removed and transferred to field operations. The only prolonged siege of note was that against much-invested Przemyśl, an Austro-Hungarian fortress in Galicia, and this only lasted so long largely because the Russians lacked heavy siege artillery. Even the 1916 Battle of Verdun, the war's longest engagement, was not primarily about capturing the town's various outlying fortresses but rather about the attrition of troops.

Right: France's Fort Vaux at Verdun was the scene of an epic five-day underground battle between its garrison and German troops in 1916. It finally fell to the latter on 7 June.

Heavy Artillery

Big guns were very much in short supply in every theatre during the first years of the war but they became the most important weapons in every country's arsenal once the fixed defences of trench warfare had developed.

The general lack of heavy artillery in 1914 partly reflected the recent experiences of the various warring nations. The French were still wedded to the idea of fast-moving warfare in the Napoleonic style of the early 19th century while the British had recently fought the elusive horse-mounted Boer commandos in the Second Anglo-Boer War (1899–1902). Neither saw the need for much more than highly mobile and rapidly deployed horse-drawn field artillery that could keep up with both infantry and cavalry.

Guns and Fortresses

The German and Austro-Hungarian planners had learned some lessons from the Russo-Japanese War (1904–5) in which the Japanese deployed heavy howitzers. Nevertheless, their armies marched to war in 1914 with a preponderance of field guns, though both of their general staffs expected to have to deal with enemy fortresses and knew they needed some heavy artillery. Prussian troops had been involved in sieges during the Franco-Prussian War and had found themselves short of the appropriate firepower. The response of the French to defeat in that war was to build or modernize a series of fortresses that might slow the fast movement of troops that Germany's Schlieffen Plan required. And Belgium, through which German troops would have to pass, had followed France's lead. Austria-Hungary had two potential major enemies – Russia and Italy – and war against either might involve fighting in the natural fortresses of the Carpathian Mountains and the Alps. In both cases shells with a plunging trajectory would be needed.

Below: A British (152mm) 6in gun position on the Western Front in 1917. This weapon fired a 45kg (100lb) shell to 12,500m (13,700yds).

60-POUNDER GUN

This British weapon was introduced in 1905 and was the standard "heavy" gun serving with British divisions at the start of the war. It remained in use throughout the conflict but by the later years had been reclassified as a medium weapon and supplemented by much heavier designs.

Calibre: 127mm (5in)
Gun weight: 4,470kg (4.3 tons)
Gun length: 4.29m (14.06ft)
Shell weight: 27.2kg (60lb)
Muzzle velocity: 634m/sec (2,080ft/sec)
Maximum range: 11,250m (12,300yds)

Above: An Austro-Hungarian Skoda-built 30.5cm (12in) "Schlanke Emma" howitzer in action.

Austria-Hungary led the way with Skoda's "Schlanke Emma" (Skinny Emma) a 30.5cm (12in) howitzer, while Germany's Krupp developed a 42cm (16.5in) weapon nicknamed "Dicke Bertha" (Big Bertha). Their combat debut was against Liège, supposedly the world's strongest fortress complex, on 12 August 1914. To the relief of the Germans and to the shock of their opponents, a dozen or so Emmas and Berthas reduced the city's supposedly impregnable concrete-and-steel fortresses to rubble in a mere four days.

As the trench lines were dug along the Western Front in late 1914, all of the combatants began fully to appreciate the need for heavy artillery to smash barbed wire, crumble trenches and bury deep dugouts in what was a new form of siege warfare, and they set about building such guns in large numbers or redeployed them from the now redundant fortresses. Little more than eight per cent of France's artillery was of the heavy types in 1914, for example, but the figure was close to 50 per cent only four years later.

Increasing Firepower

Vast numbers of different heavy artillery pieces were developed. Some were moved around on wheeled carriages but others were transported in sections and placed on reinforced beds for firing. Some types like the French Army's 220mm (8.7in) Schneider Model 1917 could fling a 90.7kg (200lb) shell out to 22,400m (24,500yds) but most of the heavy howitzer types had shorter ranges. There was a simple trade-off – the heavier the shell, the shorter the range. The overall trend was for heavier, more destructive shells. The shell of the standard German field howitzer in 1914 weighed just 6.8kg (15lb), while that of the 21cm (8.3in) Lange Mörser (Long Mortar) of 1916 was a hefty 113kg (249lb).

KRUPP 21cm MORTAR/HOWITZER

Commonly referred to as the Long 21cm Mortar, this heavy howitzer entered service in 1916. Early versions were fitted with a gun shield but these were dropped for the subsequent variants.

Calibre: 21cm (8.3in)
Weight: 6,680kg (6.57 tons)
Gun length: 2.3m (7.55ft)
Shell weight: 113kg (249lb)
Muzzle velocity: 393m/sec (1,290ft/sec)
Maximum range: 11,100m (12,150yds)

KRUPP 15cm FIELD HOWITZER

This gun made its service debut in 1913 but Krupp produced an updated model, the FH17, during World War I. It actually differed little from its predecessor, except that it was somewhat lighter due to shortages of certain raw materials. The gun remained in German service for training until World War II.

Calibre: 15cm (5.87in)
Weight: 2,200kg (2.17 tons)
Gun length: 2.1m (6.9ft)
Shell weight: 42kg (92.6lb)
Muzzle velocity: 365m/sec (1,197ft/sec)
Maximum range: 8,500m (9,300yds)

The Battles of the Frontiers

This title was the collective name given to a series of huge sprawling battles between Anglo-French and German armies that took place throughout August 1914 on or close to the French border with Germany.

France's war strategy, Plan XVII, provided that, in the event of conflict with Germany, six French armies were to concentrate along the French border from Belgium to Switzerland, roughly from Belfort to Sedan. The French also had an agreement that the British Expeditionary Force (BEF) would take up positions on the extreme left of their line. These plans brought about the Battles of the Frontiers.

Above: French medical orderlies line up with their various dogs, each of which carries vital equipment in pairs of pouches.

French Attacks

General Paul Pau's French Army of Alsace began moving towards Mülhausen (Mulhouse) in Alsace on 8 August. General Auguste Dubail's First Army and General Noël de Castelnau's Second Army pushed into Lorraine. As they advanced on the 14th, two opposing German armies, the Sixth under Crown Prince Rupprecht of Bavaria and General Josias von Heeringen's Seventh, deliberately gave ground. They turned on the 20th and launched a fierce counter-attack. A day later the French retreated – the First Army in good order but the right wing of the Second Army had been destroyed. The battle ended on the 22nd and Moltke allowed Rupprecht and von Heeringen to continue their attack, although the Schlieffen Plan called for no such action.

More French Defeats

Plan XVII also required three armies positioned north of Metz to advance eastward but the commander of the Fifth Army, General Charles Lanrezac, realized that the Germans were in Belgium in strength. He gained permission on 15 August to take

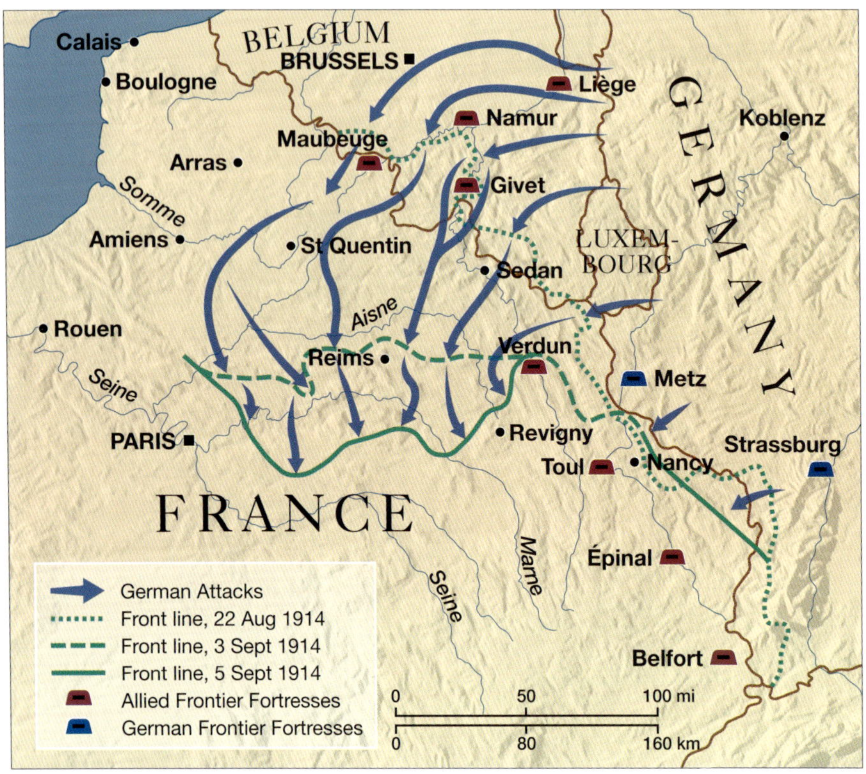

TOWARDS PARIS! Germany's advance through Belgium and into northern France.

Above: Rows of corpses await burial – a small part of the death toll in the Battles of the Frontiers.

his troops to the west of the River Meuse in southern Belgium and fall in alongside the BEF's right flank. The two remaining armies, General Ferdinand de Langle de Cary's Fourth and General Pierre Ruffey's Third, began moving on the 20th but towards the north-east and into the densely forested Ardennes.

These two French armies were hit by Duke Albrecht of Württemberg's Fourth Army and Crown Prince Wilhelm's Fifth Army on the 22nd. By the 25th the French had been forced into retreat. The Fourth fell back on Verdun while the Third crossed over the Meuse around Sedan and retreated south towards the River Marne. Meanwhile, Lanrezac had placed his Fifth Army between the Sambre and Meuse Rivers by the 20th but it was hit by two German armies, General von Bülow's Second and the Third, under General Max von Hausen, two days later. The Germans came close to enveloping Lanrezac's army during the 22nd, but he was able to withdraw the next day.

The Battles of the Frontiers were all but over and Plan XVII was in ruins. By the end of August France's armies stood on a line that ran east from Paris along the Marne to Verdun and from there south to the Swiss border. France had suffered over 210,000 casualties in four weeks, in part because its generals followed a strategy that claimed that all-out attack was always best. However, the fighting along the frontiers was not quite over as General von Kluck's 320,000-strong First Army crashed into the much smaller BEF on the 23rd.

FRANCE AND THE OFFENSIVE SPIRIT

The French Army went to war in August 1914 dressed in uniforms that would not have looked out of place on a Napoleonic battlefield and used tactics that were equally antiquated. Their troops and generals were wedded to the idea of the "offensive spirit" in which the soldiers' *élan* ("dash" or "bravery") and fixed bayonets would dominate the battlefield. Thus, in the first months of the war, particularly in the Battles of the Frontiers, the French relied on reckless offensive tactics and therefore suffered huge casualties.

Above: The army's brightly coloured uniforms were designed to foster the troops' spirit.

Reconnaissance Aircraft

Aircraft technology was very much in its infancy at the outbreak of World War I but most combatant nations did possess a few reconnaissance aircraft and these types became ever more important once static warfare had begun.

Something like 19 out of every 20 aerial sorties flown throughout World War I were reconnaissance missions. There is no doubt that such aircraft played an increasingly key role in the conflict yet there had been considerable resistance to their introduction before the war – military aviation was still in its infancy in 1914 and many generals doubted its value.

The New Cavalry?

There were also comparatively few aircraft available in 1914; many country's air arms had only recently been founded; and most senior generals had little idea of what to do with them. Traditionally cavalry units were considered an army's eyes but aircraft soon proved their worth in reconnaissance. A German two-seat *Taube* monoplane played an important spotting role during the Battle of Tannenberg on the Eastern Front in late August 1914, for example, and these aircraft soon became indispensable when trench warfare reduced cavalry to immobility all along the Western Front.

Thereafter, reconnaissance aircrafts were deemed so important that fighter aircraft were developed specifically to shoot them down or protect them. They also became more and more sophisticated. Reports delivered in person or written and dropped gave way to immediate radio messages, while bulky hand-held cameras gave way to smaller types fitted within the fuselage. Later versions were stripped of any extra weight, including weapons, to fly higher and faster. They became ubiquitous over every front – more than half of fighter ace Baron Manfred von Richthofen's 80 "kills" were of reconnaissance aircraft.

The first types had only to be stable platforms for observation and did not have to be fast or

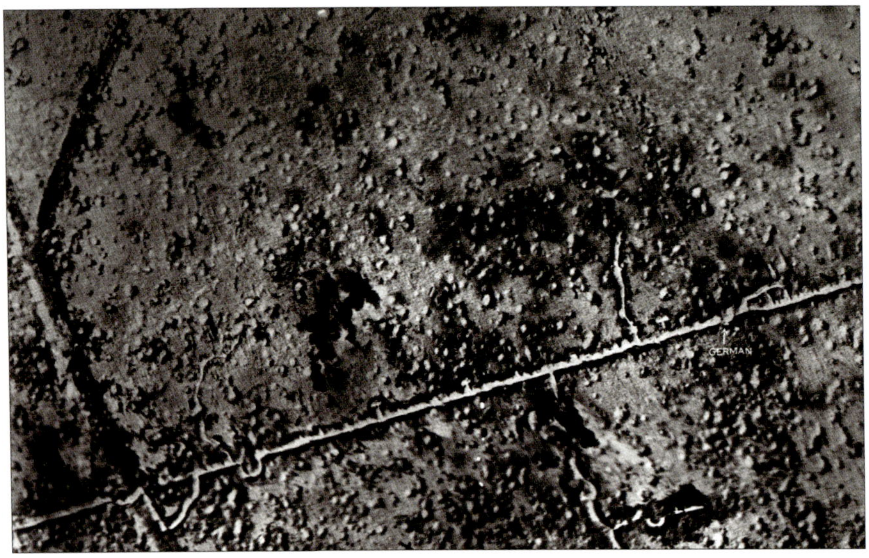

Above: Part of the Western Front photographed from a reconnaissance aircraft. Commanders increasingly relied on photo-mosaics made up of many images like this when planning attacks.

FARMAN MF-11

These French-built "pusher" aircraft were designed by Maurice Farman and were in general service in 1914. They saw action with the British and the French and fought on every front before being withdrawn from combat in 1915.

Type: Reconnaissance/bomber
Engine: 80hp Renault
Crew: 2
Ceiling: 3,000m (9,840ft)
Top speed: 96kph (60mph)
Armament: 1 x 0.303in (7.7mm) machine-gun

NIEUPORT 12

Nieuport built several designs for the French Army during World War I including the Nieuport 10 reconnaissance biplane, which made its debut in 1915. This was soon superseded by the Nieuport 12, enlarged and faster, and fitted with both rear- and forward-firing machine-guns. It was in service until early 1916.

TYPE: Reconnaissance/fighter
ENGINE: 110hp Clerget
CREW: 2
CEILING: 3,400m (11,150ft)
TOP SPEED: 160kph (100mph)
ARMAMENT: 1 or 2 x 0.303in (7.7mm) machine-guns

manoeuvrable as there was little chance of them being downed until fighters appeared. Earlier "pusher" types like the French Farman MF series or the British FE-2a, could manage no more than around 88kph (55mph) and even tractor types, like the German Albatros B-I and B-II, struggled to get above 104kph (65mph). Most of these had no weapons but they began carrying both machine-guns and bombs from late 1914.

LATER DEVELOPMENTS

The newer types that appeared in subsequent years were far more advanced. Albatros, for example, produced a whole range of increasingly advanced armed reconnaissance aircraft, including the C-I to C-III series (1915–16) and the C-V to C-XII types (1916–18). The highly successful C-X carried both bombs and machine-guns and had a top speed of around 196kph (120mph). Germany had other manufacturers, such as Aviatik, who produced the C-1 to C-III series (1915–17), and Halberstadt, who produced the C series (1917–18). Their C-V and Rumpler's C-VII were fitted with radio and cameras, making them the first truly modern photo-reconnaissance aircraft, able to record enemy positions and spot targets for artillery batteries.

Allied designers kept pace with the enemy, producing aircraft like the French Nieuport 10 and 11 (1915–16) with top speeds of around 140kph (85mph) and 155kph (95mph). Some designers opted for multi-purpose aircraft that could perform a number of battlefield functions. The British had the Royal Aircraft Factory's RE-8 (1916–18), a mass-produced multi-purpose biplane that could also undertake bombing and ground-attack missions.

Above: The *Taube* ("Owl") monoplane gained its name because of the bird-like shape of its wings. It was built both in Austria and Germany. Most were withdrawn from service by early 1915.

RUMPLER C-IV

The German company of Rumpler built many types of reconnaissance aircraft starting with the unarmed B-I, available in August 1914. This was replaced by the C-series, from early 1915. Hundreds of these were built, culminating in the C-VIIIR.

TYPE: Reconnaissance/bomber
ENGINE: 260hp Mercedes
CREW: 2
CEILING: 6,350m (20,800ft)
TOP SPEED: 170kph (105mph)
ARMAMENT: 2 x 7.92mm (0.312in) machine-guns + 100kg (220lb) bombs

Mons and Le Cateau

The British Expeditionary Force soon found itself heavily outnumbered when it pushed across the Franco-Belgian border in August 1914 and had to make a fighting withdrawal through north-east France facing repeated German attacks.

The first elements of Field Marshal John French's British Expeditionary Force (BEF) arrived in north-east France on 7 August, just three days after Britain had declared war on Germany, and the cross-Channel movement of around 125,000 men was largely completed by the 16th. The BEF concentrated around Le Cateau in north-east France but moved forward into southern Belgium on 21 August.

The BEF fought its first battle, not much more than a small skirmish between cavalry scouts, during the next day. Forty-eight hours later, however, it was struck by the full might of General Alexander von Kluck's German First Army, the extreme right wing of the Schlieffen Plan, near Mons. Kluck was somewhat caught by surprise as German intelligence had not even reported the arrival of the BEF in France.

KEY FACTS

Date: Mons (23 August 1914); Le Cateau (26 August 1914)

Place: South-west Belgium and north-east France

Outcome: The BEF escaped total destruction to participate in the Battle of the Marne.

Right: A brief respite for men of the British 11th Hussars during the retreat from Mons.

Below: A group of British cavalry photographed during the exhausting withdrawal of August 1914.

Resistance at Mons

Rapid British rifle fire inflicted severe losses on the Germans during the Battle of Mons on the 23rd and French was emboldened enough to contemplate standing his ground the next day. However, he was ordered that night to retreat in order to maintain contact with the French Fifth Army under General Charles Lanrezac that was retreating from Belgium after the Battle of the Sambre. Within a matter of days, therefore, the British were themselves falling back into north-east France down the roads that they had only recently used to move into southern Belgium. French actually wanted to withdraw to the Channel ports but he was overruled by Field Marshal Horatio Kitchener, the Minister for War, who insisted that the BEF must fall back towards the River Marne to keep contact with Lanrezac.

The retreating BEF was pursued closely by Kluck's units and fought frequent rearguard actions in the days after the Battle of Mons but on the 27th its exhausted II Corps under General Horace Smith-Dorrien stood its ground at Le Cateau and became embroiled in the biggest battle the British Army had fought in a hundred years.

THE BATTLE OF NÉRY

This battle took place as the British Expeditionary Force was retreating through north-east France in August–September 1914 and was one of the most remarkable small-scale battles of the entire war. On 1 September the rearguard of the 1st Cavalry Brigade and L Battery of the Royal Horse Artillery turned to face the might of the entire German 4th Cavalry Division. Despite having most of its guns knocked out and with many men killed or wounded, the battery's survivors fought on until all their ammunition was exhausted. Three members of L Battery received the Victoria Cross.

Above: London-born Battery Sergeant-Major George Dorrell won the Victoria Cross for his part in L Battery's heroic stand at Néry on 1 September 1914.

Above: German troops pictured in the centre of Mons after it had been abandoned by the British in August 1914. The Allies, actually Canadians, would not retake the Belgian town until 10 November 1918.

Some 70,000 British troops struggled all day against around 160,000 troops of the First Army as the latter tried to drive around both of their flanks. The battle concluded when darkness fell and the British, who had suffered some 7,800 casualties, then continued their withdrawal. They were aided in this movement by Lanrezac's Fifth Army, which was retiring on a parallel course on their right flank. Marshal Joseph Joffre, the French Commander-in-Chief, ordered Lanrezac to swing through 90 degrees and strike westward against Kluck's exposed left flank.

Kluck's Error

The ensuing Battle of Guise on the 29th did not noticeably slow the German First Army but a subsidiary attack against the German Second Army on its left caused its commander, General Karl von Bülow, considerable problems. He asked for aid from Kluck and the latter agreed, although without seeking permission from his superiors. This was to be a fateful decision as Kluck swung his army to the south-east, a route that would take his units to the east of Paris and not to the west as the Schlieffen Plan had called for. By 2 September his First Army was stretched out along the River Marne between Château-Thierry and Chantilly. Kluck mistakenly believed that there were no significant enemy concentrations on his right flank in the vicinity of Paris. It was a misjudgement that was to have profound consequences for the course of the war.

Field Artillery

Light-weight, quick-firing, field artillery guns drawn by horses were the dominant and most numerous form of artillery at the outset of the war but their importance gradually declined in favour of heavier weapons with bigger shells.

Field artillery consisted of light horse-drawn guns that could keep pace with infantry and cavalry. They were allocated at the divisional level while the distribution of heavier, slower guns was the preserve of higher formation commanders. There were two main types of field artillery – *guns* that fired a high-velocity round on a comparatively flat trajectory, mostly against targets in the open and in the firer's line of sight, and *howitzers* that lobbed a lower-velocity round on an arcing trajectory to strike targets hidden behind cover. Both types could be identified by the diameter of the barrel's bore, the usual system on the European mainland, or alternatively by the approximate weight of the shell they fired, a practice largely confined to Britain. Thus the field gun most widely deployed by the French in 1914 was the Model 1897 75mm (2.95in) while batteries supporting the British infantry relied on the Mark I 18-pounder (3.3in /84mm calibre) and the cavalry supports relied on the lighter 13-pounder (2.95in/75mm).

Rates of Fire

Most guns were quick-firers, capable of firing several rounds a minute. The best of these was the famous French "Soixante-Quinze" ("75"), the field gun that pioneered a recoil system in which only the barrel and not the whole carriage moved when fired. The "75" was phenomenally quick-firing, with a well-trained crew able to get through up to 25 rounds a minute. The crew of the not dissimilar British 18-pounder could manage only eight a minute.

Similar guns were deployed by the other combatant nations. Germany, for example, relied on the 7.7cm (3.03in) field gun, a weapon widely exported to its allies, while Russia deployed the 76.2mm (3in) M1902. Whatever the gun type, field artillery guns usually weighed

Below: British 18-pounder field guns, photographed around the Belgian town of Ypres in late 1914, with their limbers and ammunition caissons close at hand.

roughly 900–1,350kg (2,000–3,000lb). The various field guns and howitzers had a maximum range of 6,500–8,000m (7,100–8,800yds), but under battlefield conditions targets were usually engaged at shorter ranges, often at least a third less than the absolute range. There were variations in the number of guns in individual batteries but most countries deployed four. British cavalry and infantry divisions were the exception with six-gun batteries.

Above: Russian M1902 76.2mm (3in) field guns in action at the start of the war on the Eastern Front.

THE FRENCH "75" FIELD GUN

This was a revolutionary weapon when it appeared in 1897. It was light and highly mobile but most important of all it had a novel recoil system which meant that only the barrel and not the whole gun recoiled when fired. It therefore did not need to be re-laid on a target and a well-trained crew could fire an amazing 20-plus rounds in a minute. The 75 was really designed for fast-moving offensives and played a much lesser role in trench warfare.

CALIBRE: 75mm (2.95in)
GUN WEIGHT: 1,160kg (2,560lb)
GUN LENGTH: 2.7m (106in)
SHELL WEIGHT: 7.24kg (15.9lb)
MUZZLE VELOCITY: 530m/sec (1,735ft/sec)
MAXIMUM RANGE: 8,500m (9,300yds)

SHELL TYPES

There were two types of shell in service with field artillery. Shrapnel rounds, a largely anti-personnel weapon, were filled with metal balls and a bursting charge that was detonated by a preset time fuse ideally when in flight just above the enemy. High-explosive rounds had an impact fuse, which detonated when the shell hit the ground or another hard target such as a building. The force of the blast could destroy inanimate objects while both the detonation and splinters from the shell's ruptured casing were lethal to troops. Such rounds might fail to detonate if they struck soft or muddy ground.

Field artillery was essentially a weapon of mobile warfare and as such its importance on the Western Front declined with the advent of trench warfare. Shrapnel was ineffective against troops in cover and the high-explosive rounds fired by field guns were too light to make any impression on deep, strongly constructed dugouts. Despite their lack of firepower, field guns appeared in considerable numbers on the Western Front throughout the war. Improved fuses introduced later in the war meant that field guns could blast barbed-wire defences effectively. The British bombardment that preceded the opening of the Battle of the Somme in 1916 involved some 1,600 artillery pieces of which around 1,200 were either field or slightly larger medium guns. When the Germans launched Operation Michael, the first of their great offensives in 1918, they had 6,473 guns available; 3,965 were 7.7cm (3in) or 10cm (4in) field guns.

The Battle of the Marne

This titanic series of clashes during early September 1914 was masterminded by France's Marshal Joseph Joffre and proved one of the most decisive Allied victories of the war as it saved Paris and confounded Germany's Schlieffen Plan.

KEY FACTS

Date: 5 – 10 September 1914

Place: East of Paris

Outcome: The Germans were forced to retreat away from Paris across the River Marne; the Schlieffen Plan had completely failed.

The decision by General von Kluck to turn his German First Army to the south, a path that took it to the east rather than the west of Paris as the Schlieffen Plan demanded, did not go unnoticed by the Allies. Aerial reconnaissance spotted the change in direction and Marshal Joseph Joffre, the French Commander-in-Chief, fully intended to exploit the opportunity that had been presented to him. Kluck believed that there were no Anglo-French forces facing his right flank but Joffre had actually been creating a new force near Paris, the Sixth Army under General Michel Maunoury. Joffre intended to use this force against Kluck's over-exposed right flank. Most of the German armies had pushed southward across the River Marne by early September and were lying in a line that began some 48km (30 miles) to the east of Paris when Joffre struck back on the 5th.

Below: A mass grave for some of the 80,000 French soldiers who died during the Marne fighting.

The Allies Attack

The fighting around the Marne was not one but several battles that involved roughly 1 million Anglo-French and some 900,000 German troops. Maunoury was the first to attack, against Kluck's right flank. The Battle of the Ourcq (5–9 September) raged for two days before Kluck realized the danger. He pulled his First Army back across the Marne and then attacked Maunoury. The fighting was fierce but a German breakthrough was prevented once reinforcements arrived from Paris carried in many of the city's taxis.

Kluck's withdrawal left a large hole in the German line between his First and General von Bülow's Second Army. The British Expeditionary Force slowly moved into it, potentially threatening either Kluck's left or Bülow's right flanks, while the French Fifth Army, led by General Louis Franchet d'Espérey, threw itself against Bülow's Second Army along the Petit Morin. Next in line was

MARSHAL JOSEPH JOFFRE

Joffre (1852–1931) became the French Army's Chief of Staff in 1911 and was responsible for formulating the country's war strategy, Plan XVII. He was regarded as calm under pressure and imperturbable: qualities that were needed during the first months of the war. He directed the Allied victory along the Marne in September 1914 and effectively saved France from defeat. Joffre was also inflexible and launched a number of very costly attacks over the following years and, though a national hero, was sacked in late 1916.

Above: Marshal Joffre (second from left) confers with senior British officers.

General Ferdinand Foch's French Ninth Army. This attacked the German Second Army near the St-Gond marshes but quickly found itself fighting part of General Max von Hausen's Third Army as well.

The remainder of the Third Army and the German Fourth Army under Duke Albrecht of Württemberg were attacked by General Langle de Cary's French Fourth Army around Vitry-le-François. Next in line was General Maurice Sarrail's French Third Army which successfully stopped the advance of Crown Prince Wilhelm's Fifth German Army at Revigny in the Argonne. Finally, General Dubail's First and General de Castelnau's Second Armies located around Nancy and along the border with Alsace held off new and ferocious attacks from the reinforced German Sixth and Seventh Armies, commanded by Crown Prince Rupprecht of Bavaria and General Josias von Heeringen.

The Germans Retreat

By now Field Marshal Helmuth von Moltke, the German Chief of Staff, was receiving only fragmentary and contradictory reports from the Marne so he sent a trusted staff officer, Lieutenant-Colonel Richard Hentsch, to the front. Hentsch had been ordered merely to report on events but he exceeded his authority on the 9th, first by approving Kluck's unauthorized retreat and then permitting Bülow, whose own left flank was coming under more and more pressure, to pull back as well. The other German armies were forced to conform to these movements and withdrew to the line of the River Aisne over the next five days. The Battle of the Marne ended on the 10th and it was an undeniable strategic victory for the Allies though both sides had suffered approximately 25 per cent casualties.

Above: A publication celebrating the arrival of French troops by Paris taxi during the Battle of the Ourcq.

Below: French troops wait to counter-attack the Germans as the invaders begin to cross over the River Marne.

Rifles and Bayonets

The infantryman's rifle with its bayonet was the most ubiquitous weapon of the entire war and both were produced in their millions, but they were not the biggest killers – that "honour" went to machine-guns and, above all, artillery.

The rifle was the most commonly used weapon of World War I and, despite there being a sizeable number of manufacturers across Europe and beyond, all designs in service were largely similar in their mechanism and specifications. All were bolt-action, most of the straight-pull type, and all came with a magazine that allowed several shots to be fired without reloading. Some rifles had removable magazines but most were actually part of the rifle and the firer simply slotted clips of cartridges into them when reloading.

Rifles came in a rather limited variety of calibres. For example, the German Mauser Model 1898 had a calibre of 7.92mm (0.312in), while the Russian Moisin-Nagant was 7.62mm (0.3in) and the Romanian Mannlicher Model 1893 was 6.5mm (0.256in). British rifles were all 0.303in (7.7mm), while US types, like the Model 1903 Springfield, were 0.3in calibre. Most rifles were around 1.25m (50in) long and weighed some 4kg (9lb).

Magazines

Most rifles had a magazine with a five-round capacity but some, especially British and French models, could take somewhat more. The French Lebel Model 1916, for example, had an eight-round magazine, while both the British Lee-Enfield Mark I and the SMLE (Short Magazine Lee-Enfield) Mark III had a detachable ten-round magazine. Both designs reflected the British Army's belief that rapid fire would shatter an attack and its regular infantrymen were able to achieve 15 or 20 aimed shots per minute over short periods. (Most armies considered rapid fire to be 8 or 12 rounds a minute.) The Lee-Enfield's bigger, clip-fed magazine and the rifle's turn-down bolt handle were incorporated into the design to aid quick firing. Hastily trained wartime soldiers could not match the pre-war regulars' standards of speed or marksmanship, however.

Below: British recruits take part in bayonet drill. This was considered an important part of training but bayonets killed very few soldiers.

Right: A good study of a British soldier on campaign. He is armed with an SMLE (Short Magazine Lee-Enfield) rifle, first introduced in 1907.

Effective Ranges

Rifles were generally sighted up to as much as 2,560m (2,800yds) but most armies did not expect individual aimed fire to hit a specific target above 550m (600yds), a distance known as close range. Beyond this lay further zones as defined by the British Army – effective range at 600–1,400 yards (550–1,280m), long range at 1,400–2,000 yards (1,280–1,830m) and distant range at 2,000–2,800 yards (1,830–2,560m). Massed rather than individual targets could be hit at a rifle's effective range but it was not really worthwhile engaging anything at long or distant ranges.

Bayonets

There were three main types of bayonet. The most common were the ones shaped like the blade of a knife, while others were thinner needle types that were prone to snapping, and the comparatively rare knife bayonets with a serrated blade that were mostly used by the Germans. Allied propaganda claimed the serrated edge was deliberately designed to inflict even more horrendous wounds but it was actually for certain pioneering tasks.

Pre-war training manuals stressed the importance of the bayonet charge and most soldiers were inculcated with what the British termed the "spirit of the bayonet". The reality was somewhat different. Charges were extremely rare after 1914 and comparatively few people were killed or wounded by a bayonet thereafter. Bayonets were, of course, still used in trench fighting but an individual soldier faced with one was more likely to flee or surrender than fight it out. Detailed information on the precise number of bayonet wounds inflicted during the war is unavailable but it was undoubtedly extremely low compared with the big killer – artillery. British medical staff included bayonet wounds in their miscellaneous injuries category, which accounted for little more than one per cent of all casualties recorded by the British Army in the war.

GERMAN RIFLES

German infantry had two main types of rifle: the Mauser Gewehr 88 and the Mauser Gewehr 98 – first made in 1888 and 1898. The Gewehr 98 was exceedingly accurate and continued in German use until World War II.

Calibre: 7.92mm (0.312in) (Mauser Gewehr 98)
Magazine: 5 rounds
System: front-locking turn-bolt
Length: 125cm (49.25in)
Weight: 4.3kg (9.5lb)
Muzzle velocity: 870m/sec (2,854ft/sec)

SNIPING

Sniping was a valuable tool throughout the war, more so than in any previous conflict, and became especially important when static trench warfare developed. Snipers often worked as part of a two-man team with the other man being a target spotter equipped with binoculars or, more commonly, a trench periscope that protected him from enemy snipers. Snipers operated from camouflaged hides or behind metal plates with a rifle-sized slit cut into them to avoid being targeted themselves.

Right: A posed photograph of a German sniper, who would normally take up a much less exposed position.

The Race to the Sea

From late September to the end of October, the Anglo-French and German armies moved northward, attempting to swing around each other's exposed flank, but all of these attacks failed and the North Sea ultimately prevented further manoeuvres.

Failure at the Marne in early September led Moltke to order a general German withdrawal north towards the River Aisne, a decision that signalled the collapse of the Schlieffen Plan. This failure doomed Germany to what it had always wanted to avoid – a prolonged war on two fronts – and led to Moltke being replaced as Chief of Staff by General Erich von Falkenhayn on the 14th. After his victory to the east of Paris, Marshal Joffre, Moltke's opposite number, had high hopes of finishing off the German forces and ordered the Anglo-French armies to set off in pursuit. His aim was to swing round the exposed German right flank but the Germans prevented this manoeuvre at the First Battle of the Aisne (15–18 September).

Above: French troops on the march as the fighting moved northward through France during late 1914.

This fighting along the Aisne sparked off a series of attempted flanking movements that became known as the Race to the Sea. Both sides sent forces north towards the North Sea coast with the Allies trying to turn the German right flank and the latter trying to swing around the Anglo-French left. There was fierce fighting in the Picardy region during 22–26 September and then in Artois 27 September – 10 October. Thereafter, the main focus moved farther north still into Flanders where the two sides fought a number of battles but for no tangible strategic reward.

Antwerp Besieged

While the Race to the Sea proceeded, Belgium was fighting for survival. After the fall of Brussels on 20 August, most of the Belgian Army fell back on Antwerp, from where it made two sorties against the German right flank between late August and mid-September. To stymie

Below: A Belgian machine-gun detachment on the move.

Below: German troops in the last phase of open warfare in 1914.

any more threats to their lines of communication, the Germans brought up their heavy howitzers and placed Antwerp under siege on the 28th.

Antwerp's garrison, bolstered by the arrival of a British Naval Division, stood behind strong defences but the port met the same fate as Liège and Namur. The Belgian authorities surrendered on 10 October, though not before most of the garrison had retreated west along the Flanders coast, determined to maintain a toehold on Belgian soil. These Anglo-Belgian troops took up positions along the Yser Canal between Nieuport and Boesinghe. To their south lay the Anglo-French forces that had been involved in the Race to the Sea.

Last German Attacks

Although the lines were solidifying, the Germans made two more attempts to achieve victory. The first, the Battle of the Yser, was fought during 16–31 October but failed after the Belgians took the bold decision to open the sluice gates to the irrigation system that prevented flooding in this low-lying region. By the end of the month a large area stretching southward from Nieuport to Dixmude had been inundated. It was so clearly impassable that the flooded area saw no appreciable action until 1918. The Germans now turned their attention to the south of Dixmude and made their last effort to cut through the Allied lines in 1914 at Ypres.

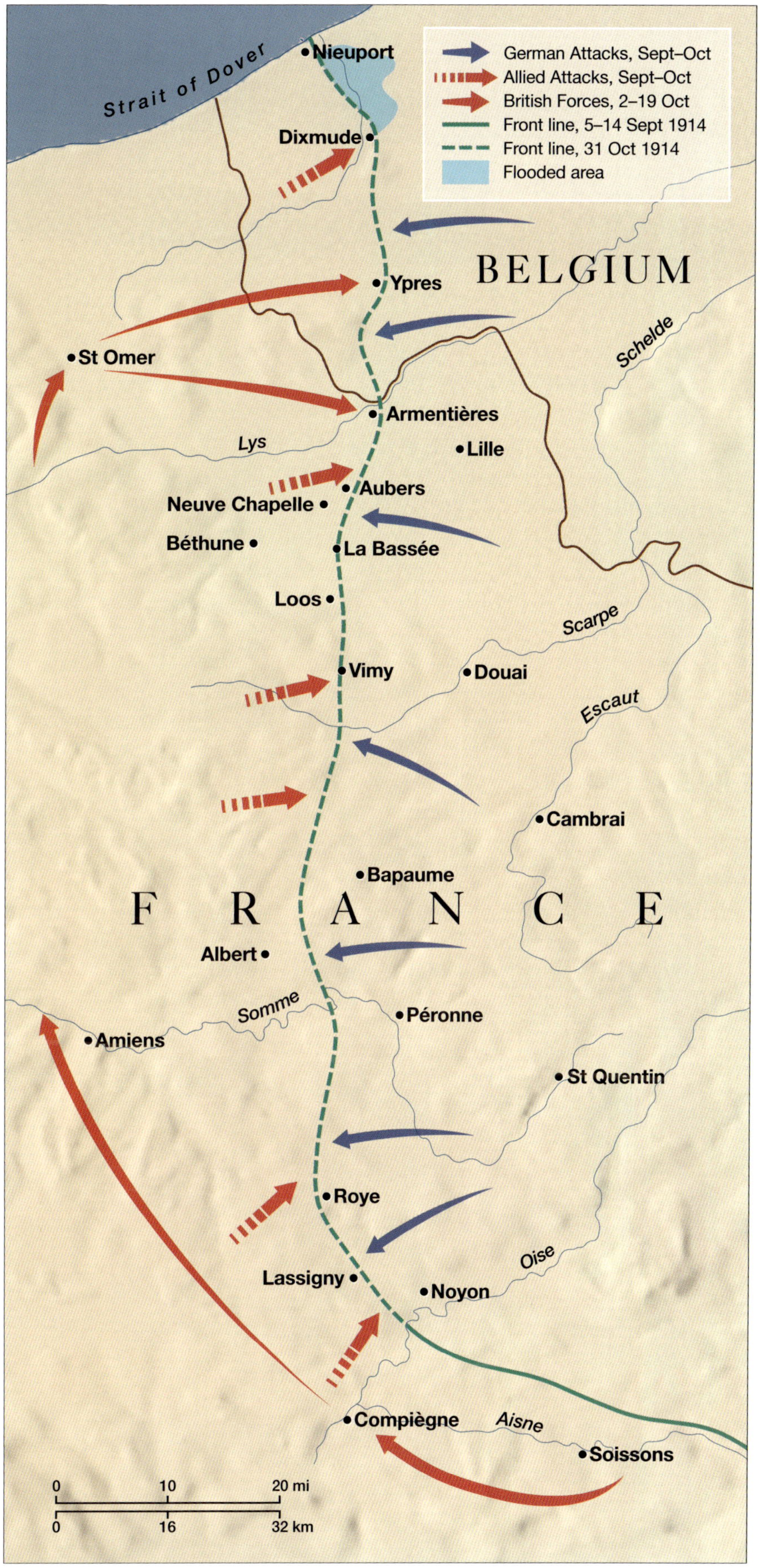

THE RACE TO THE SEA

The succession of outflanking moves in the Race to the Sea.

The First Battle of Ypres

This was the last major offensive by the Germans on the Western Front in 1914. Their attempt to break through to the Channel ports narrowly failed, although the British Expeditionary Force paid a very high price for its narrow victory.

After the Battle of the Aisne had ended in late September, the BEF under Field Marshal French had been switched to the extreme left of the Anglo-French line for the subsequent Race to the Sea. Its chief mission was to protect Boulogne, Calais and Dunkirk, Channel ports vital to the arrival of British reinforcements and supplies, by pushing into Flanders and, if possible, linking up with elements of the Belgian Army. As the Race to the Sea reached its climax in late autumn, part of the now enlarged BEF fought two battles in north-east France at La Bassée and Armentières during mid-October and early November. Some units also pushed into southern Belgium, tipping the Germans out of Ypres on 13 October after a ten-day occupation. It was in this medieval Flemish town that the BEF faced the last major German attack of 1914.

KEY FACTS

Date: 19 October – 22 November 1914

Place: South-west Belgium

Outcome: A narrow British victory bought at a high cost that led to the outbreak of static trench warfare.

THE WESTERN FRONT, 1914

The front lines after the war of movement ended in late 1914.

German Aims

The German Chief of Staff, General von Falkenhayn, was fully aware of the importance of the Channel ports to Britain. He had so far failed to take them, and time was running out, but a successful push on Ypres would likely lead to their capture and make Britain's further participation in the war doubtful. The German attacks were led by Duke Albrecht of Württemberg's Fourth Army from the 15th. British rifle fire again cut down the attackers in droves but the British also suffered heavy casualties and units to the north and south of the town were pushed back, forming a salient around the town itself.

The offensive was renewed at the end of the month with the strongest attacks being in the east and south-east. Fourth Army troops took Gheluvelt and crossed the Menin Road on the 31st, although the former was recaptured soon after. Messines Ridge, a key piece of high ground, and the outlying village of Wytschaete were overrun by 1 November, thereby making the salient even smaller. The fall of Ypres seemed imminent, so much so that Emperor Wilhelm II arrived to watch its capture, but the British held on, in part thanks to the arrival of many French reinforcements.

The Germans made two more major efforts to take the town. Matters became so critical that the Allies contemplated abandoning Ypres altogether on the 9th. The plan was rejected but the German pressure intensified, leading to the capture of St Eloi the next day and a ferocious but unsuccessful

battle to take Gheluvelt for the second time. The last German effort came on the 15th but the battle effectively ended a week later due to mutual exhaustion and increasingly bad weather.

The Casualty Toll

The Allies suffered a total of 75,000 casualties during the First Battle of Ypres – the BEF had been decimated and would need to be entirely rebuilt – while the Germans suffered losses totalling some 135,000 men. The war was a mere five months or so old and the total manpower losses were truly staggering. Belgium recorded around 50,000 men killed, wounded or missing, France 995,000, Germany 677,000 and Britain 75,000.

The French continued to attack as the year ended, launching the First Battle of Champagne on 20 December.

Right: French troops captured outside the Belgian town of Ypres.

Above: German troops man an unusually tidy trench in Belgium after the First Battle of Ypres.

The combatant nations each still believed that a decisive victory was possible but everyone knew that the war would not be over by Christmas, as had originally been hoped. The prospect of further carnage did nothing to raise the spirits of the British and German troops even though some, to the disgust of their generals, crawled out of their newly dug trenches to fraternize on Christmas Day.

THE BRITISH EXPEDITIONARY FORCE

The BEF of 1914 was tiny by European standards, a mere five divisions, but was unusual in being an all-volunteer force with numerous combat-experienced soldiers. It was also well-trained and highly motivated with the men being excellent marksmen. The BEF fought well in the first months of the war but was decimated. Thereafter, it underwent a huge expansion, first through volunteers and then through conscription. By November 1918 it contained some 61 divisions (including units from Canada, Australia, New Zealand and other parts of the British Empire).

Above: British troops prepare to move out.

The Invasions of Serbia 1914–15

Austria-Hungary planned to punish Serbia for its part in the assassination of Archduke Franz Ferdinand but its troops were repulsed and it eventually took a combined attack with both German and Bulgarian support to subdue the country.

Austria-Hungary held Serbia directly responsible for the assassination of Archduke Franz Ferdinand and issued a war declaration on 28 July. Belgrade, the Serbian capital, came under fire from Austro-Hungarian gunboats on the River Danube the next day but troops were not committed until 14 August, when more than 200,000 men under Field Marshal Oskar Potiorek crossed the Sava and Drina Rivers to the north and west of Belgrade. This move began the Battle of the Jadar River. The Austro-Hungarians were caught out when 190,000 Serbian troops led by Marshal Radomir Putnik counter-attacked on the 16th. Although the Serbs were outnumbered and fairly ill-equipped, they forced Potiorek's army back by the 21st.

After a brief interlude, the Serbians pushed into Bosnia, Austro-Hungarian territory, on 6 September but Putnik in turn was forced to withdraw when Potiorek recrossed the Drina to establish footholds on the Serbian side over the following 48 hours. The Serbians threw themselves against the Austro-Hungarian positions but after ten days of bitter fighting they were forced to concede defeat in the Battle of the River Drina. They began falling back to more defensible positions south-west of Belgrade on the 17th.

Above: Field Marshal Oskar Potiorek was sacked for mismanaging Austria-Hungary's invasion of Serbia in 1914.

Austrians Defeated

Now reinforced, the Austro-Hungarians opened another offensive on 5 November and Putnik's troops, who were short of ammunition, were forced to withdraw slowly in the hope of counter-attacking later when the Austro-Hungarians had themselves outrun their supply lines. Belgrade was occupied by the invaders on 2 December but by then Putnik had been

AUSTRO-HUNGARIAN ATROCITIES

Austria-Hungary passed the War Service Law in 1912 and it allowed for the rights of a citizen to be forfeited to the army during a national emergency. The law was first applied to Bosnia and Herzegovina on 25 July 1914 and then Serbia, where all Serbians, whether they were actually pro-Bosnia nationalists or not, became suspect. Austro-Hungarian troops systematically took hostages, burned houses and killed an estimated 4,000 civilians during their invasion of Serbia in 1914. Similar events also took place in Galicia.

Above: Austro-Hungarian troops execute Serbian civilians.

resupplied with ammunition from France and was ready to strike back. The Austro-Hungarians had the flooded River Kolubara to their rear so that when the Serbian forces pushed forward on the 3rd they were trapped. When the Battle of the Kolubara River ended on the 9th, all of the surviving Austro-Hungarian forces were back across the Danube and Sava Rivers. Belgrade was liberated on the 15th and Potiorek, who had lost some 227,000 men, was sacked and replaced by Archduke Eugene.

Above: Exhausted Serbian troops snatch some much-needed rest during their epic retreat through Serbia and Montenegro during 1915–16.

Serbia Finally Beaten

The odds against Serbia surviving a further invasion grew remote in late 1915. Germany needed the railway that ran through Serbia to send aid to Turkey after the only other viable route, through Romania, was closed by the Romanians in June. Bulgaria, Serbia's long-standing rival to the east, joined the Central Powers' cause on 6 September 1915. The German Chief of Staff, General von Falkenhayn, immediately began planning a joint attack on Serbia and command of the invasion was given to an experienced German field marshal, August von Mackensen.

Below: Serbian troops like these lacked much modern equipment but they were hardy fighters and more than a match for the Austro-Hungarian invaders.

On 6 October the Austro-Hungarian Third Army under Field Marshal Hermann Kövess von Kövesshàza and General Max von Gallwitz's German Eleventh Army crossed the Sava and Danube Rivers into Serbian territory. Five days later a pair of Bulgarian armies commanded by General Nikola Zhekov attacked westward into Serbia, making for Nish (Niš) and Uskub (Skopje). Putnik was forced to make an arduous retreat into Montenegro in the depths of winter with his forces suffering some 500,000 casualties. The survivors were all transported to Corfu in Allied warships during January 1916 and would later continue the war from Allied-occupied Salonika. Serbia, Montenegro and much of neighbouring Albania were occupied by the Central Powers until 1918.

Russia's Invasion of East Prussia

The speed of Russia's mobilization caught the German garrison in East Prussia by surprise and the Russian drive over the border caused something akin to panic in the mind of the general ordered to defend Germany's vulnerable province.

The oft-modified Schlieffen Plan was developed to prevent Germany from having to fight a war on two fronts – against France in the west and Russia in the east. It was based on many erroneous assumptions, including the belief that Russia's mobilization would be so slow that most of Germany's forces could be safely deployed against France with only a small force needed in the east. The final version of the plan, which was devised in 1914, did recognize that Russia would be able to go to war faster than had been believed. It therefore allowed for the deployment of more German forces in the east, up from 10 to 15 per cent of the manpower available.

Below: The Battle of Stallupönen, the first clash between German and Russian troops during the war. The Russians repulsed a small attack.

KEY FACTS

DATE: 15 – 23 August 1914

PLACE: German province of East Prussia

OUTCOME: A tentative Russian push into the province led to a panicked response by the local German commander.

RUSSIAN PLANS

Despite this reappraisal, the speed with which Russian forces massed against both German East Prussia and along the Austro-Hungarian Empire's Galician border in the first half of August 1914 still came as a shock to both of the Central Powers' high commands. Tsar Nicholas II actually signed the mobilization orders on 30 July; the process itself began on 4 August and the various Russian armies were largely in position by the 15th.

Russia's war-fighting strategy in East Prussia was to attack as quickly as possible to prevent Germany from defeating France and then turning its military might eastward. Two armies were immediately deployed to invade the province. East Prussia jutted into Russian territory but there were actually just two viable invasion routes. To the north and south-west strong fortifications lay around Königsberg (Kaliningrad) and Thorn (Toruń) that could not be bypassed and would take considerable time to overcome. In the centre any invader was confronted by the virtually impassable Masurian Lakes, which the Germans had made even more impenetrable by building yet more fortifications. The Russians therefore had

Above: German troops man a trench somewhere inside East Prussia's eastern border with Russia.

little option but to attack East Prussia simultaneously from the east and south-east. However, the armies would be operating in effect in isolation and, because of the distance between them, would find it difficult to coordinate their actions.

The 150,000-strong Russian First Army under General Paul von Rennenkampf took up positions in the east, while far to the south-east General Alexander Samsonov deployed his larger Second Army below the Masurian Lakes. In total the two generals mustered some 29 divisions and were opposed by just 13 divisions of General Maximilian von Prittwitz's German Eighth Army. Rennenkampf moved first with the intention of drawing Prittwitz towards him so that Samsonov, who was to begin moving two days later, could come up behind the Germans and trap them in a pincer movement. The plan appeared sound but both Rennenkampf and Samsonov were far from optimistic as their forces were under-equipped and relied on a poorly organized supply system.

Early Russian Success

Nevertheless, morale among the First Army was raised shortly after it entered East Prussia when a German raid was beaten off at Stallupönen on the 17th and then a much larger attack at Gumbinnen was defeated three days later. Prittwitz panicked and ordered an unauthorized retreat to the River Vistula, a move that meant abandoning most of the province. His superiors soon countermanded his decision and replaced him with Generals Paul von Hindenburg and Erich Ludendorff on the 23rd. They resolved to strike against first one and then the other of the opposing Russian armies.

Left: Colonel, later General Maximilian Hoffmann, a senior staff officer of the German Eighth Army in East Prussia.

RUSSIAN MOBILIZATION

Germany's war strategy, the Schlieffen Plan, was in part formulated in the belief that Russia's mobilization would be ponderous but this view became less and less tenable in the years before 1914. General Vladimir Sukhomlinov, the Russian Minister for War from 1909, undertook a root-and-branch reform of the country's war machine. He secured greater military spending and began to expand the rail network on which mobilization relied. The expansion was to have been completed by 1916 and this so alarmed the Germans that they were even more willing to contemplate war in 1914.

Above: Russian troops gather around Tsar Nicholas II as they prepare to march off to war.

Cavalry

Most armies had significant numbers of cavalry at the outbreak of the war and, although they were relegated to a secondary role on the Western Front for much of the conflict, they performed well elsewhere, especially in Palestine.

Cavalry units were found in every army, and sometimes in considerable numbers, at the outbreak of World War I. Russia had a staggering 29 divisions, Germany 11, France 10 and Britain just 1, yet they had become virtually irrelevant in most if not all theatres by 1918. At the outset many generals expected that horsemen would play their traditional roles: opposing other cavalry, conducting reconnaissance missions and pursuing a defeated and disorganized enemy. Most cavalrymen continued to carry swords and, to a lesser extent, lances but the vast majority had also been trained to fight on foot with modern firearms.

Above: A German cavalryman – if not his mount – is prepared to deal with a gas attack later in the war.

The Western Front

Cavalry on the Western Front were largely bystanders once trench warfare had begun in late 1914. There were cavalry clashes initially – the British 9th Lancers charged the German 1st Guard Dragoons at Moncel on 6 September, for example, but the omens were not good. Some 70 German cavalrymen charged a dismounted squadron of the 18th Hussars at Faujus a few days later and were hit by a hail of rifle fire. Virtually every attacker was killed or wounded. For the next three years or so the cavalry stood behind the lines waiting to exploit breakthroughs that never came. Mud, machine-guns and barbed wire had effectively denied them use of their greatest asset – mobility.

A measure of open warfare broke out in 1918 but by then cavalry numbers had been greatly reduced. Many units had been disbanded and their men transferred to other duties. The remaining cavalry did occasionally mount up to move to the scene of the action but invariably fought on foot. There were

Below: A column of Indian cavalry on the Western Front in late 1914. Indian mounted units later served with distinction in Palestine.

even British plans to use cavalry in conjunction with Whippet light tanks, but the marriage was an unhappy one. Whippets could not keep up with the cavalry and the cavalry were far too vulnerable to enemy machine-gun fire to press ahead of the bullet-proof tanks.

Other Theatres

Cavalry units were used more frequently and for longer elsewhere during the conflict. Austria-Hungary, Germany and Russia all deployed them on the Eastern Front largely because warfare there was often more open because of the huge distances involved. It was impossible to build or man trenches that would have had to stretch from the Baltic Sea to the Romanian border. Thus, there was a greater degree of mobility than on the Western Front.

It was in Palestine that cavalry saw the greatest action. The British Empire forces deployed a number of mounted units, particularly ones raised in Australia and New Zealand, and these usually rode into action but fought on foot as the 2nd and 3rd Australian Light Horse did at the Battle of Beersheba in late 1917. Yet, on the same day, two other units, the 4th and 12th Australian Light Horse, actually charged a double line of Turkish trenches some 2,750m (3,000yds) to their front. The Australians had not been issued with swords so instead galloped forward with bayonets drawn and the sight so unnerved the Turkish defenders that most took flight.

By 1918 the Allies had a full corps of cavalry in Palestine with units from Australia, New Zealand, Britain itself, India and France. Britain's Arab allies were almost entirely mounted on horses and camels during their campaign against Turkey in Arabia and into Palestine.

Above: Belgian lancers move out to protect their homeland from German invasion in August 1914.

Below: A detachment of Bulgarian cavalry moves through a town somewhere in the Balkans.

The Battle of Tannenberg

The German victory at Tannenberg in late August 1914 relied on the swift movement of troops by rail across East Prussia so that one of two strong but mutually isolated Russian armies could be overwhelmed.

The Russian invasion of East Prussia in August 1914 began to go wrong shortly after General Rennenkampf's First Army's minor victory at Gumbinnen on the 20th. Rennenkampf was meant to continue menacing the German Eighth Army to his front, while the Second Army under General Samsonov advanced from the south-east. Rennenkampf's slowness was noted by the German Eighth Army's chief of operations, General Max Hoffmann, who came up with a bold plan to defeat first one and then the other of the invading armies. His outline was adopted by the new commander of the Eighth Army, General von Hindenburg, and his deputy, General Ludendorff, when they arrived at the front during the 23rd.

Below: German troops advance through a burning town during the Battle of Tannenberg.

KEY FACTS

Date: 26 – 30 August 1914

Place: South-east East Prussia

Outcome: The Germans achieved an overwhelming victory that smashed the Russian Second Army in just a few days.

German Advances

A screen of cavalry was left facing the virtually immobile Rennenkampf, while one of the Eighth Army's four corps was rushed to the south-east by train to take up positions on Samsonov's exposed left flank. Two other German corps marched south from Gumbinnen to take up positions on the Second Army's other flank, while a fourth corps remained where it was near the village of Tannenberg, which now stood directly in Samsonov's path. Samsonov's troops began to push beyond Tannenberg from the 22nd and made some forward progress over the next six days, yet they were becoming over-extended and increasingly short of all kinds of supplies.

Above: A Russian child soldier pictured with his comrades somewhere in East Prussia, 1914.

The German attacks on the Second Army's exposed flanks began developing during the 26th and 27th. It took no more than three days virtually to destroy Samsonov's isolated command – more than half of his 230,000-strong force was either killed, wounded or captured. The defeated general disappeared into a forest and committed suicide on the last day of the month. Hindenburg's

FIELD MARSHAL PAUL VON HINDENBURG

Hindenburg (1847–1934), who had retired in 1911 but returned to service three years later, was the archetypal senior Prussian officer, being both aristocratic and commanding. He had an air of calm authority, some said it was actually vacuity, and was something of a self-publicist. Much of the credit for his efforts should have gone to others, not least General Erich Ludendorff, with whom he effectively ran Germany's war effort from late August 1916. Hindenburg again retired in June 1919 but was President of Germany 1925–34.

Above: Field Marshal Hindenburg adopts a suitably martial pose.

losses totalled no more than 20,000 men and Tannenberg was portrayed as a great victory in Germany, one that made both Hindenburg and Ludendorff into household names. The battle was also seen as a disaster by both Britain and France, but the truth was that the Russian Army could still call on vast reserves of manpower.

New Attacks

The Germans had fought an essentially defensive battle to overwhelm Samsonov and they now launched an offensive operation to crush Rennenkampf and remove the final threat to East Prussia. To do this, large numbers of troops were transferred from the Western Front at a critical point in early September, a strategic decision that undermined the Schlieffen Plan. The First Battle of the Masurian Lakes opened on the 7th and troops from the German Eighth Army were launched against Rennenkampf's right flank as he belatedly began to push deeper into East Prussia. The attack scythed through the Russian lines south of the lakes but Rennenkampf was just able to retreat before the trap closed.

The battle left Hindenburg a little way inside Russia by the 13th but his army was by now exhausted and suffering from acute supply shortages, while Rennenkampf was safely back across the River Nieman and being reinforced by the Russian Tenth Army. These forces launched a counter-attack, the Battle of the Nieman, on the 25th and after three days of heavy fighting Hindenburg finally called off his advance. Russian casualties reached 125,000, but Germany, too, had suffered, with around 100,000 killed, wounded or missing in East Prussia since August. Yet, for all the bloodshed, the strategic situation along the northern sector of the Eastern Front was largely unchanged.

Below: German troops man a well-camouflaged position in the vicinity of the Masurian Lakes.

Operations in Poland and Galicia

Austria-Hungary launched a largely unsuccessful attack on the Russians at the outbreak of the war and the empire had to call on its German ally for military aid to prevent a near collapse on the Eastern Front.

At the outbreak of war the Austro-Hungarian Chief of Staff, Field Marshal Franz Conrad von Hötzendorf, concentrated three armies in Galicia for a major offensive into the south of Russian Poland, an area that was defended by General Nikolai Ivanov's South-western Army Group. Conrad began to advance on a 320km (200 mile) front on 23 August. In the north General Victor Dankl's First Army defeated the Russian Fourth Army at the Battle of Kraśnik during the first two days and General Wenzel von Plehve's Russian Fifth Army was driven back by Field Marshal Moritz Auffenberg's Fourth Army at the Battle of Zamosc-Komarów (26 August – 1 September).

Above: Although probably posed, this image shows the type of siege lines that the Russians threw around the fortress of Przemyśl during the fighting in Galicia.

Below: The remains of one of Przemyśl's forts after Russian shelling. The town fell in March 1915 but was later recaptured.

Russian Victories

Matters were very different in the south. Two Russian armies took on the Austro-Hungarian Third Army, which had been slightly reinforced by some units from the Second Army freed from service in Serbia. The Third Army was forced to withdraw towards the fortress of Lemberg (Lvov) after the Battle of Gnila Lipa (26–30 August) and was decisively beaten at the Battle of Rava Russkaya (3–11 September). Lemberg fell and the Austro-Hungarian forces retreated some 160km (100 miles) to the Carpathian Mountains. As more and more Russian troops began arriving in the north, the two Austro-Hungarian armies there also retreated so that the greater part of Galicia was lost by early October. Only the fortress of Przemyśl held out.

The Germans now intervened, largely to prevent a Russian thrust through Russian Poland into Silesia, one of

Germany's great mineral-producing and industrial areas. The Ninth Army under General Paul von Hindenburg was assembled by rail at great speed around Cracow (Kraków) by late September. Hindenburg launched a spoiling attack into south-west Poland on the 28th but was checked around Ivangorod (Dęblin) by more powerful Russian forces on 12 October. He withdrew but his efforts had inflicted a major delay on Russia's preparations to invade Silesia and Hindenburg's reward came on 1 November. He was promoted to field marshal and made commander-in-chief on the Eastern Front with General Ludendorff named as his deputy.

FIELD MARSHAL FRANZ CONRAD VON HÖTZENDORF

Conrad (1852–1925) was the Austro-Hungarian Army's Chief of Staff from 1906 and had a justified reputation as an arch-militarist, urging attacks on his country's neighbours. When war came in 1914 his plans were bold and optimistic but were far beyond the capabilities of the forces he led. Conrad was increasingly marginalized, especially after the disastrous Trentino Offensive in Italy during 1916, and was sacked in March 1917. He then served in Italy but was dismissed from his post on 15 July 1918.

Above: Conrad had grandiose plans but lacked forces of the quality needed to execute them.

There were no reinforcements available for a follow-up offensive but Ludendorff devised a bold plan that relied on speed of manoeuvre. The Ninth Army, soon to be commanded by General August von Mackensen, was spirited away in a week, again by rail, to the comparatively lightly defended north-west border with Poland. Mackensen struck south-east towards Lódz on 11 November. He drove between General Rennenkampf's First Army and General Schiedmann's Second. Rennenkampf was soon reeling after an attack on his over-extended left wing but an attempted envelopment of the Second Army was checked by the arrival of Plehve's Fifth Army. The battle ended in stalemate on 25 November.

Below: The ruins of a town somewhere in Galicia give a good indication of the fighting's ferocity.

GERMANY IN CONTROL

Lódz can be considered a narrow Russian victory but it was Germany that reaped the strategic rewards. The Russian Commander-in-Chief, Grand Duke Nicholas, called off the invasion of Silesia, not least because he had lost close to 1.8 million men in 1914 and was very short of all manner of war supplies by the year's end. Russia never again threatened an invasion of Germany. The Germans had lost around 275,000 men and their high command was now fully aware that Austria-Hungary, which had suffered close to 1 million casualties, was incapable of independent action. Henceforth, German forces would have to take the lead on the Eastern Front.

Operations in China and the Pacific

Germany's far-flung colonies in the Pacific and Far East were far too isolated and vulnerable to stand alone and they were all captured by various Allied expeditions in the first few months of the conflict.

Germany was never in the same league as either Britain or France when it came to the acquisition of overseas colonies. By 1914 it controlled a handful in Africa, a number of Pacific islands that were used as coaling and radio stations, and part of New Guinea. Its most important possession was Tsingtao (Qingdao), a port on China's Shantung (Shandong) Peninsula. This was acquired during 1898 in compensation for the murder of Lutheran missionaries and was home to the most powerful German naval force outside Europe in 1914. The port had a 4,000-strong garrison but the key element was the East Asiatic Squadron, a flotilla of two armoured cruisers and five light cruisers. Its orders were to attack British shipping and underwater communications cables when war was declared.

Above: Senior Japanese officers and their lone British counterpart stand among the Tsingtao siege lines with a piece of heavy artillery in the background.

Tsingtao Besieged

Yet Germany's Pacific possessions were actually in a hopeless position. They were too far from home to expect any aid and they faced a considerable number of enemies. Britain had a sizeable number of warships stationed at bases such as Hong Kong, while in the south-west Pacific Australia and New Zealand had both declared war. France had bases in Indochina and an even more significant threat came from Britain's ally Japan, a country with ambitions to create a Pacific empire of its own. Recognizing that Germany was unable to defend Tsingtao in any meaningful way, the Japanese government demanded that the port be evacuated on 15 August. Germany refused and Japan declared war eight days later.

By late August a largely Japanese fleet had blockaded Tsingtao and on 2 September the first troops landed on the peninsula to begin the siege

Left: The oil depot at Tsingtao, Germany's only toehold on the Chinese mainland, goes up in flames during the British and Japanese siege that ended with the port's capture on 7 November 1914.

Right: Japanese troops, some of the 24,000 men involved in the siege of Tsingtao, are put ashore on 2 September 1914.

operations. It was an unequal fight as the garrison faced some 23,000 Japanese troops and a smaller 1,300-strong British expeditionary force. The defences took a pounding from Allied warships and artillery, though progress was slow due to bad weather and fierce resistance, but the attackers had reached the garrison's last line of defence by early November. The port finally surrendered on the 7th.

Germany's other Pacific possessions – the Carolines, Marianas, Marshalls, Palaus and Samoa, as well as part of the Solomon Islands and New Guinea – soon fell to the Allies. Australian and New Zealand forces occupied Samoa without firing a shot; British troops faced minimal resistance in the Solomons; while the Japanese finally took the Marshalls in November. Germany had lost virtually all of its Pacific colonies by December 1914 and, after early successes, the East Asiatic Squadron had also been largely destroyed at the Battle of the Falklands.

CHINA AT WAR

China actually declared war on Austria-Hungary and Germany on 14 August 1917 and even offered 300,000 troops for overseas service but the country was so riven by political factionalism that such an effort was beyond its means. It therefore had little direct impact on the Allied combat effort beyond sending a military mission to Europe. China's greatest contribution was the 230,000-plus skilled and unskilled labourers who worked behind the lines in France and elsewhere to keep the machinery of war supply rolling.

Left: Some of the thousands of Chinese who toiled on the Western Front for the Allies are seen here building a light railway.

EMDEN IN ACTION

One of its light cruisers, *Emden*, had separated from the squadron on 8 September and embarked on a brief but spectacular commerce-raiding cruise in the Indian Ocean that saw it sink some 70,000 tons of shipping. It also bombarded oil facilities at Madras on the 22nd and went on to sink an old Russian cruiser, *Zhemchug*, and a French destroyer, *Mousquet*, on 28 October. However, time was running out for *Emden*. Some 14 Allied warships had been detached to hunt it down and its supply ships were being sunk one by one. The end came on 9 November, when it was tracked down by the more powerful Australian cruiser *Sydney*. In a brief battle at Direction Island, part of the Cocos and Keeling group in the southern Indian Ocean, *Emden* was destroyed by long-range gunfire in the first battle ever fought by an Australian warship. Most of the crew were captured but 50 who were ashore when the battle started later made their way back home.

Surface Raiders

The Imperial German Navy intended to launch a variety of surface ships against Britain's maritime trade routes which stretched across the globe but most of the raiders were sunk, lost or interned during the first months of the war.

Crippling an opponent by destroying his maritime trade and merchant fleet was a well-established naval strategy by 1914. As submarines were still an unknown quantity and as those available did not have the range to operate globally, many navies earmarked other vessels to undertake such duties. These were either purpose-built or converted civilian craft and the three main types were generally known as commerce raiders, armed merchant cruisers and auxiliary commerce raiders. They mostly operated far from home and relied on colonies, specially designated freighters or neutral ports for resupply.

Commerce Raiders

Germany had eight commerce raiders. Seven of these were with the East Asiatic Squadron in the Pacific and one, *Karlsruhe*, was in the West Indies. Four of the Pacific raiders were sunk at the Battle of the Falkland Islands in December 1914 while a fifth, *Dresden*, was scuttled in March 1915. The squadron's remaining pair had equally brief careers. *Emden* successfully cruised the south-west Pacific and Indian Ocean between August and early November 1914 but then succumbed to the Australian cruiser *Sydney*.

The squadron's final cruiser, *Königsberg*, headed into the western Indian Ocean intending to sink Allied ships using the Suez Canal. It sank just two ships before the British found its hiding place in the River Rufiji's delta in German East Africa (now in Tanzania). An old ship was scuttled across the river's mouth to prevent any escape and the raider was eventually damaged by fire from two British monitors and then scuttled on 11 July 1915.

The cruiser stationed in the West Indies, *Karlsruhe*, sank three vessels in the mid-Atlantic shortly after the outbreak of war and then sailed into the South Atlantic where it netted some 14 freighters between 31 August and 14 October 1914. *Karlsruhe* then headed into the Caribbean, with the intention of hunting through the Bahamas but succumbed to an unexplained internal explosion while at anchor on 4 November.

Right: *Seeadler*, a German merchant raider, made one successful cruise beginning in December 1916 and captured 15 Allied merchant ships in the Atlantic and Pacific in 225 days.

Seeadler was a three-masted windjammer built in Scotland as the *Pass of Balmaha*.

The ship was wrecked on a reef in the South Pacific and the crew eventually interned in Chile.

The interior was modified with the addition of facilities for prisoners, better crew quarters and hidden gun positions.

The hull was built in steel by the Robert Duncan Company, Port Glasgow.

SMS *SEEADLER*

Type: Converted sailing ship
Laid down: 1888
Displacement: 1,571 tons
Crew: Not known
Speed: Variable
Main armament: 2 x 10.5cm (4.1in) guns

Armed Merchant Cruisers

Armed merchant cruisers (AMCs) were usually fast passenger liners converted for military use by being fitted with armaments. They were used by Britain, France and Germany. The British had the greatest number and their 10th Cruiser Squadron consisted of 20 AMCs that protected the sea lanes between Britain and Iceland until 1917. The Allied AMCs proved to be vulnerable both to mines and torpedoes, and losses were unacceptably high – the British lost 12 and the French 13. The survivors were mostly converted to troop transports and hospital ships from 1916.

Germany used its AMCs exclusively in the aggressive role of commerce raiding but they were largely unsuccessful. Some had brief but spectacular careers, like the fast liner *Kaiser Wilhelm der Grosse*, which sank several ships before 26 August 1914 when it was scuttled by its crew after it had been disabled by the British cruiser *Highflyer* off Spanish Morocco. A second, *Cap Trafalgar*, was sunk by a British AMC, *Carmania*, in the South Atlantic on 14 August 1914. Two others, *Prinz Eitel Friedrich* and *Kronprinz Wilhelm*, were interned by the US authorities in March and April 1915, respectively.

Armed Commerce Raiders

Auxiliary commerce raiders were essentially civilian craft fitted with hidden weapons. Germany's were often auxiliary minelayers converted to look like Scandinavian freighters, usually sailing under a neutral flag. Around ten saw service in the war and some were highly successful.

Möwe is considered the most renowned. It sank 34 merchant ships in two sorties and one of its mines sank the British pre-dreadnought battleship *King Edward VII* in January 1916.

Below: HMS *King Edward VII* sinking after hitting *Möwe*'s mine.

SMS *EMDEN*

Emden's career was brief but spectacular. During August – November 1914 it sank 18 British merchant ships, captured 5 and sank a Russian cruiser and a French destroyer. *Emden* is shown below wrecked on Direction Island after being tracked down by Allied ships.

Type: Light cruiser
Laid down: 1908
Displacement: 3,650 tons
Crew: 321
Speed: 24.5 knots
Main armament: 10 x 10.5cm (4.1in) guns

SMS *KÖNIGSBERG*

Königsberg undertook operations off the coast of East Africa, sinking just two ships, including *Pegasus*, an old British cruiser. *Königsberg* took refuge in an East African river delta and was tracked down and sunk in 1915.

Type: Light cruiser
Laid down: 1907
Displacement: 3,400 tons
Crew: 350
Speed: 23.5 knots
Main armament: 10 x 10.5cm (4.1in) guns

Germany's West African Colonies

Germany's three colonies in West Africa were only lightly defended, could expect little outside help and were largely surrounded by colonies belonging to various of the Allies so it was unsurprising that they soon fell.

Germany's appetite for building a colonial empire came rather late in the 19th century and at a time when the other leading European powers, especially Britain and France, had carved up most of the world between themselves. Thus, by the outbreak of World War I, Germany controlled only a number of island groups in the south-west Pacific, the concession port of Tsingtao in China and, most importantly, four colonies in Africa – Togoland (Togo) and Kamerun in West Africa, German South-West Africa (Namibia) and German East Africa (Burundi, Rwanda and mainland Tanganyika). The African colonies had been acquired in 1884–5 but by 1914 were only lightly garrisoned, despite having some useful port facilities and important radio stations that were capable of intercepting Allied messages and relaying them to Berlin.

Above: A South African train takes on water while carrying troops into German South-West Africa in 1915.

Below: Colonial troops like these spearheaded Britain's war effort against Togoland and Kamerun.

Allied Superiority

The German colonies were largely isolated from their motherland and were ripe for invasion, not least because they were invariably adjacent to Allied colonies that could muster greater forces. The first to come under attack were Togoland, South-West Africa and Kamerun. Togoland was largely surrounded by French-controlled Dahomey (Benin) as well as the Gold Coast (Ghana), a British possession. Togoland was defended by some 300 European troops and 1,200 locally raised *askaris* (native troops) and was the first to fall. The local general abandoned the vulnerable coast and fell back inland to the radio station at Kamina. An attack by Anglo-French troops was beaten off on 22 August 1914 but the station was destroyed on the approach of a large Allied force and the surviving German garrison surrendered four days later.

German South-West Africa was in an equally exposed position as the largely pro-British Union of South Africa lay to the south and the British Bechuanaland Protectorate (Botswana) was to the east. To the north was Angola, a colony of the then neutral but pro-British Portuguese. Although the ports of Swakopmund and Lüderitz with their radio stations were strategically important, they were soon abandoned and the colony's 9,000-strong garrison concentrated around the inland capital, Windhoek.

During 1914 there were Allied landings at Lüderitz on 19 September and Swakopmund on 25 December. South African troops were roundly beaten at Sandfontein on 26 September and it was not until

AFRICA IN 1914

The African colonies of the various belligerent powers in 1914.

1915 that the main assault began. The delay was partially due to a pro-German, anti-British revolt in South Africa by a small number of Boer nationalists that was only defeated in February 1915. One column under General Jan Christiaan Smuts pushed east out of Lüderitz and then turned north to inflict a defeat on the Germans at Gibeon on 26 April. The second column, under General Louis Botha, moved out from Swakopmund and took Windhoek on 17 May. The last detachments of the colony's garrison surrendered at Tsumeb on 9 July.

Kamerun

Despite being surrounded by Allied colonies, the garrison in Kamerun survived the longest. The Allies advanced at several points in August 1914 and took the port of Duala with its radio station in late September. The German commander retreated into the interior and in 1915 three Allied columns were sent to track him down. Progress was slow for much of the year but the fall of the town of Yuande on 1 January 1916 signalled the end. Some 800 German troops and 7,000 *askaris* fled into Rio Muni, a Spanish enclave, and the northern town of Mora, the last pocket of resistance, capitulated to Allied forces on 18 February 1916.

Below: German troops are escorted into captivity after the fall of Togoland in August 1914.

Naval War in the North Sea

There were no major clashes between the bulk of the British and German fleets during 1914 but both sides were able to claim some notable propaganda victories from actions at sea in the first months of the naval war.

At the outbreak of war the Royal Navy's main force, the Grand Fleet, took station at various bases in south-east England, eastern Scotland and the Orkneys, while the rival German High Seas Fleet concentrated at Wilhelmshaven and Kiel. Despite public expectations, neither fleet was specially keen to risk a major battle. The British did not want to see their numerical advantage reduced by mines or torpedoes, while the Germans did not want to see the disparity grow. Nevertheless, both sides were willing to undertake sorties if they might yield results out of proportion to the forces deployed.

The first significant battle of the naval war took place on 28 August. British cruisers made a sweep into German home waters in an attempt to draw out some of the Imperial German Navy's warships and lead them towards the guns of Vice-Admiral David Beatty's powerful squadron of battle-cruisers. The Battle of Heligoland Bight did not entirely go to plan as the British light cruisers ran into a more powerful force than expected. Only the arrival of Beatty's battle-cruisers saved the day. Three German light cruisers, *Ariadne*, *Köln* and *Mainz*, and a destroyer were sunk, while the British *Arethusa* was also heavily damaged.

Above: A German U-boat on patrol in the North Sea with the crew keeping watch for Allied warships.

U-boats in Action

In fear of further losses, the freedom of action of Germany's surface warships was curtailed after the battle by Emperor Wilhelm II but his ruling did not apply to the small U-boat fleet. He had authorized submarines and torpedo boats to carry out limited offensive sweeps as early as 6 August but the submariners' performance

Below: The battle-cruiser HMS *New Zealand* fought in three battles – Heligoland Bight, Dogger Bank and Jutland – and survived the war.

Below: British sailors look on as the German light cruiser *Mainz* begins to settle in the water during the Battle of Heligoland Bight in late August 1914.

Above: The British destroyer *Lurcher* (left) approaches *Mainz* to take off survivors. *Mainz* sank just one hour after being put out of action by a torpedo hit.

was not at all good. Three days after receiving permission to commence operations, *U-15* was caught on the surface of the North Sea and rammed by a British warship, *Birmingham*. The U-boats also failed to sink any of the vessels transporting the British Expeditionary Force across the English Channel in the middle two weeks of the same month.

Their performance improved somewhat in September. HMS *Pathfinder*, a cruiser, became the first major warship to fall victim to a torpedo attack in open waters when it was sighted by *U-21* in the Firth of Forth on the 5th.

This victory was soon overshadowed by a much greater feat. British warships, mainly destroyers and cruisers, were patrolling the waters of the southern North Sea as part of the campaign to protect troop transports crossing the English Channel. The patrolling destroyers had to be withdrawn due to bad weather in late September but the cruisers remained on station.

Weddigen's Triumph

On the 22nd, three elderly cruisers, *Aboukir*, *Cressy* and *Hogue*, were spotted by Captain Otto Weddigen's *U-9* as they sailed slowly north along the coast of Holland. *Aboukir* was torpedoed first and sank within 30 minutes. The other cruisers' captains foolishly stood by to rescue survivors and each ship was torpedoed in turn. The loss of three obsolete warships did not significantly upset the naval balance in the North Sea but the sinkings and the death of some 1,400 sailors at the hands of a submarine shocked the British public. It also troubled the admirals of the Royal Navy and they immediately instigated much more stringent anti-submarine procedures.

U-9's success showed sceptics in the German Navy what U-boats were capable of, but there was still much to prove. The boats were not yet the great hunters of merchant ships that they would later become. By year's end 100 Allied or neutral freighters had been sunk but only four by U-boats. Five U-boats had been lost.

CAPTURING GERMANY'S NAVAL CODES

This was one of the most valuable gifts to fall into the hands of British intelligence during the war. The German cruiser *Magdeburg* ran aground in the Gulf of Finland on 26 August 1914. It was shelled by two Russian warships and boarded. The boarders seized code-books and cipher tables and these reached the British by mid-October. *Magdeburg* was scuttled and the German Navy, believing the books and tables had gone down with it, made no alterations to their codes. They remained unaware of their loss until 1918.

Anti-submarine Barriers

Britain struggled to fight German U-boats in the early days of the war. Barriers of steel-net mesh were moored to the seabed in the hope of entangling the U-boats, while mines and fast warships were used to blow up the boats.

No ship-mounted weapons were capable of sinking submerged submarines when war broke out in August 1914. The British, who had the most to fear from submarines, soon began building maritime net barriers, commonly referred to as barrages. These either forced submarines to the surface, where they could be tackled by naval gunfire or rammed by warships, or left them at the mercy of tethered mines positioned with the nets. Perhaps the most successful barrages were those developed to prevent German U-boats from reaching their hunting grounds in the eastern Atlantic by way of the English Channel or through the North Sea. All U-boats had to pass through these areas on their journeys between their patrol areas and their home bases in occupied Belgium and in Germany itself.

Above: A mine of the type used in the Allied North Sea barrage built during 1918.

Blocking the Channel

The British first built a barrage between Dover and the Belgian coast to prevent attacks on their troopships crossing to France in August 1914. This initial effort was deemed inadequate and a 25km (15.5 mile) barrage stretching between Dover and Ostend was begun the following February. The line comprised indicator nets – lengths of steel mesh up to 100m (110yds) long that were positioned by drifters, set at various depths and moored to the seabed. Any U-boat that became entangled in one would either have to surface or drag the netting and its easily identifiable surface buoys away with it. The drifters were in radio contact with fast warships that could then be directed to the target and tackle the submarine with gunfire or by ramming when it had to surface for air.

Below: A German U-boat at sea. This is the *U-9* which sank three elderly British cruisers off the Dutch coast on 22 September 1914.

Right: A British depth charge explodes during a hunt for a U-boat. Aggressive countermeasures would ultimately prove superior to the passive anti-submarine barriers.

The system, which gradually became more and more extensive and began to incorporate mines, was far from foolproof. The early contact mines were unreliable, while U-boat captains were often able to avoid the nets by travelling on the surface at night. The Dover Barrage did have its successes. U-boats were briefly prohibited from passing through the Channel for 12 months after April 1915, while better mines, more frequent night patrols and searchlights all played their part in improving the barrage. At least 12 submarines were lost in the barrage and the U-boats finally ceased using the Channel route in August 1918.

The route into the North Atlantic by way of the North Sea was not tackled until mid-July 1917. The building of a huge barrage between the Orkneys and the Norwegian coast was largely the brainchild of an American naval officer, Admiral Henry Mayo. He successfully argued that his country's new magnetic mine, which exploded when a submarine entered its magnetic field rather than needing direct contact, was appropriate for the task. The mine-laying took place during June–October 1918 and it was largely undertaken by US crews, who laid more than 80 per cent of the 69,000 mines deployed. Yet for all that effort only three U-boats were confirmed sunk in the minefields.

Otranto Barrage

The third great Allied barrage was built in the Mediterranean as a way of preventing Austro-Hungarian and German surface warships and submarines from entering the sea from their bases in the northern and eastern Adriatic. It stretched across the Strait of Otranto from the heel of Italy to Valona (Vlorë) in Albania. Construction of the barrage began in late 1915 but the 100km (60 miles) of anti-submarine nets patrolled by numbers of warships were never wholly secure and only one U-boat was destroyed.

Right: An aerial photograph of the anti-submarine barrage at Scapa Flow in the Orkneys, the Royal Navy's most important base and home of the bulk of the Grand Fleet.

Coronel and the Falklands

The fortunes of the German and British naval squadrons operating in the South Atlantic and south-east Pacific swung dramatically in 1914 with the British eventually emerging victorious after the Battle of the Falklands.

At the outbreak of war the greater part of the Imperial Germany Navy was based in home waters, but a handful of warships were overseas. Among these were various cruisers, armed merchant cruisers and auxiliary commerce raiders poised to attack Allied shipping and the small Mediterranean Squadron based at Pola (Pula). The largest and most powerful force was Admiral Maximilian von Spee's East Asiatic Squadron based at Tsingtao in China. Spee's squadron comprised two armoured cruisers, *Gneisenau* and *Scharnhorst*, five light cruisers, *Dresden*, *Emden*, *Königsberg*, *Leipzig* and *Nürnberg*, and various support ships. Spee's orders were to cruise the Pacific, attacking British shipping for as long as possible before eventually heading back to Germany.

Commerce Raiding

Spee's light cruisers operated independently during the first two months of the war, making use of Germany's Pacific island colonies for resupply, radio intelligence of possible targets and news of the 30 or so Allied warships hunting them. The *Emden* and *Königsberg* continued their commerce-raiding cruises until sunk in November 1914 and July 1915, respectively, but the remainder of the squadron reunited at Easter Island between 12 and 18 October 1914. They then headed for the west coast of South America. British intelligence identified their general position in the south-east Pacific and the task of destroying Spee was given to the warships of Rear-Admiral Christopher Cradock's South American Squadron based in the Falklands Islands.

Battle of Coronel

Cradock took into action two armoured cruisers, *Good Hope* and *Monmouth*, the light cruiser *Glasgow*, and an armed liner, *Otranto*. With the exception of *Glasgow* his squadron was older, slower and wholly outgunned. The two squadrons finally met off Coronel, a Chilean port, late

Below: The German light cruiser *Leipzig* succumbs to fire from the British armoured cruiser *Cornwall* during the Battle of the Falklands.

Above: The Battle of Coronel on 1 November 1914 saw a weak British squadron outclassed by Germany's East Asiatic Squadron.

Above: Vice-Admiral Frederick Doveton Sturdee (1859–1925) led the victorious British squadron during the Battle of the Falklands.

on 1 November. *Otranto* was ordered away immediately but Cradock tried to bring his other ships into action even though they were outranged. It took just 40 minutes to reduce *Good Hope* and *Monmouth* to blazing wrecks that quickly sank with all hands. *Glasgow* was struck five times but escaped. Spee's ships were undamaged.

Once Cradock's fate became known back in Britain, there was a public outcry and the press demanded that those responsible for the defeat be sacked. First Lord of the Admiralty Winston Churchill, the political head of the Royal Navy, and the military head, Admiral Prince Louis of Battenberg, were targeted. Churchill survived but German-born Battenberg, who had to endure particularly vitriolic attacks because of his background, did not. He was replaced by Admiral John Fisher.

Revenge on Spee

The British sent a powerful task force to the Falklands, including the battle-cruisers *Inflexible* and *Invincible*, two armoured cruisers, three light cruisers, including the *Glasgow*, and an armed merchant cruiser. Spee, unaware of their presence, approached Port Stanley in the Falklands at dawn on 8 December intending to destroy its facilities. The British squadron under Vice-Admiral Sturdee sailed out to meet him. Spee was outgunned and his warships slower so he tried to manoeuvre his way out of trouble but British fire finally told. *Scharnhorst* and *Gneisenau* were sunk first, followed by *Nürnberg* and *Leipzig*. *Dresden* escaped but was scuttled three months later. The East Asiatic Squadron ceased to exist.

ADMIRAL MAXIMILIAN VON SPEE

Spee (1861–1914) was a career admiral in the Imperial German Navy and commanded its powerful East Asiatic Squadron at the outbreak of war. He was widely thought of as one of his country's finest admirals and his command was equally highly regarded, the ships having won several pre-war gunnery contests. Spee was based in China, a long way from home, and was eventually hunted down by the British after his victory at Coronel. He and his two sons were killed at the Battle of the Falklands in December 1914 when most of the ships of his squadron were sunk.

Above: A formal portrait of Admiral Maximilian von Spee.

Battle-cruisers

Inspired by Admiral Fisher, the Royal Navy developed battle-cruisers in what proved to be a rather flawed attempt to create a new class of warship that was armed like a dreadnought battleship but had the greater speed of a cruiser.

Although cruisers were a long-established type of warship by the outbreak of World War I, the larger battle-cruisers were a relatively new concept and had not been tested in action. The idea came from the fertile brain of Britain's Admiral John Fisher, who was also responsible for the powerful dreadnought type of battleship. Fisher wanted a class of warships that could act independently, or form the nucleus of a detached squadron, or work in conjunction with the main battlefleet of dreadnoughts. In this last mission, battle-cruisers were to act in the scouting and reconnaissance role, seeking out the enemy's main fleet and reporting back on its position. Their heavy armament, which was comparable to that of a dreadnought, meant that they could destroy smaller warships, while their high speed meant they could outrun bigger opponents. Battle-cruisers were originally known as fast armoured cruisers but took on their more common name in 1912.

Below: A close-up of one of the turrets of the British battle-cruiser *Tiger* – an early attempt to provide the warship with a means of aerial reconnaissance and firepower.

First Battle-cruisers

Britain launched its first three battle-cruisers, HMS *Invincible*, *Indomitable* and *Inflexible*, during 1909. These, and a second group of three, carried eight 12in (305mm) guns (dreadnoughts mostly had ten) and displaced 17,250 tons. Later classes carried larger guns. *Renown* and *Repulse*, launched in 1916, each had six 15in (380mm) guns. The Royal Navy had most battle-cruisers with 12 built in 1908–17. Only Germany and Japan copied the design and had them available in 1914.

Battle-cruisers did have successes. *Invincible* and *Inflexible* sank two less-powerful German armoured cruisers during the Battle of the Falklands in late 1914, while on detached service from the main battlefleet. Germany's own battle-cruisers also enjoyed some successes while acting independently, not least when they severely dented the British public's faith in the Royal Navy by bombarding a number of towns on Britain's east coast. Yet these victories

HMS *TIGER*

Class: Only ship of its type
Laid down: 1912
Displacement: 28,500 tons
Crew: 1,185
Speed: 30 knots
Main armament: 8 x 13.5in (343mm) guns

masked some serious technical and design shortcomings, especially in Britain's battle-cruisers, that were only fully exposed in larger fleet actions.

Part of the problem was that their name was perhaps misinterpreted by some officers and led them to believe mistakenly that battle-cruisers could take their place in the main line of battle. Their armament suggested they could take on similarly armed battle-cruisers or dreadnoughts but their armour, which had been reduced to give them their higher speed, actually meant that they could not stand punishment from the heavy guns carried by either.

SMS *DERFFLINGER*

SMS *Derfflinger* was completed in mid-1914 and took part in raids along the east coast of England and the Battle of the Dogger Bank in early 1915 before being badly damaged during the Battle of Jutland in 1916.

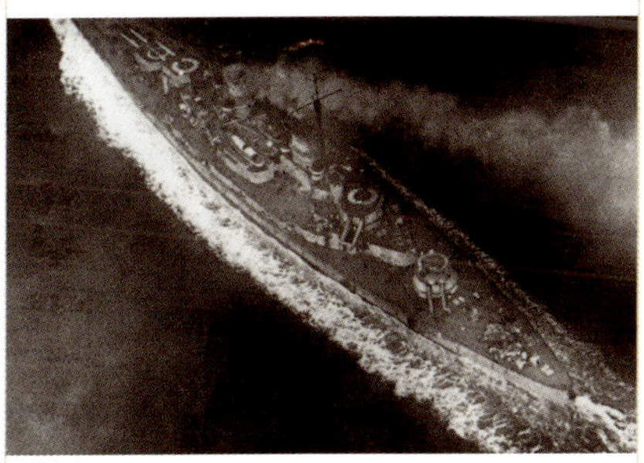

Sister ships: *Hindenburg, Lützow*
Laid down: 1912
Displacement: 28,000 tons
Crew: 1,112
Speed: 28 knots
Main armament: 8 x 30.5cm (12in) guns

SMS *GOEBEN*

Goeben was handed over to the Turkish Navy in August 1914, although still German-crewed. It operated in the Black Sea against Russia and later in the Mediterranean. Damaged by mines in January 1918, it spent the rest of the war in dry dock.

Sister ship: *Moltke*
Laid down: 1909
Displacement: 22,640 tons
Crew: 1,053
Speed: 29 knots
Main armament: 10 x 28cm (11in) guns

Problems in Action

The Battle of Jutland in May 1916 revealed the truth. Three British battle-cruisers, *Invincible*, *Indefatigable* and *Queen Mary*, were sent to the bottom in quick time, blown apart in an instant by single salvoes of shells. The shells easily penetrated their overly thin armour and then exploded causing a fire that detonated ammunition that was being stored incorrectly. Germany's own battle-cruiser squadron did not escape without loss or damage either. The *Lützow* was sunk and all of the other ships were hit repeatedly, not least the *Seydlitz*, yet all reached their home port. Their survival was partly due to luck, but also to good seamanship and design precautions to prevent secondary internal explosions during the heat of battle. Neither Britain nor Germany lost any more battle-cruisers during World War I. Their vulnerability was clear to all but the growth of naval aviation gradually removed the need for them to act in the reconnaissance role for the main battlefleet.

SMS *SEYDLITZ*

Class: Only ship of its type
Laid down: 1911
Displacement: 25,000 tons
Crew: 1,068
Speed: 30 knots
Main armament: 10 x 28cm (11in) guns

The Caucasus Front 1914–16 Wounded Turkish soldiers taken prisoner by the Russians.

Zeppelins A group of German airships sets out on a bombing mission to England.

Winter Offensive Against Russia Troops of the Russian Army march off to the front.

1915 – TRENCH WARFARE

The year opened with both sides confident that victory could still be achieved. The German High Command opted to go on the defensive in the west and strike eastward against Russia, in part because Austria-Hungary was proving a very poor ally. France and Britain would be attacked indirectly at sea by Germany's increasingly important U-boats. The Allies, joined by Italy in May, had a far from clear-cut war plan. The French were wedded to evicting the Germans from their home soil and determined to launch a series of offensives on the Western Front. The British could offer little help as their small army had been virtually destroyed in 1914.

The British were split on where to deploy their meagre resources. Most generals saw the Western Front as the decisive theatre but some politicians, appalled by the blood-letting of 1914, argued for an indirect strategy against the weaker Central Powers. The defeat of Austria-Hungary, Bulgaria or Turkey would, they argued, bring about the collapse of Germany. The Allies opened up a number of subsidiary battlegrounds, chiefly on the Gallipoli Peninsula, in Palestine and in Mesopotamia (Iraq) and forces were also poured into Salonika in the south Balkans to confront the various Central Powers.

Home Fronts British women at work on a farm having taken over jobs done by men now in the army.

Four Battles Along the Isonzo Italian Bersaglieri ready for action on the Isonzo front.

Pre-Dreadnought Battleships The French ship *Suffren* served in the Dardanelles.

The Second Battle of Ypres

The German Army deployed gas on a large scale for the first time in spring 1915 against the Allied positions around the Belgian town of Ypres in an attempt to eradicate a salient and test the new weapon's capabilities.

Germany's military leaders had decided to concentrate on knocking Russia out of the war during 1915 and were content to remain largely on the defensive on the Western Front. However, the high command's Chief of Staff, General von Falkenhayn, gave permission for a limited spoiling offensive in mid-spring when it was discovered that the British and French were preparing another major attack, even though they had only recently closed down two efforts – the British-led Battle of Neuve Chapelle (10–13 March) and the French Army's Battle of the Woëvre (6–15 April). The German target was Ypres, scene of heavy fighting in late 1914 that had left an Allied-held salient in the German line to the east of the Belgian town. The main German aims were to clear the salient, taking high ground that would give their troops a local advantage, and to test the effectiveness in action of the newly developed but untried chlorine gas.

KEY FACTS

Date: 22 April – 25 May 1915

Place: Ypres, south-west Belgium

Outcome: Germany s only major attack on the Western Front in 1915 reduced the Ypres salient by two-thirds.

Below: The badly damaged centre of Ypres pictured in early 1915 after several months of bombardment.

Gas Attack

The fighting was left to the German Fourth Army under Duke Albrecht of Württemberg. The action opened on 22 April with a brief artillery barrage. When that ended, the chlorine gas was released from its canisters and drifted over a section of trench north of the town held by French and Algerian troops. Soon many were dying in great pain, unable to breathe. They were completely unprepared for this new threat and fled in terror, leaving a large hole in the defences. The German assault troops were wearing an early form of gas mask and had advanced some 3.2km (2 miles) by the next day but thereafter were halted by counter-attacks from units of General Smith-Dorrien's British Second Army.

New Attacks

This brought only a temporary respite to the Allies and the Germans attacked again on the 24th, but this time against Canadian troops to the north-east of the city. The fighting quickly spread along most of the east and south-east of the salient as far as Hill 60. Smith-Dorrien believed that further attempts to regain the lost ground would be futile and costly in lives so he requested permission for a general withdrawal to better,

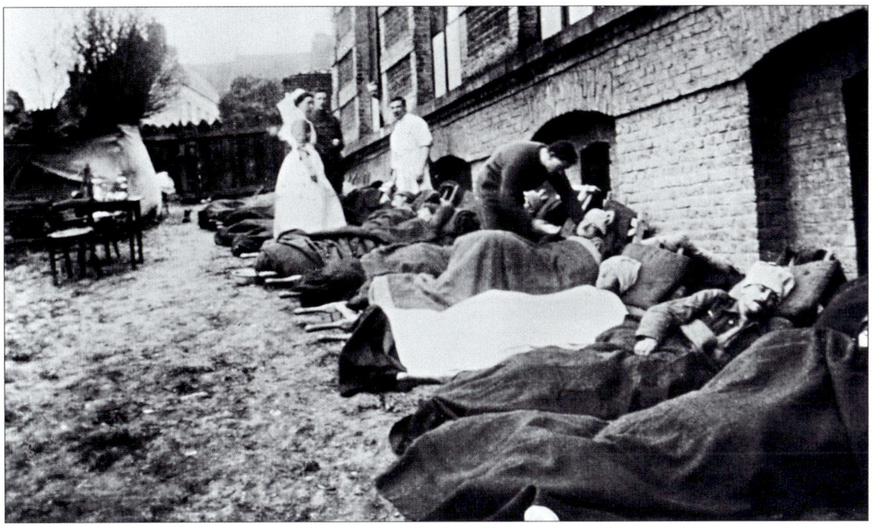

Above: Medical staff tend the wounded, just a few of the 60,000 casualties that the British forces suffered in the battle.

more defensible ground nearer Ypres. This was refused by the BEF's commander, Field Marshal French, and Smith-Dorrien was replaced by General Herbert Plumer. He, too, urged withdrawal and his plan was eventually accepted, but not until a French counter-attack had failed on 29 April. The realignment took place in early May but fighting and gas attacks continued to the 25th.

Duke Albrecht's increasingly exhausted troops did gain some more ground during these final weeks of battle, particularly between 8 and 14 May, and this left them in possession of a line of high ground not much more than 3.2km (2 miles) outside Ypres from where they now looked down on the battered town and would do so until the Battle of Passchendaele in 1917.

In a month or so of fighting the Germans had captured around two-thirds of the salient and inflicted some 60,000 casualties on the British and 10,000 on the French. The German Fourth Army, which had lost some 35,000 men, was exhausted and lacked the manpower to continue offensive operations but its artillery began methodically to raze what remained of Ypres to the ground, making life a misery for the Anglo-French troops left holding the now reduced salient.

Below: A panoramic view of a much fought-over sector of the Ypres battlefield known as Hill 60.

THE DANGER OF SALIENTS

Salients, whether big or small bulges in the front line, were a tricky prospect for both attacking and defending forces. Troops holding a bulge that pushed into an enemy's line could be fired on from the front and both sides of the salient, while attacking troops often found they had punched a salient into the defenders' line and thus came under crossfire. The most infamous salient of the war was that around Ypres, which was formed in late 1914 and not fully eradicated until 1918.

Right: Men of 1st Australian Division in a trench near Gheluvelt, Ypres Salient, 20 September 1917.

Gas Warfare

Gas was deployed in considerable quantities during the war by most of the combatant nations and, although it became lethal and could produce truly horrible injuries, it was never a war-winning weapon.

Gas had been considered as a weapon before the outbreak of war but there was a general consensus that it was wholly "uncivilized". Yet all that changed with trench warfare, a development that sparked a wide-ranging search for technologies that could break the deadlock. Gas became acceptable and the types used changed from mere irritants with only short-term medical impact to ones with almost immediate lethality. Most were not long-lasting on the battlefield but a few were.

First Uses

The Germans were the first to use gas on the battlefield close to Neuve Chapelle on the Western Front in October 1914 and next in January 1915 near Bolimov on the Eastern Front.

Above: British artillerymen pose for a photograph while preparing gas shells for use.

The amount of gas used was small and the results were not promising. At Neuve Chapelle the small quantity of the irritant gas released was not noticed by the targeted French troops while at Bolimov the xylyl bromide, a form of tear gas, froze due to the cold weather and therefore did not disperse. Nevertheless, the Germans persevered and introduced much more dangerous gases and these did have a significant effect.

Chlorine gas, which destroys the respiratory organs in a few seconds, was used to devastating effect during the Second Battle of Ypres in April 1915.

In the war as a whole Germany was the greatest user of gas (68,000 tonnes), while France manufactured 37,000 tonnes and Britain 25,000 tonnes.

Below: German stormtroopers undergo realistic training by advancing through a cloud of gas.

Left: British troops blinded by gas in April 1918 await medical treatment and evacuation to the rear.

Below: Three early respirators, including a German Rahmenmaske (framework mask) and its carrying can (left).

Types of Gas

The most widely used types were the aforementioned chlorine gas and the almost odourless mustard gas, a slow-acting agent that causes internal and external bleeding and vomiting and frequently leads to death. Some proponents of gas warfare concluded that lethality was neither necessary nor desirable. They reasoned that gas casualties who survived with considerable infirmity were a constant drain on medical facilities and detrimental to enemy morale in the long term.

Gas was dispersed in two ways. It was released in vapour form by fixed canisters positioned in or near the front line, a technique that wholly relied on the wind blowing in the right direction and one that meant that gas was effectively a short-range weapon. Artillery shells filled with an agent in liquid form that evaporated after a small explosive charge burst the shell open were widely used from 1916. Gas was also put in high-explosive rounds in small quantities for a "mixed" effect. Artillery shells gave gas greater range and much better accuracy, but some problems still remained insoluble.

Gas was not a truly effective weapon as it needed a long list of ideal conditions. It often failed due to adverse weather, especially the strength and direction of the prevailing wind and the temperature. It was quite common for gas to be blown back into the attackers' faces by contrary winds.

All sides quickly developed gas masks and these became more and more sophisticated. Early ones consisted of thick cotton pads soaked in bicarbonate of soda, to cover the mouth and nose, and separate goggles, but these gave way in all armies to the more familiar combined mask and respirator types. Filters were usually filled with charcoal or chemicals to neutralize the gas.

Below: Both men and animals needed protection against gas attack. The British Army began issuing horse respirators in 1916.

The Second Battle of Artois

The French Commander-in-Chief, Marshal Joffre, launched a major offensive in Artois to drive the Germans from French soil but, despite some early successes, the fighting soon became stalemated and a breakthrough never materialized.

Even as the Second Battle of Ypres was being fought to a conclusion, Marshal Joseph Joffre, the French Commander-in-Chief, launched yet another major offensive with the intention of making a decisive breakthrough. His chosen battlefield was in Artois.

British Attacks

The British First Army under General Douglas Haig was first committed either side of Neuve Chapelle with the aim of pushing Crown Prince Rupprecht's Sixth Army beyond Aubers Ridge and Lille. The attack, the Battle of Aubers Ridge, opened on 9 May and was heralded by a mere 40-minute preliminary bombardment due to a shortage of shells. When the British infantry advanced, they found the German trenches largely undamaged and an alert enemy waiting. Haig called off the attack and the fighting ended next day with the British losing around 11,500 men.

The British tried again on the night of the 15th after Joffre had requested a further effort. This time Haig struck to the south of Neuve Chapelle. This attack, the Battle of Festubert, was preceded by a four-day barrage and did make some initial progress before becoming bogged down. The battle was halted on the 25th by which time the Sixth Army was driven back a mere 730m (800yds) at a cost of some 16,500 casualties. The German losses were around 5,800 men.

Joffre unleashed General Auguste Dubail's Tenth Army on 9 May after a four-day bombardment from more than 1,000 guns had fired 690,000 shells on the German trenches. The main effort took place between Arras and Lens on a 10km (6 mile) front approaching Vimy Ridge, a commanding piece of high ground. A corps in the centre led by General Philippe Pétain broke through and made 5km (3 miles) in the first 90 minutes but that was the high point of the attack. A lack of reserves and the prompt arrival of German reinforcements prevented any further exploitation

KEY FACTS

Date: 9 May – 18 June 1915

Place: Artois region of north-eastern France between Arras and Lille

Outcome: The French-led attack ended in failure and heavy casualties.

Right: The crew of a French heavy mortar pose for a photograph in their artillery emplacement.

Below: The devastation produced by increasing artillery bombardments, near Festubert, March 1915.

Above: A somewhat bizarre remedy to one of the more common problems encountered in trench warfare – a rowing boat used to overcome flooding.

of Pétain's gains. Heavy but inconclusive fighting continued until the 15th and briefly flared again between 15 and 19 June but to no great advantage for either side. The battle officially ended on the 30th by which time French casualties had reached around 100,000 men.

SHELL SCANDAL

The shortage of ammunition for Haig's artillery had wider political repercussions. The Liberal government of Prime Minister Herbert Asquith had seriously underestimated the volume of war supplies needed by the British Army at a time when it was expanding rapidly and had not undertaken sufficient measures to ensure that the country's economy was up to the job being asked of it. Matters reached a crisis point on 14 May when a report in *The Times* newspaper bluntly stated that the initial failure at Aubers Ridge was due to a serious lack of high-explosive shells.

The article had, in fact, been sanctioned by a powerful anti-Asquith cabal that included the newspaper's influential owner, Lord Northcliffe, various senior politicians and commanders on the Western Front. The "Shell Scandal" seriously damaged the prime minister's position and he was forced to form a coalition government, largely composed of leading Liberals and Conservatives but with one socialist member. Ammunition supply now became the responsibility of the new Ministry of Munitions which was placed under the dynamic Liberal cabinet member David Lloyd George, who had himself been one of the leading anti-Asquith conspirators.

DEFENCE IN DEPTH

This was a battle tactic developed by the Germans but later adopted by the British though not always by the French. Most defenders in the front line would pull back to prepared positions during the opening stages of an enemy offensive and then launch counter-attacks once the latter had pushed beyond their largely static artillery cover and become increasingly immobile. The tactic proved effective against the Allied offensives of 1916 and 1917 but ultimately could not prevent the defenders from suffering losses comparable to those of the attackers.

Below: A French infantry detachment takes much-needed water up to the front during a lull in the Artois fighting.

Trench Systems

Trench warfare developed on the Western Front in late 1914 and, although types of trenches varied considerably largely due to the impact of the local terrain, they became progressively deeper, wider and more complex as the war continued.

Trench systems were to some extent a reflection of local conditions, and the continuous lines most associated with the war were by no means their only form. In very mountainous terrain, as on much of the Italian Front or, indeed, in the Vosges region of France, the lines were generally less complete and might consist of a series of mutually supporting mountain-top strong-points. Not all trench systems were below ground but might rather be built up. This could be because the bedrock was near the surface and too difficult to dig through or the water table might be too near the surface so that sunken trenches would be waterlogged. This was true especially on the most northerly part of the Western Front in Belgium, where there was a high water table and the Belgians had deliberately flooded much of the low-lying area near the coast in 1914.

Trenches evolved as the war progressed. They were originally little more than connected scrapes in the ground and not designed for permanent occupation but, once the fronts had become static in late 1914, the defence systems became deeper and more complex. The Germans – probably the most skilled exponents of trench building – began digging second trench lines from late 1915 and a third was added thereafter.

Below: Trench systems everywhere were plagued by rats and hunting them down was a task performed on a regular basis by all sides.

Trench Layouts

The most typical type of system consisted of three lines about 730m (800yds) apart connected by communication trenches. The first line, the one nearest the enemy, was the fire trench, the main line of resistance; the second was the support trench; and the third was the reserve. All trenches usually zigzagged or had angular firebays to minimize the impact of shellfire and prevent an enemy from firing directly down them. Dugouts, either deep underground or just shelters cut into the trench sides, were constructed to give troops even greater shelter and a measure of comfort. Sandbags were added for more protection, wooden shoring placed to prevent the sides from collapsing, and duckboards laid to aid drainage. Repair work to dugouts was needed on an almost constant basis.

Deeper Defences

Although this system held good for much of the war, it did change and the lines became more complex from 1916 onward, when the Germans adopted "defence in depth". The line nearest the enemy consisted of relatively modest defensive outposts – strong-points based on large shell-holes or prefabricated concrete pill-boxes – that were not designed to stop an enemy advance but rather delay him or channel him into more exposed "killing zones". Next, up to 1.5km (1 mile) away, came the front line. Again this was not necessarily continuous but a system

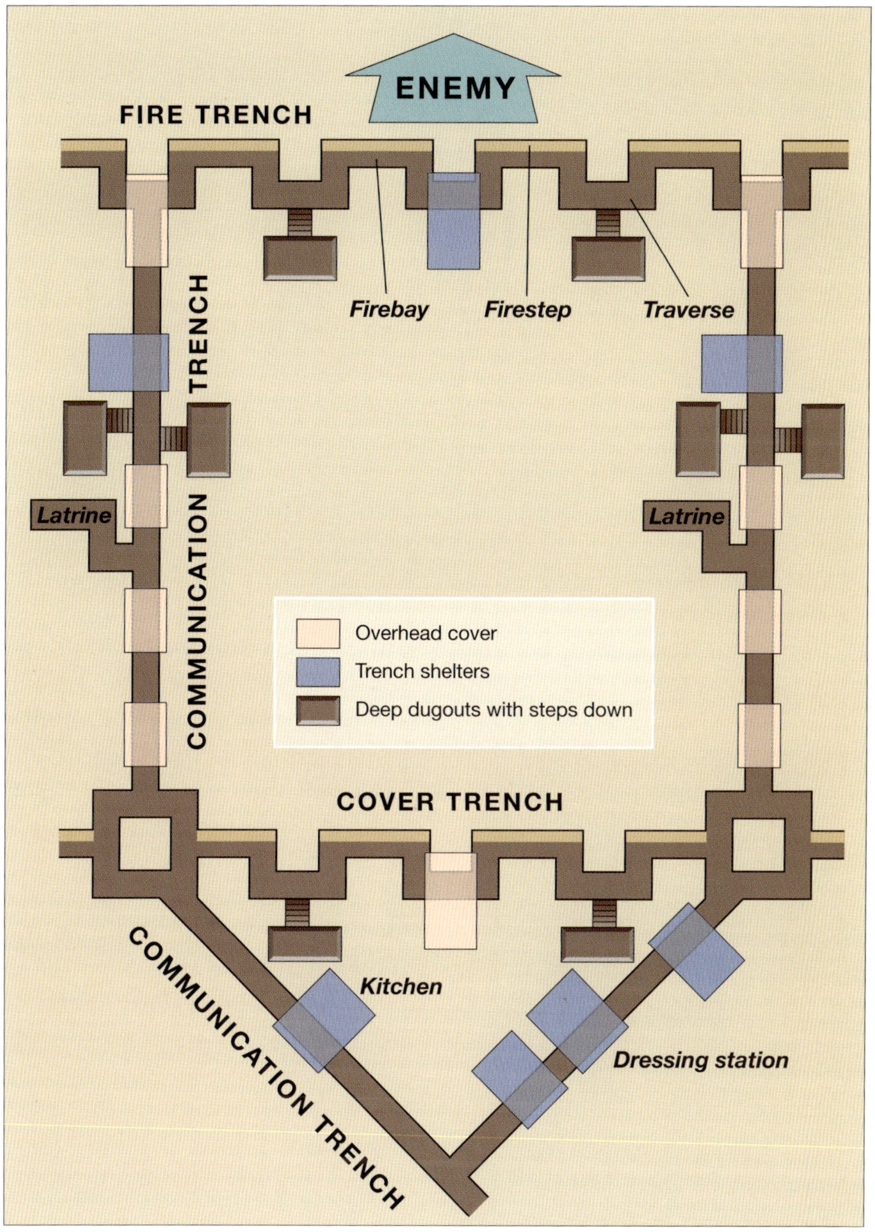

A TYPICAL TRENCH SYSTEM A standard three-line trench system of the sort used on every war front.

SAPPING

This was a technique used to approach an enemy position without being exposed to fire. Small, narrow trenches, or "saps", were first dug out into No Man's Land and at a certain point the diggers would turn towards each other, thus creating a new trench line. Individual saps were also used as listening posts, particularly by the British who had a philosophy of dominating No Man's Land. Sapping was a tried-and-trusted technique but it was extremely slow and involved much back-breaking work.

The most formidable example of defence in depth was the Hindenburg Line, which ran along the northern and central sector of the Western Front. It was begun in September 1916 and was still under construction in late 1918. It actually comprised a number of large, mutually supporting fortified positions that had a depth of up to 16km (10 miles).

of mutually supporting strong-points that could be fired into from the rear if captured. Next came what was known as the "battle zone", an area perhaps 2km (1.2 miles) wide that consisted of a maze of short trenches and numerous strong-points capable of all-round defence. Behind this was the beginning of the "reserve zone" which might include yet more defensive trench systems and hold prepared emplacements for the artillery.

Below: Some of the dense rows of barbed war that protected the German Hindenburg Line.

Battles in Champagne and Artois

This action by the British Expeditionary Force was part of a joint Anglo-French offensive in late 1915. It made progress at first but was soon halted by a lack of reinforcements and several German counter-attacks.

In autumn 1915 the French Commander-in-Chief, Marshal Joseph Joffre, launched another attempt to crack open the Western Front with both his own expanded forces and Field Marshal French's reinforced BEF. The great effort comprised two simultaneous but geographically separate attacks. The first, known as the Second Battle of Champagne, involved 500,000 French troops attacking on a 16km (10 mile) front in the Argonne area of eastern France. Joffre enjoyed a three-to-one superiority in manpower and the offensive commenced on 25 September after a four-day preliminary bombardment from 2,500 guns. The outnumbered Germans held the high ground and had been forewarned of the offensive. Consequently, the attack made little progress in the first critical days and, despite two attempts to regain the momentum over the following weeks, the battle ended in stalemate on 6 November. The French recorded some 144,000 casualties in the fighting, while the Germans suffered 85,000.

KEY FACTS – LOOS

Date: 25 September – 16 October 1915

Place: Loos, north-eastern France

Outcome: Superior German defensive tactics defeated the British offensive.

Above: German prisoners captured by French forces during the Second Battle of Champagne.

The second of Joffre's attacks was a joint Anglo-French affair in the Artois region in the north-east. The French forces engaged in the Third Battle of Artois were largely assigned to capture Vimy Ridge, a piece of crucial high ground that dominated the low-lying plains around Arras. General Dubail's Tenth Army pushed forward on 25 September and soon ran into trouble against the ridge's formidable defensive system which was manned by units from Crown Prince Rupprecht's Sixth Army. Casualties were extremely high. One division did manage to claw its way to the summit on the 29th but this brief success was not matched elsewhere. The attacks continued fitfully due to periods of awful weather but the Third Battle of Artois ended in early November.

Battle of Loos

The British pincer of this two-pronged effort in the north-east was directed against Loos. Six divisions of General Douglas Haig's First Army advanced on 25 September and made some progress against numerically inferior opponents on the first day, especially on the northern

Left: A typical scene of devastation on the Artois battlefield during 1915.

Above: A contemporary artist's view of Scottish troops charging the German defences at Loos.

flank. Despite difficult going and the ongoing shell shortage that had been plaguing the British for months, Loos was captured and troops were on its far outskirts before problems began to arise. Much to Haig's fury, the BEF's increasingly indecisive and demoralized commander withheld much-needed reserves and there were immense difficulties in getting vital supplies to the leading units. The British were forced back by strong German counter-attacks the next day and did not regain any momentum until early October. However, they had suffered heavy losses for precious little gain and thereafter bad weather so blighted the battle that it was finally called off on the 8th.

THE FIGHTING IN 1915

By the end of 1915 the Western Front had hardly moved, despite the series of Anglo-French offensives in Artois and elsewhere. Casualties had been high on all sides. The Artois and Loos fighting between September and November had cost the French around 48,000 casualties and the British some 60,000. German losses were less than half the total Allied figure, a statistic that reflected the undoubted dominance of the defence over attack. Total Western Front casualties for 1915 were enormous – 960,000 French, 295,000 British and approximately 650,000 German soldiers had been killed, wounded or taken prisoner. This scale of loss impacted on the British command structure and Haig replaced French as the BEF's commander-in-chief in December. Joffre was also being criticized for the costly failure of his offensives.

FIELD MARSHAL JOHN FRENCH

French (1852–1925) was a cavalry officer who was made Commander of the British Expeditionary Force at the outbreak of war. He was under orders to keep his command intact but was not really up to the task. French's mood swings were notoriously bad; he was often seized by doubt and rarely showed any drive. He was also unable to establish a working relationship with the French High Command and even with some of his own officers. He was dismissed in December 1915 after mismanaging the Battle of Loos.

Below: A panoramic view of the Loos battlefield. The various trench lines can be identified by white lines of material dug out to form them.

Early Fighters

The idea of arming aircraft to shoot down other aircraft only truly evolved in the first months of World War I, when it was soon recognized by air power advocates that reconnaissance aircraft were a vital weapon in modern warfare.

There were no purpose-built fighter aircraft in existence in 1914 but they were quickly developed once the trenches had been dug. Their first roles were to protect the increasingly important reconnaissance aircraft that had taken the place of redundant cavalry and to shoot down those of the enemy.

The earliest types, some of them monoplanes but mostly biplanes, were usually conversions of two-seater reconnaissance aircraft that had been fitted with a single machine-gun operated by the observer from the rear of the cockpit. The chief problem was that the machine-gun was easiest to aim when firing forward but most aircraft were of the "tractor" type. The propeller was at the front of the fuselage and there was no means of firing through its arc without shooting the wood to bits.

FOKKER E-TYPES

These German Army Air Service aircraft were designed by the Dutchman Antony Fokker and are regarded as the first true fighters. They saw action from mid-1915 and took a terrible toll of Anglo-French machines until spring 1916.

TYPE: E-III monoplane fighter
ENGINE: 100hp Oberursel
CREW: 1
CEILING: 3,650m (12,000ft)
TOP SPEED: 140kph (85mph)
ARMAMENT: 1 or 2 x 8mm (0.315in) machine-gun(s)

Pusher Fighters

There was one exception: "pusher" aircraft had the propeller to the rear with the crew positioned at the front, but such aircraft had a much poorer performance. The British Vickers FB-5, which made its appearance in July 1915, was of this type but its top speed of 112kph (70mph) was not especially impressive.

Deflector Gear

A French pilot, Roland Garros, came up with a solution to the tractor problem. In March 1915 he fitted steel plates to the propeller of a Morane-Saulnier L Parasol, a two-seater monoplane, so that bullets would be deflected away without causing damage. France's first dedicated fighter, the Morane-Saulnier N Scout, appeared shortly thereafter. This "deflector gear" gave the Allies an edge in the race to develop better fighters but this advantage was soon lost.

MAX IMMELMANN

Immelmann was one of the first *Experten* (or "aces") of the German Army Air Service. He shot down 15 Allied aircraft before his death in June 1916. He invented the Immelmann turn, an aerobatic manoeuvre still used by pilots. This is a combined backward loop and roll that can allow a fighter pilot who is being pursued to turn the tables on his pursuer.

Above: Max Immelmann, the "Eagle of Lille", one of the first fighter aces, who became a popular hero in Germany.

MORANE-SAULNIER TYPE N

This French fighter made its debut in late 1914 and was one of the first true fighters on the Western Front. Early models were fitted with deflector gear but later models carried the more advanced interrupter gear. It also saw service with Britain (as shown) and Russia.

Engine: 80/110hp Le Rhône
Crew: 1
Ceiling: 4,000m (13,100ft)
Top speed: 160kph (100mph)
Armament: 1 x 8mm (0.315in) machine-gun

The Germans captured an example of the deflector gear in April 1915 and set about making a better version. Fokker, a Dutch company, came up with interrupter gear, a device that prevented a machine-gun from firing when a propeller blade passed immediately in front of its barrel. It was first tried out on the Fokker E-I monoplane and it had transformed air warfare by late 1915. Some 300 E-types, especially the single-seat E-III with a top speed of around 140kph (85mph), shot down more than a thousand Allied aircraft and took an especially heavy toll of the Vickers FB-5 in what was known as the "Fokker Scourge". The E-types were pre-eminent until the arrival of comparable Allied fighters in the spring of 1916.

VICKERS FB-5

This "pusher" fighter was the first ever British fighter and began arriving on the Western Front in mid-1915. It was soon outclassed by the Fokker E-types and production ended in early 1916 after some 100 aircraft had been built.

Engine: 100hp Gnome Monosoupape
Crew: 2
Ceiling: 2,700m (8,800ft)
Top speed: 112kph (70mph)
Armament: 1 x 0.303in (7.7mm) machine-gun

AIR COMBAT TECHNIQUES

As fighters gradually appeared, leading pilots began to develop the tactics of air combat. Complex dogfighting was rare and victory usually went to the pilot who exploited the sun and clouds to sneak up behind his opponent and open fire at close range. Pilots recorded their successes, or "kills", and those who achieved more than five became recognized as "aces". Many were soon killed, however.

Right: Roland Garros (in beret) flew the first Allied aircraft to be fitted with deflector gear.

Winter Offensive Against Russia

German forces scored a notable victory over the Russians during the Second Battle of the Masurian Lakes in early 1915 but Austro-Hungarian forces suffered horrendous losses in a botched offensive through the Carpathians.

Germany decided to concentrate on the Eastern Front during 1915, aiming to knock Russia out of the war. The plan was to make two attacks, one in the north and one in the south of the front. The first thrust was to be made from East Prussia by the 100,000 troops of the German Eighth and Tenth Armies. The offensive was preceded by a diversionary attack on 31 January. The German Ninth Army made a feint push towards Warsaw that led to the Battle of Bolimov, noteworthy for one of the first uses of poison gas. The main event in East Prussia began on 7 February, when General Otto von Below's Eighth Army advanced through a blinding snowstorm to hit the left flank of the isolated Russian Tenth Army, thereby initiating the Second Battle of the Masurian Lakes.

Indecisive Attacks

Below's advance, which pushed his opponents back 96km (60 miles) in a week, was joined on the 9th by an attack on the Russian right flank by General Hermann von Eichhorn's Tenth Army. The Russian Tenth Army crumbled, and began a retreat towards Kovno (Kaunas). Three corps were virtually surrounded but one put up a desperate fight in the Augustovo Forest until the 21st that allowed the others to make good their escape. Yet, for all their initial successes, the Germans gained little and they fell back to the East Prussian border in the face of counter-

RUSSIAN DEFEATS, 1915

The Central Powers' advances in Poland and Galicia.

Below: Russian troops moving off to the front.

attacks by the Russian Twelfth Army under General Plehve. In all the Russians lost some 200,000 men during the battle, including 90,000 prisoners.

Carpathian Battles

The second thrust was made by three armies positioned along the Carpathian Mountains. The main force was General Alexander von Linsingen's Austro-German South Army. His mission was to strike northwest through the Carpathians in the direction of Lemberg to relieve the besieged fortress of Przemyśl. The Austro-Hungarian Third Army, commanded by General Svetozar Boroevic von Bojna, was on the South Army's left flank while General Karl von Pflanzer-Baltin's Austro-Hungarian Tenth Army was on the right flank. Both were detailed to act in a supporting role.

Pflanzer-Baltin scored an early success by taking Czernowitz (Cernovcy) with 60,000 prisoners from General Alexei Brusilov's Eighth Army on 17 February but his push was then halted by strong counter-attacks. South Army made little progress, coming to a halt amid the snowbound mountains. The Przemyśl fortress and its garrison surrendered to the Russians on 22 March after a 194-day siege. The Russians launched various local counter-attacks in the following weeks but these ended on 10 April, due to supply difficulties and the arrival of German reinforcements under General Georg von der Marwitz. The Carpathian fighting was a disaster for Austria-Hungary and cost it 800,000 casualties, most due to the appalling weather. The Chief of Staff, Field Marshal Conrad von Hötzendorf, was forced to call on Germany for even more military aid as his demoralized and increasingly ethnically divided army began to disintegrate before his eyes.

Above: Russian supply carts pulled both by horses and slow-moving oxen somewhere in the Carpathians during their spring offensive of 1915.

THE SIEGE OF PRZEMYSL

Przemyśl was a major Austro-Hungarian fortress complex in Galicia. It was briefly besieged by the Russians in September 1914, then relieved for a few weeks in October, and then placed under siege once again. Its salvation became something of a national cause in Austria-Hungary but the failure of the relief operation in early 1915 sealed its fate. The 120,000-strong garrison held out until 22 March but then surrendered. The Russian victory was short-lived as the fortress was retaken by Austrian and German forces on 4 June and never again threatened.

Right: German troops escorting Russian prisoners captured at Przemyśl, June 1915.

Mortars

Trench mortars, a type of specialist artillery that could fire explosive shells in a high trajectory, were not new, having been around for centuries, but the stagnation of trench warfare saw them become one of the most important weapons of the war.

Mortars are short-range infantry-support weapons designed to lob shells in a high arc on to a target. They were originally designed in the 18th century to hit targets sheltering behind either natural features such as hills or constructed defences like fortress walls. Although they had fallen out of fashion somewhat before World War I, several armies soon recognized that they were ideal weapons for hitting enemy troops sheltering in trenches. Germany, France and Britain were the major manufacturers and sold their various designs to their allies.

Below: British armourers prepare a huge number of "toffee apple" rounds for the early type of 2in (51mm) mortar.

9.45IN MORTAR

As the war progressed Britain deployed a wide-range of mortars including the 9.45in type, seen here being loaded with its large projectile, commonly known as the "Flying Pig". Although very effective, these heavier mortars were difficult to manhandle around the battlefield.

Type: Heavy smoothbore mortar
Calibre: 9.45in (240mm)
Weight: 866kg (1,910lb)
Maximum range: 1,600m (1,750yds)
Crew: 9

German Superiority

The Germans had the edge in the quality and provision of mortars for much of the early part of the war, largely because they had recognized that these weapons had played an important part in the siege warfare of the Russo-Japanese War. Consequently, the German

Army had a number of excellent *Minenwerfer* (mine-thrower) types from the outset. Around 150 had been delivered by August 1914. They were bigger, heavier and less portable than later mortars, largely because they had been designed specifically to take on the concrete and steel of France's frontier fortresses. They used a propellant charge to fire a variety of ammunition – explosive, incendiary and gas – that had a range of around 1,000m (1,100yds). Rifling made them quite accurate and their range was increased in later models by lengthening the barrel.

MINENWERFER

The smallest of Germany's late war *Minenwerfer* types is pictured here being pulled by part of its crew. All three calibres had wheeled carriages, which were usually removed before the weapon was used in action.

Type: Light rifled mortar
Calibre: 76mm (3in)
Weight: 100kg (220lb)
Maximum range: 1,000m (1,100yds)
Rate of fire: 20rpm
Crew: 6

They came in a variety of calibres, defined as light, medium and heavy, that fired projectiles weighing 4.08kg, 49.44kg and 95.26kg (9lb, 109lb and 210lb) respectively. The mortars were not really man-portable in the modern sense as most were very heavy. As they could not be broken down into various parts, they were moved about on two-wheeled carriages (the larger types normally horse-drawn) from which they could be fired if required but they were usually found mounted on a steel plate in the trenches. The Germans did attempt to resolve their mobility problem by introducing much smaller *Granatenwerfer* (grenade-thrower) types. These fired a finned grenade out to ranges of 230–275m (250–300yds) and were much lighter.

Allied Designs

France and Britain had no modern mortars in 1914. The French resorted to bringing ancient ones out of retirement while the British experimented with contraptions that would not have looked out of place at a medieval siege. Some looked like miniature siege engines; others were large crossbows, such as the British Leach that could lob a small grenade up to 180m (200yds). One early design of 2in (51mm) calibre fired a bomb that looked like a large toffee apple.

True mortars began to arrive in 1915. The French developed the Batignolles, a series of heavy mortars. Arguably the best and certainly the most modern-looking mortar of the war was the British Stokes design. It was named after its creator, Sir Wilfred Stokes, and began to appear in 1916. These came in a variety of calibres and fired a rocket-shaped grenade. Like all British and French mortars they were smoothbore designs. These were truly man-portable as they broke down into three sections – barrel, baseplate and adjustable bipod.

STOKES MORTAR

The British Stokes mortar could be easily moved by its crew. It was eventually made in 4in (101mm) and 6in (152mm) versions in addition to the most usual 3in calibre.

Type: Light mortar
Calibre: 3in (76.2mm)
Weight: 49kg (108lb)
Max. range: 730m (800yds)
Rate of fire: 22 rounds/min
Crew: 2

Above: An Australian-crewed 3in Stokes Mortar in action in a captured trench near Villers-Bretonneux in July 1918.

Germany's Gorlice–Tarnów Offensive

Germany's major offensive on the Eastern Front in mid-1915 was one of the most successful of the whole war, pushing the Russian Army back hundreds of miles and inflicting more than two million casualties on it in a matter of just five months.

Although Germany had decided to attack Russia in 1915, the first effort during February and March had not delivered a definitive victory. It also revealed that the Austro-Hungarian Army was in poor shape and that German forces would have to shoulder the greater burden of the fighting henceforth. Despite his personal misgivings, the German Chief of Staff, General von Falkenhayn, was persuaded in mid-April to release troops from the Western Front for a second major offensive. Both he and other members of the high command moved eastward to Pless in East Prussia to supervise the operation.

Below: A German soldier gives a wounded Russian soldier a drink on a Galician battlefield, June 1915.

German troops grouped in East Prussia were first used in a diversionary attack north and east into Kurland, the coastal plain bordering the Baltic Sea. The operation began on 26 April with the small German Nieman Army pushing towards Libau (Liepaja), a threat that drew in ever more Russian troops over the following weeks. Due to successes in Galicia during May and June, these operations were extended and led to the fall of the fortress of Kovno (Kaunas) on 17–18 August. A renewal of these operations, the Vilna (Vilnius) Offensive, led to the capture of that city on 26 September but at a high cost.

Capturing Poland

The main, two-pronged attack was against a great salient that included eastern Russian

Above: General August von Mackensen, German commander during the Gorlice–Tarnów Offensive.

Poland and Russian-occupied Galicia, actually part of the Austro-Hungarian Empire. General Max von Gallwitz's German Twelfth Army was poised to strike south-east towards Warsaw itself but the main attack was to be undertaken by some 120,000 men transferred from the Western Front. These formed the German Eleventh Army under General August von Mackensen and the army was located to the south between Gorlice and Tarnów.

The offensive opened on 2 May and Mackensen's troops smashed through the northern flank of the weakened Russian Third Army on a front of nearly

PRELIMINARY BOMBARDMENT

Extensive programmes of shelling before (rather than during) an offensive were the most commonly used type of bombardment. They required an attacker's artillery to fire on the enemy positions in the hope that this deluge would overwhelm the defenders. Such bombardments grew longer and involved more and more heavy guns but it became clear that they could not do what was being asked of them. Worse, they also alerted the defenders to the likelihood of attack and created a devastated landscape in No Man's Land that seriously impeded the progress of the attackers.

Right: A British 60-pounder gun in action during a bombardment near Ypres in April 1918.

48km (30 miles). The Third Army had ceased to exist as a fighting force by the 10th, when it was finally granted permission to withdraw to the River San after losing some 200,000 men, including 140,000 prisoners. The Russian high command, STAVKA, was reluctant to send reinforcements to Galicia because of the developing German attacks in the north.

Despite Russian counter-attacks during 19–25 May, the German-led advance continued – Przemyśl was recaptured on 4 June, the Russians began evacuating most of Galicia from the 22nd and Lemberg was retaken two days later. The offensive in the south wound down in the last days of the month by which time the Germans had taken a staggering 250,000 prisoners and suffered just 90,000 casualties. There was little better news for the Russians in the north of the salient. Gallwitz's Twelfth Army took Warsaw in early August, captured Brest-Litovsk on the 25th and overran Grodno on 2 September.

THE NEW FRONT LINES

The German-led attacks on the Eastern Front between May and September pushed the Russians back up to 480km (300 miles) and showed that in the east at least mobile warfare was still possible. They also established a front line from north of the Pripet Marshes to the Baltic Sea, which would remain unchanged until late 1917, and to the south, which would remain fixed until June 1916.

The Eastern Front had seen losses on an unparalleled scale in 1915 – Germany suffered around 250,000 casualties, Austria-Hungary over 715,000 and Russia around 2.5 million, including a million prisoners.

Right: A small part of the million or more Russians captured during the Gorlice–Tarnów fighting.

Balloons

Balloons played a number of vital roles in the war, such as protecting vulnerable sites from being attacked by aircraft, but their most important role was that of aerial observation despite the advent of reconnaissance aircraft.

Balloons, lighter-than-air, gas-filled envelopes lacking a metal or wooden frame, were widely used during World War I and were kept aloft by either hot air or a gas. They had two main roles – observation of the enemy on land or at sea, or as components in fixed anti-aircraft defence systems.

Artillery observation balloons were cheap to build and their wicker baskets offered a generally more stable viewing platform than an aircraft. They were tethered to the ground by wire(s) attached to a winch or winches and positioned behind friendly lines so that their crews could look for suitable targets or check the fall of artillery fire and correct it if necessary. They usually operated in groups of two or three to make the triangulation of a target more precise. Communication with the ground was initially by semaphore flags or even by dropping weighted messages before the arrival of portable radio sets. These types of balloon were in service for much of the war, particularly up to 1917, but were increasingly replaced by better reconnaissance aircraft and aerial photography.

Above: The aircraft carrier HMS *Furious* with a Sea Scout Z anti-submarine balloon on its rear flight deck. *Furious* began life as a battle-cruiser but was successively updated for its new role.

Attacking Balloons

The crews of observation balloons were vulnerable both to ground fire and attacks by fighters, and they were the only British airmen to be issued with parachutes as a matter of course

Left: British warships in Scapa Flow, the Grand Fleet's main base. A tethered balloon keeps watch for submarines or other hostile activity.

OBSERVATION BALLOONS

Such balloons were used to watch enemy activity behind the front line or to spot targets and correct the aim of the artillery. Conditions for the spotter were tolerable in good weather but abysmal in other circumstances.

Below: A British balloon is lowered to the ground at the end of a mission on the Western Front.

Above: A row of tethered balloons holding a wire barrage, designed to slice through the wings of any aircraft whose crew failed to spot the wires in time, pictured around north-east London.

as it took such a long time to winch them to the ground in an emergency. Yet pilots detested missions to destroy balloons as they involved flying behind enemy lines into areas usually heavily protected by anti-aircraft batteries and fighters.

Balloons were not easy to shoot down. Before the advent of incendiary or explosive bullets, standard rounds from a fighter's machine-gun would often pass harmlessly through the envelope. There was also a good chance that a fighter, which had to get very close to a balloon to make its machine-guns count, might become fatally entangled in, or have a wing sheared off by, the various steel wires that routinely dangled below the target. Destroying a balloon was such a feat of arms that all of the warring air forces designated it a "kill" in the same way as shooting down an enemy aircraft.

Balloon Barrages

Balloons linked together with chains from which wires dangled to ensnare any attacking aircraft were also deployed to protect vulnerable airspace over valuable targets such as major cities and industrial sites. London was the most prominent case because of the frequent airship and heavy bomber raids it had to endure during the war. These tethered balloons were positioned to the north and east of the capital and were part of a defensive system that included fighter aircraft patrols, anti-aircraft batteries and searchlights.

Aside from their use in land operations, balloons were deployed in anti-submarine warfare, mostly by Britain's Royal Naval Air Service. They largely operated in the English Channel or Irish Sea and had the endurance and speed to act as lookouts for convoys. Several types were developed but the most common were the 70 designated Sea Scout Z (SSZ). These entered service in May 1915 and comprised a balloon from which the fuselage of a BE-2C biplane was suspended. The final development of the Sea Scout was termed the Coastal-class Airship, a design that could stay aloft for up to 24 hours and in which the BE-2C fuselage was replaced by a purpose-built gondola.

Four Battles Along the Isonzo

The River Isonzo was effectively the frontier between north-eastern Italy and the Austro-Hungarian Empire and after the Italians sided with the Allies in 1915 it was the site of the first four great – if unsuccessful – Italian offensives of the war.

The Dual Alliance between Germany and Austria-Hungary had been signed in 1879 but it became the Triple Alliance when Italy joined in 1882. While the document was supposed to bind the three powers together, relations between Austria-Hungary and Italy were never good and deteriorated further over the following decades. The alliance was renewed in December 1912 but by then Italy had established close relations with the Entente powers. The chief problem between Austria-Hungary and Italy was territorial. There was a sizeable Italian-speaking population in the Trentino (South Tyrol) region and also around Trieste, but both areas were controlled by Austria-Hungary. Italian irredentism, an ardent nationalist movement dedicated to recovering these lands, was a powerful force in the country's turbulent politics.

KEY FACTS

Date: 23 June – 2 December 1915

Place: Along the River Isonzo, north-eastern Italy

Outcome: The attacking Italians lost more than 180,000 men for little gain.

Right: The Italian Commander-in-Chief July 1914 – November 1917, General Luigi Cadorna.

Below: Italian Bersaglieri, elite light infantry, with their distinctive headgear, on the Isonzo front, 1915.

A New Alliance

Sensing an opportunity, British and French diplomats worked tirelessly to prise Italy away from the Triple Alliance once war had been declared in August 1914. Germany also courted Italy but the Allies won the day. Their promises of significant territorial gains from Austria-Hungary once victory had been achieved led Italy to sign the Treaty of London on 26 April 1915. Italy announced that it was leaving the Triple Alliance on 3 May and then declared war on Austria-Hungary on 23 May; a declaration against Bulgaria followed on 20 October but Italy did not declare war on Germany until 28 August 1916.

Italy's Commander-in-Chief, General Luigi Cadorna, opted to conduct a largely defensive campaign in the South Tyrol and concentrated his efforts against Trieste in the hope of breaking through near there and then driving on to Vienna. His first objective was the town of Gorizia, a little way inside Austro-Hungarian territory on the far side of the River Isonzo. The local terrain, an area of sometimes mountainous

Above: Austro-Hungarian troops refill their water bottles during a lull in the fighting.

ITALIAN IRREDENTISM

Italy's pre-war political life was strongly influenced by irredentism, the fierce nationalist desire to take control of parts of the Austro-Hungarian Empire, especially the Trentino (South Tyrol) and Trieste areas, where sizeable percentages of native Italians lived. The arch-irredentist was the poet Gabriele d'Annunzio (1863–1938), who was also a sparkling orator and became something of a war hero. Dissatisfied with the peace treaties signed in Paris, he led a small force of irredentists to capture Fiume (Rijeka) in 1919 but they were forced to surrender by the Italian Navy in early 1921.

plateaux dissected by river gorges, was difficult in the extreme. The 875,000-strong Italian Army also lacked much modern equipment, especially large stocks of ammunition, artillery and transport.

Opening Offensives

The First Battle of the Isonzo in 1915 was spearheaded by 200,000 men and 200 guns, from the Italian Second and Third Armies under General Pietro Frugoni and Emanuele Filiberto, Duke of Aosta. The Austro-Hungarian Army had extended its border defences in the months before war had been declared and the Italians made virtually no impression on them between 23 June and 7 July. Cadorna tried again between 18 July and 3 August. More artillery had been brought up but shells were still in short supply and his troops again failed to make any worthwhile gains. The two battles cost the Austro-Hungarian Army some 45,000 men while the Italians lost around 60,000.

The Third Battle of the Isonzo began on 18 October after Cadorna had rushed much more artillery up to the front. Yet even the firepower from 1,200 guns made little difference and Gorizia still lay out of reach when the fighting ebbed away on 4 November. There was no change during the Fourth Battle fought between 10 November and 2 December. Italian losses in the Third and Fourth battles reached 117,000 and the Austro-Hungarians lost around 72,000 troops. Cadorna would launch further battles along the Isonzo, however.

Right: Italian troops use a military ferry to cross over the River Isonzo in 1915.

Attacking the Dardanelles

The British attempt to force the narrow channel of the Dardanelles was devised to knock Turkey out of the war and create a new supply route to Russia but it ended in abject failure and led to the disastrous Gallipoli land campaign.

Britain and France wanted to send war supplies to Russia's large but ill-equipped armies. The only sea route possible was the difficult North Sea–Arctic passage to ports such as Murmansk and Archangel. The southern route by way of the Mediterranean to the Black Sea was blocked by the narrow Turkish-controlled Dardanelles sea lane.

A pre-war British feasibility study had concluded that it would be possible – if difficult – for warships to bludgeon a safe passage through the Dardanelles and this appeared to be confirmed in November 1914, when a British naval squadron inflicted major damage on the Narrows' outer forts. These were actually undermanned and extremely poorly equipped at the time. However, Turkey responded by strengthening the defences with German aid.

KEY FACTS

Date: 19 February – 23 March 1915

Place: The Dardanelles in the eastern Mediterranean

Outcome: Heavy losses were inflicted on Allied warships largely by Turkish mines.

Above: An illustration from a contemporary French magazine. In reality it was impossible to locate many of the Turkish batteries.

Allied Strategy

The Dardanelles' issue was raised by Britain's First Lord of the Admiralty, Winston Churchill, in January 1915. He was a strategic "Easterner", one of those who thought that breaking the stalemate on the Western Front would cost too many lives and that Germany might be more easily defeated by crushing its allies first. A naval breakthrough in the Dardanelles might, he believed, deliver a decisive blow against Turkey and thus Germany. Churchill won approval for an Anglo-French operation at the end of the month. The Royal

Below: Battleships from the Anglo-French fleet line up across the entrance to the Dardanelles.

Navy provided a task force based around Britain's newest dreadnought, *Queen Elizabeth*, 3 battle-cruisers and 12 older pre-dreadnoughts, under Admiral Sackville Carden, while a smaller French fleet was led by 4 pre-dreadnoughts.

First Naval Attacks

The bombardment of the outer forts began on 19 February 1915 but was ineffective. The ships had to move in closer to complete the attack on the 25th but the Allies still faced problems. Mobile Turkish howitzers were difficult to knock out and these, backed by searchlights, were frustrating night-time attempts by minesweepers to clear the minefields that blocked the Narrows. It was decided that troops would be needed to clear the howitzers, thus leading to the Gallipoli land campaign, but the naval effort was renewed after intelligence reports suggested (correctly) that the Turks were short of ammunition.

Churchill urged Carden to risk all with a charge through the Narrows, but the admiral was ill and collapsed from nervous exhaustion. His deputy, Admiral John de Robeck, oversaw the next attack on 18 March. What followed was an unmitigated disaster. The Allied ships did manage to knock out a few shore batteries but the survivors brought down a heavy fire. Minesweepers were unable to complete their task and several capital ships ran into minefields. The French pre-dreadnoughts *Bouvet* and *Gaulois* were sunk and *Suffren* badly damaged, while the British lost the *Ocean*. No Allied warships remained in the Narrows by dark and the naval attack was abandoned.

The next stage was to assemble land forces to attack the Gallipoli Peninsula and clear the way to Constantinople, but that would prove to be an equally difficult proposition.

WINSTON CHURCHILL

Churchill (1874–1965) was made First Lord of the Admiralty in 1911 and oversaw the continuing reform of the Royal Navy. He was seen as dynamic but prone to impulsive gestures. Churchill's senior appointments upset some naval officers and his interference in operational matters irked others but his reputation was seriously tarnished by the Gallipoli fiasco, which he had promoted. He was sacked in May 1915. Thereafter, he served as a junior minister and as an officer on the Western Front before returning to the heart of government as the Minister of Munitions and then Minister of War.

Above: Winston Churchill, the driving force behind the attempt to force the Dardanelles and the subsequent Gallipoli campaign.

Left: The crew of HMS *Irresistible* passing a tow to HMS *Albion* after the *Albion* ran hard aground during a bombardment off Gaba Tepe in the Dardanelles on 24 May 1915.

Pre-dreadnought Battleships

Although they no longer had the speed and gunpower to lead a battlefleet into a full-scale action, ageing pre-dreadnought types were still able to perform many vital roles to play in the battle for naval supremacy.

When the Royal Navy's HMS *Dreadnought* was launched in 1906, its gunpower made every other battleship in existence obsolete and sparked a worldwide naval arms race. Yet no navy was going to scrap its very costly pre-dreadnought battleships. Consequently many outdated pre-dreadnoughts remained in use when war broke out in 1914.

Numbers in Service

On the Allied side, the Royal Navy had 29 operational pre-dreadnoughts with 20 in mothballs, the French had 17 largely based in the Mediterranean, Italy 8 and Russia 9. Two countries that subsequently joined the Allied cause, Japan and the USA, had 23 and 16 respectively. The fleets of the Central Powers also contained pre-dreadnoughts – Germany had more than 20, Austria-Hungary 12 and Turkey 2.

The pre-dreadnoughts came in a variety of designs and were of varying ages. The Royal Navy and Germany, for example, had such ships that had been built between 1892 and 1908 and, while they differed in detail, they did have some similarities. They typically displaced 10,000–14,000 tons, with the more recent ships being larger. They usually carried four main guns of 28cm (11in) calibre (Germany) and 12in (30.5cm) (Britain) and had secondary armaments of 10–14 lighter guns. Although the pre-dreadnoughts' firepower seemed impressive, they were wholly outclassed by the dreadnoughts, and most naval strategists agreed that the former would take a terrible pounding from the latter in a full-blown fleet action.

At War

The German Navy needed all the large warships it could muster to oppose the British in

Below: The French *Suffren* dated back to 1899 but was torpedoed and sunk by *U-52* off Lisbon in 1916 after service in the Dardanelles.

HMS *Formidable*

HMS *FORMIDABLE*

FORMIDABLE CLASS
TYPE: Pre-dreadnought battleship
LAID DOWN: 1898
DISPLACEMENT: 15,000 tons
CREW: 780
SPEED: 18.5 knots
ARMAMENT: 4 x 12in (305mm) + 12 x 6in (152mm) guns

the North Sea so its High Seas Fleet retained some of its pre-dreadnoughts. The gamble paid off, because the fleets only met once and only one German pre-dreadnought was lost to enemy fire – SMS *Pommern* at Jutland in 1916. Other German pre-dreadnoughts did give valuable service in the Baltic but largely in support of ground operations.

The Royal Navy adopted a slightly different plan. Its pre-dreadnoughts were quickly removed from the main Grand Fleet but many were sent on subsidiary missions like shore bombardments, or to theatres where they were unlikely to meet more powerful enemy dreadnoughts. Most ended up in the Mediterranean operating against Turkey.

In all, Britain lost 11 pre-dreadnoughts in the war. France and Russia each lost 4, Italy 2 and Japan 1. The Central Powers also had losses but not on the same scale. Aside from Germany's *Pommern*, the Turkish Navy had two sunk and Austria-Hungary one.

Right: The pre-dreadnought *Pommern* was one of six German pre-dreadnoughts at the Battle of Jutland in 1916. *Pommern* was sunk with all hands by a torpedo from the British destroyer *Faulknor*.

Gallipoli – The Landings

The Gallipoli landings were a British-led effort to put ashore a force that could drive up the peninsula and take the Turkish capital, Constantinople, but they went wrong from the beginning, not least because the campaign was badly managed.

The Gallipoli campaign of 1915–16 grew out of a belief among some leading political figures in Britain that the fighting on the Western Front was stalemated and that Germany might be fatally weakened by adopting an indirect approach, a strategy that knocked out one of its allies. Turkey was chosen largely because its defeat would also open the Dardanelles seaway so that the western Allies would be able to supply Russia's large but under-equipped armies more easily. The campaign was actually the brainchild of the then First Lord of the Admiralty, Winston Churchill, but not all agreed with his views. Senior military figures were very lukewarm and believed that the war could only be won on the Western Front.

KEY FACTS

Date: 25 April 1915

Place: Gallipoli Peninsula, European Turkey

Outcome: British and Commonwealth forces met unexpectedly strong resistance from the Turkish garrison.

Allied Plans

The campaign began as a naval operation but the joint Anglo-French attempt to drive through the Narrows ended in abject failure in March 1915 and it was decided that troops, mostly British but with some French support, would have to be committed. The plan was to land them on the Gallipoli Peninsula and then push rapidly northward to capture the nearby Turkish capital, Constantinople (Istanbul). However, the movement of troops and equipment to the eastern Mediterranean was ponderous and did not go unnoticed by the Turks, who began increasing their garrison on the peninsula.

The Invasion

The landings took place on 25 April at five points on Helles, the southern tip of the peninsula, codenamed S, V, W, X and Y, and at Gaba Tepe, more than 19km (12 miles) farther along Gallipoli's west coast. This last was officially known as Z Beach but was commonly referred to as ANZAC Cove, after the Australian and New Zealand Army Corps troops who landed there. The results were

ANZACS AT WAR

The soldiers of the Australian and New Zealand Army Corps (ANZACs) proved to be some of the best troops to serve with the Allies. They fought with considerable distinction at Gallipoli, in Palestine and on the Western Front. Something like 322,000 Australians served overseas out of a population of 5 million and some 60,000 of them were killed and 220,000 wounded. New Zealand sent some 100,000 men abroad, around 10 per cent of its population, and suffered some 58,000 casualties, including 17,000 killed.

Right: An ingenious rifle mount and a trench periscope used by a two-man Australian sniper team.

mixed. At ANZAC Cove the troops came ashore at the wrong point and had to scale cliffs to advance inland; they did not take Chunuk Bair, a height that dominated the entire peninsula. The landing at Y Beach was unopposed but there was fierce resistance at the other beaches. By nightfall the attackers had seized a foothold on the tip of the peninsula and the ANZAC troops were holding a perimeter that was destined to remain largely unchanged.

The Turkish defenders at Helles withdrew on the morning of the 26th and established positions a little south of the village of Krithia and near to an important piece of high ground known as Achi Baba. The British now attempted to break through this line. The First Battle of Krithia on 28 April cost them 3,000 casualties for no gains and the Second Battle (6–8 May) saw the British push forward a mere 730m (800yds). The Third Battle took place on 6 June and again resulted in very heavy casualties and no real progress.

The Allied campaign was thus in disarray by the end of the first week of June and a form of trench warfare was developing that made a rapid advance on Constantinople unlikely. The greatest problem was that neither Achi Baba nor Chunuk Bair had been taken, meaning that the British and ANZAC positions were overlooked. The Turks had also been able to mount various small counter-attacks, thanks in large part to the energy of a young officer called Mustafa Kemal, that frequently frustrated the attackers. It was also evident that the landings had gone ahead with insufficient troops and a lack of artillery shells. Withdrawal might have been the best option but the opposite course was taken. More troops were sent to Gallipoli and new attacks and landings attempted over the following months.

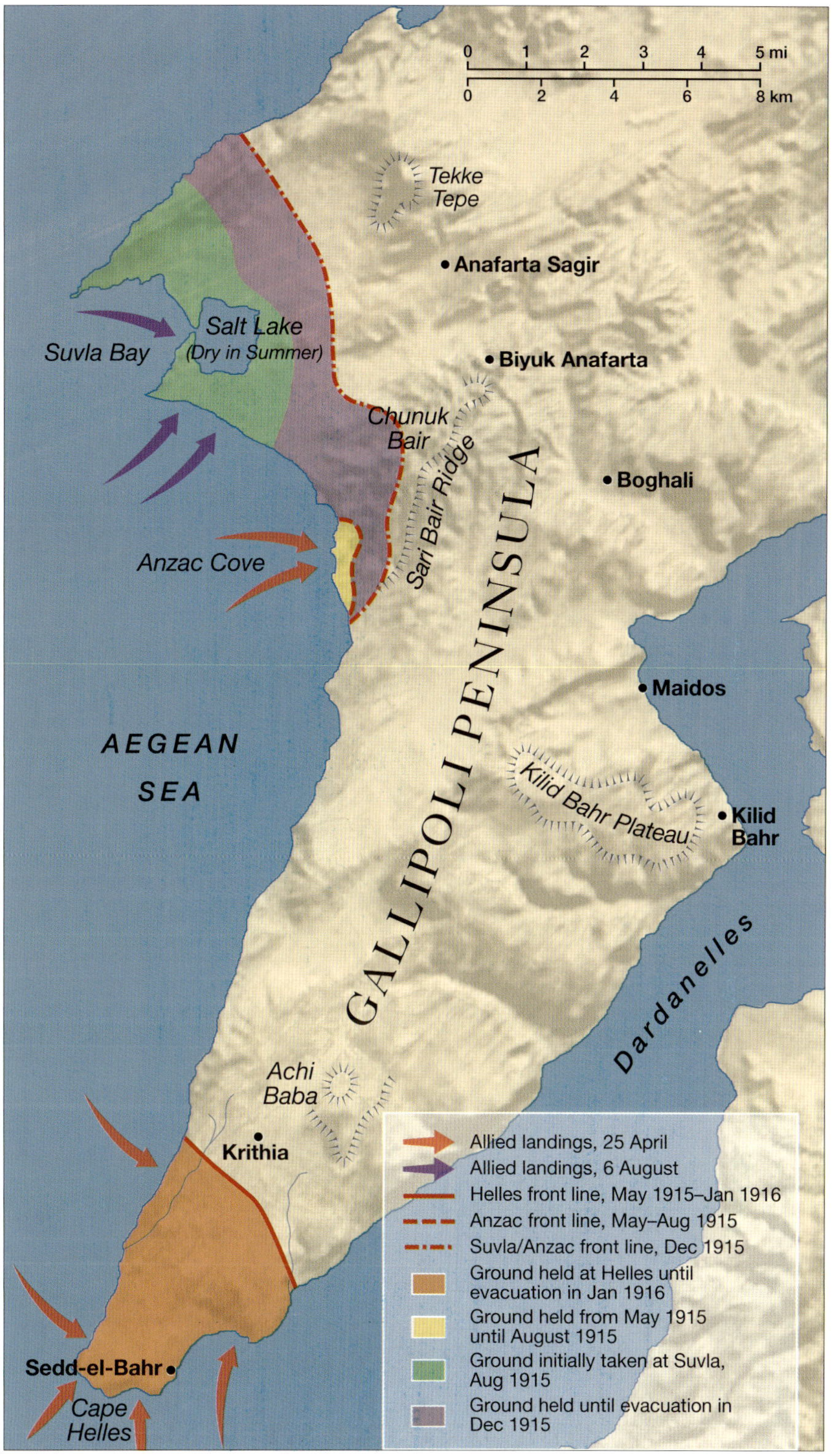

THE GALLIPOLI LANDINGS

The landings and the fighting ashore until the withdrawal in 1916.

Seaplanes and Flying Boats

Amphibious aircraft were an unknown quantity at the outbreak of war but they proved invaluable as they performed several roles including those of reconnaissance and bombing from both coastal bases and warships themselves.

Seaplanes, aircraft fitted with floats so that they can take off and land on water, and flying boats, aircraft with waterproof hulls that can perform similarly, were used by most nations in World War I. Their main role was maritime reconnaissance but they also engaged in air-to-air combat, made anti-shipping sorties and raided coastal installations. Most seaplanes operated from coastal air stations but some, British examples in particular, operated from ships known as seaplane tenders.

However the aircraft were launched and recovered, maritime aviation was still in its infancy and the available aircraft could only be used in calm conditions. Bombs were the main anti-ship weapon. Britain and Germany experimented with torpedoes but found that they were usually too heavy for existing engines to cope with.

In British Service

British seaplanes were operated by the Royal Naval Air Service (RNAS), the largest maritime air force of the conflict, which came into being on 1 January 1914. It eventually had some 50 squadrons that operated from a similar number of coastal stations. The RNAS deployed a variety of seaplanes. The twin-engined Norman Thompson NT-4 and NT-4A equipped several squadrons and carried light bombs for anti-submarine work. One of the most successful later designs was the Felixstowe F-type flying boat, which began operating from 1917. Although slow at 150kph (95mph), these four-man aircraft handled well and could stay aloft for up to 10 hours. An F-type shot down the German airship *L.62* in May 1918 and

Below: A German Friedrichshafen floatplane. The company produced floatplanes during World War I.

Below: A pre-war seaplane built by the German company Albatros. Their main contribution to naval aviation during the conflict was the W-4 single-seat fighter.

Above: A pre-war version of the British Sopwith Tabloid of the type that, with some modification, served as a naval reconnaissance and light bomber aircraft during the war.

five F-2As with a Curtiss H-12 took part in one of the very few battles between seaplanes. On 4 June 1918, they saw off 14 German aircraft after a dogfight, destroying 6 for the loss of just the Curtiss.

The first successful launch of an aerial torpedo was in July 1914 from a British aircraft and the world's first torpedo-bomber was the two-seat Short 184, which entered service with the RNAS in 1915. A 184 flying off Gallipoli from the seaplane tender *Ben-My-Chree* in August 1915 became the first aircraft to sink a ship with a torpedo. Despite this success, using torpedoes remained dangerous for the dropping aircraft and in the case of the Short 184 and the later 320 their use was discontinued. Other major British seaplanes were Sopwith's Schneider (1915) and Baby (1916).

German Designs

Germany developed its own naval aviation service. It largely relied on a handful of manufacturers, such as Friedrichshafen, which produced the FF-33 series from late 1914. The main reconnaissance model, the FF-33e, was fitted with a two-way radio and carried a load of hand-thrown bombs, while the FF-33l was the seaplane fighter version. These types were superseded by the FF-49 from May 1917, a more robust aircraft that was better suited to the harsh conditions likely to be encountered in the North Sea. Other types included the Albatros W-4 floatplane fighter and the Hansa-Brandenburg series – the CC, KDW, W-12 and W-29.

Both Austria-Hungary and Italy deployed maritime aviation units. The former relied on German types, like the Hansa-Brandenburg CC, but did also produce the two-seat Löhner L flying boat, one of which sank the French submarine *Foucault* on 15 September 1916. The Italians produced several such aircraft including the Macchi M-5 biplane fighter.

SOPWITH SCHNEIDER

The British Schneider, seen here being recovered by HMS *Undaunted*, was based on a pre-war design that had won the 1914 Schneider trophy. The military version appeared in early 1915 and was largely used for anti-submarine and Zeppelin patrols. Some 136 were built before it was replaced in early 1916.

Type: Patrol floatplane
Engine: 100hp Gnome Monosoupape
Crew: 1
Ceiling: 3,000m (9,850ft)
Top speed: 148kph (92mph)
Armament: 1 x 0.303in (7.7mm) machine-gun

The Caucasus Front 1914–16

The fighting in the remote Caucasus of north-eastern Turkey swung backwards and forwards between 1914 and 1916 but by the close of the latter year the Russians held a sizeable portion of Turkish territory in Armenia.

Turkey and Russia held long-standing animosities towards each other, not least over the Balkans, and these soon led to hostilities in World War I. When Turkey went to war against the Allies on 31 October 1914, its navy bombarded Odessa, Sevastopol and Theodosia, ports on Russia's Black Sea coast, the same day. The Russian government then issued its own declaration of war the next day. The main battlefield between the two for the next three years or so would be the mountainous Caucasus.

Right: Germany's Emperor Wilhelm II greets Turkish Minister of War Enver Pasha aboard the battlecruiser *Goeben*.

Turkey had long craved the Russian Caucasus, a region that lay just over its own north-east border, and Enver Pasha, the country's Minister of War, was set on invading the inhospitable area despite the advice of the head of the German military mission, General Otto Liman von Sanders, who strongly opposed the plan.

Opening Battles

Russia actually struck first, crossing the border into Turkish Armenia at several points, but the advance towards Erzerum was largely halted in late November 1914. Enver took personal command of the Turkish forces in Armenia on 14 December and launched his own major attack a week later, just days after the first heavy snows of winter had fallen. The advance towards Kars was opposed by 100,000 Russian troops, and these inflicted severe casualties on the Turks at the Battle of Sarikamish fought from 26 December 1914 through January 1915. Only 18,000 Turkish troops out of an initial 95,000 survived the battle and the freezing conditions during the retreat to Erzerum. Enver returned to Constantinople.

The Turkish leadership suspected that the Christian Armenians had been covertly

Left: Wounded Turkish soldiers in the Caucasus are treated by their Russian captors.

supporting the Russian invaders and initiated a series of vicious crackdowns that set off a full-blown revolt in April and May. Armenians seized Van on 20 April and held it until Russian forces arrived on 18 May. The Turks struck back in July. General Abdul Kerim crushed a Russian corps at the Battle of Malazgirt (10–26 July) north of Lake Van and retook the town itself on 5 August. His cautious advance was halted in its tracks by a Russian counter-attack a few days later.

YOUNG TURKS

"Young Turks" was the name commonly used to describe members of Turkey's radical and highly nationalistic Union and Progress Party. Turkey was a democracy and a UPP-dominated government was formed in early 1913. The Young Turks, led by War Minister Enver Pasha and Interior Minister Talaat Pasha, effectively held the reigns of power from 1914 onwards. They allied with Germany and oversaw the country's increasingly botched war effort but mostly remained above criticism until mid-1918. The UPP was dissolved on 20 October that year.

Above: Talaat Pasha (centre) on his visit to Austria, when he was prime minister during the war.

Russian Attacks

Grand Duke Nicholas, uncle of Tsar Nicholas II, was appointed to the position of viceroy of Caucasia on 24 September and he laid plans for a major effort in early 1916. This broad-front offensive into Armenia by some 200,000 troops was actually commanded by General Nikolai Yudenich and opened on 11 January 1916. The main thrust was from Kars towards Erzerum. Kerim's Third Army was decisively beaten at Köprukoy a week later and Erzerum itself fell on 16 February after a three-day siege. Yudenich had also made a smaller thrust along the Black Sea coast, which was aided by troops landed from Russian warships, and this culminated in the capture of Trebizond (Trabzon) on 18 April.

In response Enver ordered a two-pronged counter-offensive. The Third Army, now led by Vehip Pasha, pushed along the Black Sea coast but was routed by Yudenich at Erzinjan by 28 July. The second Turkish attack, by Ahmet Izzim Pasha's Second Army, enjoyed some initial success. A corps commanded by Mustafa Kemal of Gallipoli fame captured Mus and Bitlis on 15 August but Yudenich soon retook the two towns, leaving the Russians holding much of Armenia as fighting died down for winter.

Left: Russian troops push forward through a mountain pass during the fighting in the Caucasus. Bitter winters here often led to a seasonal suspension of operations.

Palestine 1914–16

The Middle East, and Egypt in particular, was crucial to Britain's war effort not least because the Suez Canal, the country's major supply route to India, was highly vulnerable to attack from Turkish troops based in neighbouring Palestine.

Turkey's attacks on the Allies in late October 1914 prompted a swift response from the British government. Britain annexed Cyprus on 5 November, sent cruisers to shell Turkish forts at the entrance to the Dardanelles on the 30th and declared a protectorate over Egypt on 18 December. Egypt's Suez Canal was vital to Britain's interests as the main route to India, cornerstone of the empire. British and Empire troops were soon arriving to defend the canal and General John Maxwell was put in command.

The Turks were aware of the canal's strategic importance and in early 1915 made an attempt to capture it. A 22,000-strong force drawn from the Fourth Army, under Minister of Marine, Djemal Pasha, set out from Beersheba in Palestine on 14 January. That it successfully crossed the waterless Sinai Peninsula was largely due to the organizational skills of Djemal's German Chief of Staff, General Friedrich Kress von Kressenstein. The Turkish force made an attempt to cross the canal on pontoons on 2–3 February but the attack was easily broken up by the defenders' fire and Djemal withdrew back to Beersheba. For the remainder of the year the canal zone remained something of a backwater, not least because both sides were far more concerned with events at Gallipoli and in Mesopotamia.

Above: A lone Turkish cavalryman pictured somewhere in Palestine. Attempts by the Turks to capture the Suez Canal were largely half-hearted and ended with defeat at the Battle of Romani in 1916.

Battles in 1916

The British were preoccupied by two matters in 1916 – a Turkish attack in Sinai and a revolt to their rear. A new commander, General Archibald Murray, had pushed the canal's defences into the Sinai Peninsula and this involved building communications, setting up various forts and developing a satisfactory system for supplying water. For the most part this work went on without the Turks responding in force, although there was some skirmishing against the 3,500-strong Turkish Desert Force led by Kress von Kressenstein.

The Turks finally made a larger effort to disrupt Murray's work in July 1916. This time Kress von Kressenstein commanded some 16,000 troops and was supported by various German machine-gun, artillery and anti-aircraft detachments as well as a dozen aircraft. By mid-July the largely Turkish force was positioned outside Romani, a town some 32km (20 miles)

Left: An Indian Vickers machine-gun detachment pictured in Palestine. Such troops made up a sizeable proportion of the British war effort in the region.

Right: Turkish artillerymen manhandle a field gun into position. Such light weapons were better suited to the campaigns in the Middle East, which generally were more fluid than the Western Front.

east of the canal that marked the farthest extent of Murray's advance. The battle began with a surprise attack by the Turks on 4 August that gained some ground but the gains had been lost by the next day. Kress von Kressenstein was then forced to retreat 96km (60 miles) back to El Arish due to growing water shortages. The Battle of Romani cost the Turks roughly 8,000 casualties and the British little more than 1,000. The British victory permanently removed the Turkish threat to the Suez Canal.

Below: A few German troops, like these cavalrymen, fought alongside the Turks in Palestine.

THE CALL OF JIHAD

On 14 November 1914, in a speech given in Constantinople, Sheikh-ul-Islam, a senior Muslim cleric, declared a holy war against the then Allies – Britain, France, Montenegro, Serbia and Russia. He also preached that those Muslims who lived in Allied countries or under their rule and did not heed his call would either burn in hell or suffer unspecified "painful torment". Much of this anti-Allied sentiment stemmed from a well-received visit to the Middle East by Germany's Emperor Wilhelm II in 1898 and the subsequent use of agents to stir up anti-Christian feeling.

SENUSSI REVOLT

The British did face another problem, however. Germany and Turkey had convinced Sidi Ahmad es Sherif, the leader of the Senussi people of western Egypt and Italian-controlled Tripolitania and Cyrenaica (Libya), to rise against the British in late 1915 and had provided them with various modern weapons by submarine.

The Senussi were opposed by the initially small Anglo-Egyptian Western Frontier Force (WFF) but it was finally able to inflict a decisive defeat on them at Aqqaqia on 26 February 1916. The Senussi resorted to guerrilla warfare that eventually tied down some 60,000 Italian troops and the 35,000-strong WFF. Ahmad was largely beaten by late 1916 to early 1917 but his raids continued into the last year of the war, even though the flow of supplies from Germany and Turkey had long since dried up.

The Mesopotamian Campaign 1914–16

The first part of the prolonged and probably unnecessary British campaign in Turkish-controlled Mesopotamia was characterized by poor planning and bad management and also saw one of Britain's most shocking defeats of the war.

British and Indian troops had been sent to protect some of the Persian Gulf's oil installations shortly after the war in Europe began and responded to Turkey's war declaration in late October 1914 by capturing the port of Basra in Turkish-controlled Mesopotamia (Iraq) on 23 November. The same troops had pushed northward to take Qurna, the point where the Euphrates and Tigris rivers meet, by early December.

British operations in Mesopotamia were originally conceived on a small scale but after two Turkish attacks on Qurna and Ahwaz were easily repulsed in April 1915, Major-General Charles Townshend was ordered to explore the possibility of taking Baghdad. Townshend set off from Basra up the Tigris at the head of a reinforced division and naval flotilla and captured Amara on 3 June. Even better news came when a force under Major-General George Gorringe that was moving along the Euphrates to protect Townshend's western flank inflicted a further defeat on the Turks at Nasiriya on 24 July.

Above: A detachment of Indian troops on anti-aircraft watch with a Lewis machine-gun.

Townshend resumed his own advance in August and made for Kut-el-Amara, a town two-thirds of the way to Baghdad held by 10,000 troops under Nur-ud-Din Pasha. The British units were becoming over-stretched because they had to protect lines of communication that stretched 480km (300 miles) down the Tigris back to Basra. Townshend's 10,000 men won the Battle of Kut on 27–28 September but suffered more than 1,200 irreplaceable casualties in the process.

Reluctant Advance

With Baghdad almost in sight, Townshend was ordered to push on, although he justifiably complained that he lacked both the manpower and supplies needed. He moved forward on 11 November and ran into an extensive line of defences that Nur-ud-Din had built outside Ctesiphon. The Turks could muster some 18,000 troops and 45 guns, while Townshend had scraped together 11,000 troops and 30 guns. The British attacked on the 22nd but Townshend was forced to retreat after four days as Turkish reinforcements had arrived in

Left: Turkish casualties await evacuation from an Indian Army first-aid station near Tikrit.

strength. The British losses at Ctesiphon totalled 4,600 men, while the Turks lost some 6,200.

Surrender at Kut

The Turks did not pursue the British closely and the retreating force reached Kut on 3 December. However, four days later, the town was placed under siege. Townshend had two months' supplies and awaited relief with some confidence but his faith was misplaced. Two British generals, Fenton Aylmer and Gorringe, led expeditions to break the siege in January and March 1916 but both were repulsed, the latter on 7 March by the Turkish Sixth Army under a German commander, General Kolmar von der Goltz. Townshend and nearly 10,000 troops surrendered on 29 April and went into a captivity that many would not survive. The relief expeditions had suffered some 21,000 casualties.

The British High Command and the War Office now debated the next move. While a new commander, General Frederick Maude, kicked his heels in Basra, some argued for withdrawal, while others backed a renewed advance towards the capital, Baghdad. Finally, on 3 December, Maude led his 166,000-strong Anglo-Indian force back into Mesopotamia along both banks of the Tigris. The campaign was no longer a minor sideshow.

Above: An aerial view of Kut, the site of the humiliating British surrender in April 1916.

WAR IN PERSIA

Oil-rich Persia (Iran) was a relatively undeveloped country in 1914 but it had also been a long-established and highly sensitive strategic buffer zone between the Russian Empire and British-controlled India. It had been split by them into two zones of interest, a British south and Russian north, in 1907, but Germany tried to undermine Anglo-Russian authority once war had been declared. Weapons and money flowed to various dissident Persian nationalist groups and they came close to taking over the country in 1915 but were largely defeated by Russian forces during the following year.

Left: A British 18-pounder (84mm) field gun in action in Mesopotamia.

The Wider War at Sea

The Battle of the Dogger Bank was the sole major clash between surface warships in 1915 but German submarines were becoming a greater menace in the North Atlantic and were also sinking neutral ships in what proved a dangerous strategy.

There was only one major engagement in the North Sea between units of Britain's Grand Fleet and Germany's High Seas Fleet during 1915. The Battle of the Dogger Bank on 24 January came about when British intelligence discovered that Vice-Admiral Franz von Hipper's battle-cruiser squadron intended to raid the English coast and sink fishing trawlers. Hipper was surprised by Admiral David Beatty's battle-cruiser squadron and the German flagship, *Seydlitz*, was badly damaged and *Blücher* sunk in a running fight. Dogger Bank was not a major fleet engagement but it did have considerable consequences. The High Seas Fleet was smaller than the Grand Fleet and the loss of just one major vessel worried the German establishment. The commander of the High Seas Fleet was sacked and Emperor Wilhelm II ordered his fleet to avoid further unnecessary risks.

Above: The killing of civilians during U-boat attacks was used for propaganda purposes by the Allies.

If the High Seas Fleet could not be risked, the Imperial German Navy would have to use other means to strike back at Britain, chiefly by intensifying the campaign against Britain's trade. The German Navy did not rely entirely on U-boats for this as they were still a relatively untried technology and did not have the endurance of surface ships. Auxiliary commerce raiders and armed merchant cruisers could range much farther and for longer. Some of these were successful but their impact lessened as many were sunk or interned and by spring 1915 U-boats were playing the greater part in the campaign against British shipping. Coastal submarines operated in the North Sea and English Channel, freeing larger boats for service in the Western Approaches.

Below: The mortally wounded German battle-cruiser *Blücher* rolls over during the Dogger Bank action.

U-boat Attacks

A key moment came on 4 February 1915, when Germany announced it would initiate *Handelskrieg* (trade warfare). This allowed its 30 or so submarines to sink Allied merchant ships sailing around Britain and Ireland without warning from the 18th. The decision had not been taken easily and was only reached after bitter argument. The military case was clear-cut but Germany's political leaders knew that unrestricted submarine warfare was a contravention of international law. It would hand the Allies a major propaganda victory as such a strategy would almost certainly lead to

Above: Britain's war effort very much relied on merchant ships like this one, here being manoeuvred into dock, and such vessels were the U-boats' main target.

the sinking of neutral vessels and the death of citizens from neutral states.

Neutral Losses

German U-boats sent roughly one million tons of shipping to the bottom in 1915 and just 17 submarines were lost. Yet, as those opposed to *Handelskrieg* had predicted, these successes had a high political price. The first neutral target of the campaign was the Norwegian tanker *Belridge*, which was damaged on 19 February but a later victim caused wider repercussions. The United States had already issued stern warnings but on 1 May the US tanker *Gulflight* was torpedoed and two crewmen killed. An even more vehement response was required after the British passenger liner *Lusitania* was sunk on 7 May and 128 US citizens died.

Even this did not prevent further loss of US lives – two more civilians died when another British liner, *Arabic*, was lost on 19 August. Germany now decided to back down and on the 30th announced that merchant ships would not be attacked without warning – but the damage had been done and the prohibition on *Handelskrieg* was destined not to last.

ADMIRAL DAVID BEATTY

Beatty (1871–1936) was probably Britain's most flamboyant and well-known senior naval officer of the war. He had been made commander of the Grand Fleet's Battle-cruiser Squadron in 1911 and led it in action at Heligoland Bight (1914), Dogger Bank (1915) and Jutland (1916), battles in which his seeming rashness cost his squadron several warships. The losses were not entirely his fault, however, and in late 1916 he was made Commander-in-Chief of the Grand Fleet over the heads of more senior officers. He essentially continued the cautious strategy of his predecessor until the German fleet surrendered in 1918.

Below: The sinking of the *Lusitania* and the death of 128 US nationals led to a suspension of Germany's U-boat campaign.

Gallipoli – The Withdrawal

The British persisted with the stalled Gallipoli campaign throughout the summer of 1915, even making further landings in August, but with the onset of winter it was clear to all that there was no other option than complete withdrawal.

When the British-led amphibious assault on Gallipoli was made on 25 April 1915 the immediate intention was to push along the mountainous peninsula to capture Constantinople and knock Turkey out of the war. Yet these hopes were soon dashed and by early June the campaign had degenerated into the bitterest form of trench warfare. The British had captured Helles, the southern tip of the peninsula, and an even smaller area farther along its west coast held by the Australian and New Zealand Army Corps and christened ANZAC Cove. The Turks held the high ground and could readily call down artillery fire on the beaches.

Above: ANZAC troops pictured by one of the many dugouts that were built into the cliff and valley sides that typified the Gallipoli Peninsula.

Below: One of the beaches across which all of the British and ANZAC supplies had to be ferried – often under Turkish gunfire.

Landings at Suvla

General Ian Hamilton, the British commander, tried to break the stalemate by making another landing on the west coast behind the main Turkish lines. While the troops at Helles launched a diversionary attack, the ANZACs were to break out and then swing northward to link up with troops landed at Suvla Bay. The operation took place on 6–10 August and, while the diversionary attack was successful, the ANZACs became bogged down and were unable to cut through the Turkish lines. The force that landed at Suvla, commanded by General F. Stopford, was unopposed but

Above: The British and others made numerous attacks but they were increasingly localized and caused the Turks no great problems.

foolishly failed to push inland at once. The Turks reacted quickly and were soon overlooking the beach in strength.

Suvla was effectively the last throw of the dice for Hamilton and his request for further reinforcements was largely rejected because they were needed elsewhere. The general had also lost the support of his superiors and was relieved of his command on 15 October. His replacement, General Charles Monro, arrived on the 28th, toured the various beaches, and recommended total withdrawal the next day. After various other options were discussed, Monro was finally given permission to evacuate all three of the embattled and claustrophobic beachheads on 3 December.

Secret Withdrawal

In stark contrast to the landings, the two-stage withdrawal was a masterpiece of excellent planning, meticulous staff work and orderly execution. Pessimists in the Allied camp expected a casualty rate of around 50 per cent but they were wholly wrong – just three casualties were reported in all. Suvla Bay and ANZAC Cove were the first to be abandoned. Some 105,000 men, 5,000 animals and 300 guns were removed under cover of darkness between 10 and 20 December. Thanks to a variety of ruses that suggested the trenches were still being manned and first-rate noise discipline, the 100,000 Turkish troops around the two beaches never discovered what was actually taking place. The withdrawal from Helles followed a similar pattern between late December and 9 January 1916, when 35,000 men and 3,700 animals were spirited away.

Below: These barges, known as "Beetles", proved invaluable throughout the fighting for bringing in supplies, not least water, and evacuating the wounded to hospital ships lying offshore.

The multinational campaign had cost the Allies some 276,000 casualties, many of whom were invalided home because they had contracted various sicknesses. Turkish losses are problematical but probably totalled at least 250,000. The Gallipoli fiasco had both political and strategic repercussions in Britain. Its failure led to the resignation of the dynamic First Lord of the Admiralty, Winston Churchill, who had been the driving force behind the campaign. It also meant that there would be no supply route opened to Russia through the Dardanelles to the Black Sea.

The advocates of the strategy to undermine Germany's war effort by knocking out its weaker allies, the so-called "Easterners" like Churchill, were now largely discredited. "Westerners", mostly generals who believed the war could only be won by crushing Germany on the Western Front, were instead in the ascendancy, although the debate would continue.

German Submarines

The Imperial German Navy began the war with very few submarines but they started to grow in importance and eventually became the main weapon in the campaign to bring Britain to its knees by strangling its maritime trade routes.

Germany deployed the most technically advanced and largest fleet of submarines of all during World War I but actually had none in service before 1906. Its navy had around 30 submarines available in August 1914 but by the end of the war a further 350 or so had seen active service. Their operational peak came in June 1917 when 61 were at sea.

The Imperial German Navy actually produced very few different types of boat during the war as its planners rightly believed that concentrating on fewer types made production, maintenance and the training of crews much more straightforward. Larger boats designed for long-range operations were given U- numbers, and there were smaller, short-range UB- and UC-boats that usually operated in shallower coastal waters.

Above: Crewmen watch over the engine room machinery in a U-boat. The image gives a good idea of the cramped working conditions aboard a World War I submarine.

Below: A UB-III class U-boat slices through rough seas off the German island of Heligoland in the south-eastern North Sea.

U-boat Types

The term U-boat derives from *Unterseeboot* ("submarine boat") and these spearheaded the operations against British maritime commerce. They were built in batches and each differed in some way but overall became larger and more powerful as the war progressed. The

UC-1

UC-1 (illustrated) was Germany's original mine-laying submarine, the first of a class of 15, and appeared in 1915. It carried 12 mines which were deployed downwards through hatches in the keel. Surface armament was one machine-gun. It was 55m (180ft) long and had a surface speed of 6.5 knots (5 knots submerged). The *UC-1*'s chief weakness was its endurance, a mere 1,280km (800 miles) at 5 knots. It had a 16-man crew. The boat was lost on 19 July 1917 off Nieuport, Belgium, somewhat ironically probably to a mine.

650-ton *U-21* launched in 1913 had a surface speed of around 15 knots and some 9 knots submerged. It had a crew of 35 and carried four torpedo tubes and an 8.6cm (3.4in) deck gun. *U-140*, launched in late 1917, was much bigger. It displaced 1,930 tons and could cruise on the surface at nearly 16 knots or submerged at close to 8 knots. It had a crew of 64 and its weapons comprised six tubes and two 15cm (5.9in) deck guns. Its range was also more than three times that of *U-21*.

Cargo U-boats

The biggest of the U-boats were the Deutschland class, which appeared in 1916 and started out as unarmed cargo-carrying vessels. *Deutschland* itself caused something of a stir when it sailed as a merchant ship from Kiel to Baltimore in the then-neutral USA, partly to return with war materials but also as a propaganda mission. It arrived at its destination on 9 July and returned home with a cargo of various key metals. The seven vessels, *U-151* to *U-157*, were later converted into fighting submarines. They had two tubes and a 15cm (5.9in) deck gun. Two of them were sunk but *U-155* proved to be very successful, sinking a total of 19 Allied vessels on its first sortie to the Azores area in June–September 1917.

UB-boats became operational from spring 1915. The earliest batches, *UB-1* to *UB-17*, were found to be unsuitable for even the most basic anti-shipping role and were superseded by the larger UB-II class boats, *UB-18* to *UB-47*. These were faster, 9 knots rather than 6, and had a much greater range. The boats were first commissioned in 1915. The next UB-III class (*UB-48* to *UB-136*) did not emerge until the last year of the war. These were larger still, roughly four times the displacement of the first batch, with five torpedo tubes and one deck gun.

UC-boats were similarly conceived for short-range tasks but operated as minelayers. These first appeared in the English Channel in mid-1915 and also served in the Baltic, Black and Mediterranean Seas. Larger UC-II boats, numbers *UC-16* to *UC-79*, began operating in 1916 and they carried 18 rather than 12 mines and had an impressive range. A third batch, the UC-III class, was ordered in 1917 but did not see action.

UB-1

This small submarine was the lead boat in a class of eight. They were all transported in sections to either Belgium or the Adriatic Sea where they operated for the duration. *UB-1* itself was wrecked in the Adriatic Sea and scrapped.

Type: Coastal submarine
Laid down: 1914
Displacement: 127 tons
Crew: 14
Speed: 6.5 knots (surfaced)
Main armament: 2 x 45.7cm (18in) torpedo tubes

Home Fronts

The civilian populations of the various combatant nations largely backed the war when fighting broke out in 1914 but by the conflict's later stages many were suffering from war weariness and many faced very real privations.

Although the various home fronts were different in many ways, they also had some startling similarities. When war broke out in August 1914, for example, it was greeted with widespread enthusiasm in all of the capitals of the major combatant nations, where crowds took to the streets in their thousands. There were exceptions, especially among left-wingers like France's Jean Jaurès, but they were marginalized and faced much public ire. Jaurès was assassinated in a Paris café on 31 July for his anti-war views.

War enthusiasm also meant that people accepted – at least at the outset – tighter state control. This took many forms, not least tight limits on union activity. There were restrictions imposed on enemy aliens or those opposed to the war, especially in the United States where the Espionage Act (1917) and the Sedition Acts led to the imprisonment of 1,600 people. Britain enacted the Defence of the Realm Act in 1914 and restricted access to alcohol, a policy that was also followed in many other countries. Russia took the most extreme measure and banned both the production and consumption of vodka in August 1914. The United States introduced Prohibition in 1918, although it did not begin to operate for another two years.

Below: German civilians riot – a not uncommon sight as food became increasingly scarce.

Food Rationing

Hunger was another common problem. Many Germans suffered because of Britain's naval blockade while the German submarine campaign severely curtailed the movement of foodstuffs to Britain by ship. Bad harvests and poor distribution systems also contributed to the problem. Although it was kept from the public, Britain was just a few weeks from starvation in spring 1917 and nationwide ration books for meat and dairy produce were introduced in July 1918. Britain's allies also suffered. Moscow's supply of food was something like 60 per cent below what was required by January 1917. The French government encouraged "meatless days" at around the same time and then introduced rationing of some foods and fuel in early 1918. German civilians suffered to an even greater degree, particularly during the harsh

Above: British women at work on a farm, replacing men conscripted into the armed forces.

"turnip winter" of 1916–17, and some estimates suggest that 700,000 Germans had died of malnutrition by 1919.

Women at War

The war also brought women into the workplace as never before, despite their facing discrimination and hostility. In Britain there were 175,000 in war production by late 1914; by August 1917 some 750,000 were working in jobs formerly held by men and a further 350,000 were employed in work directly created by the war economy. A further 240,000 women were working in agriculture by 1918.

The picture was similar if patchier in France, Italy and the USA, but Germany lagged behind. Women were not encouraged to enter war-related employment until the introduction of the Hindenburg Programme in late 1916.

Civilians did die through enemy action during the war, but on a small scale compared to World War II. However, the Armistice in 1918 did not halt the suffering as the world was confronting an influenza pandemic. It broke out in spring 1918, lasted for a year or so and cut a swathe through Europe and elsewhere – 229,000 died in Britain, 166,000 in France and 225,000 in Germany. The worldwide figure was an estimated 20 million and 70 per cent of the victims were under 35.

Above: A French magazine celebrates the twin female roles of motherhood and war-factory work.

Below: A long but orderly queue of British women and children seeking rationed produce.

PACIFISM

The clamour for war was overwhelming in 1914 but a few figures in many of the combatant nations did oppose the war, often at much risk to themselves. There were two types of pacifism at the outbreak of war. First there was personal pacifism in which an individual opposed violence on moral or religious grounds. Second was political pacifism in which either internationalist or left-wing groups believed war was a capitalist conspiracy against workers or liberal isolationists felt that war was none of their country's business. Pacifism also acquired a third definition referring to those who wanted to bring the ongoing war to an end not through victory but by an immediate peace settlement.

Zeppelins

German Zeppelins and other airship types carried out dozens of raids against Britain, France and Russia during the war but the British bore the brunt of their attacks, with 53 raids in total between 1914 and 1918.

In World War I rigid-frame airships were used most extensively by the German Army Air Service and the Imperial German Navy, in both reconnaissance or night-time bombing roles. Germany built two main types, the well-known Zeppelin and the little known Schütte-Lanz (SL). Both of these were kept aloft by highly pure but potentially explosive hydrogen, though they had different types of rigid frame.

Above: German airships head out on a mission over England. The first attack came in January 1915 but the raids tailed off dramatically from 1917 onward.

Airship Variants

The more common design was the Zeppelin, which was developed by Graf Zeppelin and was first accepted into German military service in March 1909. Zeppelins had a metal (duralumin) frame and came in a variety of designs. The early *L.3* was around 158.5m (520ft) long, was crewed by 16 men, and had a top speed of 72kph (45mph), while the more advanced R-type measured some 200m (650ft), had a crew of 19 and a top speed of 96kph (60mph).

The smaller Schütte-Lanz type was named after its designers, Professor Schütte and Doctor Lanz. SL airships had the drawback that their plywood frames tended to absorb atmospheric moisture too easily in flight. This made them difficult to control and they became unpopular with their crews.

The German Army put great store in its airships but its faith was shattered in the first weeks of the war. They were deployed

Left: French troops stand watch over the burnt-out remains, mostly twisted metal, of the German airship *L.39* on 6 April 1917.

on daylight reconnaissance missions over heavily defended areas of Belgium and France, and in August 1914 alone four were lost to ground fire and one was destroyed when a British fighter attacked it in its shed. The Army lost interest in airships from late 1916 and then abandoned them altogether in June 1917.

Long-range Raids

The German Navy, which had always led the way in airships, thereafter dominated operations and increasingly turned to night-time bombing. In total the German Naval Airship Division operated 73 airships during the war (59 Zeppelins, 8 Schütte-Lanz and 6 other types, such as the Parseval) and these made 342 bombing and 1,191 reconnaissance flights. Their main bombing targets were in England, especially London and other industrial areas, and Paris, although there were attempted raids on targets in Russia, including Baltic naval bases and the capital Petrograd (St Petersburg). Perhaps the most ambitious Zeppelin operation was that undertaken by *L.59* in late 1917. It was ordered to fly supplies from Bulgaria to German forces in East Africa. The mission (21–25 November) was aborted in mid-flight but *L.59* and its 22-man crew spent some 95 hours in the air and made a round trip of 6,750km (4,200 miles), braving violent storms and mechanical failures.

Zeppelins and SLs were in reality not as menacing as was believed. Their raids over England in particular did cause alarm but little damage and, in truth, they were very vulnerable; 77 out of 115 Zeppelins were destroyed or damaged beyond repair, for example. Many crashed due to adverse weather – high winds and ice were especially dangerous – while others were shot down by ground fire or, increasingly, by high-altitude fighters. Sometimes bombs were dropped on airships from above, while some fighters like the French Nieuport 17 and the British Sopwith Camel were equipped with incendiary rockets, such as the French Le Prieur that appeared in 1916. Rockets were supplanted by incendiary bullets and their use was largely discontinued by 1918.

ZEPPELIN *L.32*

The German naval Zeppelin *L.32* was commissioned on 7 August 1916 but made only 11 flights including two raids on England. It failed to bomb anything significant on 24 August and on 24 September it was first hit by anti-aircraft fire and then downed by a fighter.

Type: "Super Zeppelin"
Engines: 6 x Maybach HSLu
Length: 198m (650ft)
Gas volume: 55,000 cu m (1,950,000 cu ft)
Top speed: 100kph (60mph)
First flight: 4 August 1916

Accidents were also not uncommon. The worst came in January 1918 when five airships were destroyed in a fire at their base while they were undergoing maintenance.

THE LARGEST ZEPPELIN RAID

The biggest German airship raid on England took place on the night of 2 September 1916 and involved 11 Navy and 3 Army airships, most of them Zeppelins. A further two turned back early in the mission. The raiders struck up and down the East Coast, dropping 261 high-explosive and 202 incendiary bombs that did little damage but did kill 4 civilians and injure 12. One airship, *SL.11*, was shot down by a BE-2 fighter over Cuffley in Hertfordshire, just north of London.

Below: The spectacular end of a German airship. It was very rare for crew members to survive the downing of Zeppelins because of their combustibility.

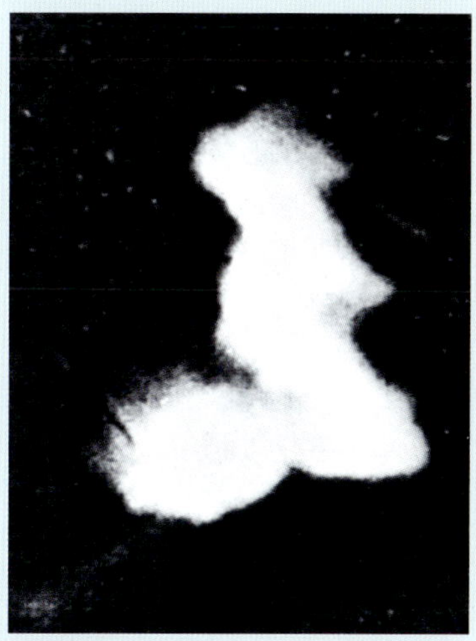

Civilians Under Fire 1914–18

The distinction between civilian and military personnel and property became blurred during World War I. In previous wars civilians might be at risk when the fighting armies were nearby; now cities far from the front were targets.

Above: Bomb damage to a street in London's West End following a visit from a German Zeppelin.

Although many French and German civilians died due to deliberate enemy action, their British counterparts faced the most sustained onslaught. The first major naval attack on Britain took place on 16 December 1914, when German warships bombarded the ports of Hartlepool, Whitby and Scarborough. Housing and other property were destroyed while casualties amounted to 122 dead and 433 injured. German warships returned to the East Coast in April 1916, hitting Lowestoft and Great Yarmouth. The loss of life was small and the damage minimal but, once again, civilian morale suffered and faith in the Royal Navy weakened. German naval raids left 157 dead and 641 injured in all.

Zeppelin raids on Britain usually involved two or more airships and concentrated on the south-east coast, the industrial North and the Midlands and, above all, London. They began on 19/20 January 1915 and London was hit for the first time on 31 May. There were a further 19 missions that year, 22 in 1916, 7 in 1917 and just 4 in 1918. Most were conducted in darkness and more than 5,750 bombs were dropped. The biggest raid occurred in September 1916 and involved 16 airships. In all some 556 British civilians were killed and 1,350 injured by bombs dropped from Zeppelins during the war.

Aircraft Attacks

Although there had been aircraft raids on south-east England since October 1914, true strategic bombing did not begin until early 1917. The main campaign involved heavy bombers, chiefly the Gotha G but also the larger Riesenflugzeug from late October. The first raid against London took place during daylight on 27 May and seven more followed, but in late August heavy losses forced the bombers to turn to night operations. There were a further 19 raids with the final attack coming on 19/20 May 1918. Gothas made 383 sorties and 43 were lost, while Riesenflugzeug types made just 30 sorties with 2 lost. Although the bombers caused little damage, civilian casualties totalled around 850 dead and over 2,000 injured. Morale did suffer until the anti-aircraft defences were improved.

Although British civilians bore the brunt of the German strikes, the French also suffered from such attacks, including 30 air raids on Paris. Parisians also had to endure long-range bombardment by the so-called "Paris Gun" in 1918; almost 900 were killed or injured.

Above: A German airship is manoeuvred out of its shed prior to a mission over England.

Attacking Germany

Germany was also the target of strategic bombing from late 1917 but the raids peaked in the final months of the war. The effort was largely conducted by Britain's Independent Air Force, which was founded in June 1918 under Major-General Hugh Trenchard. It soon began striking targets located in the industrial heartland of western Germany from airfields in eastern France and dropped some 558 tons of bombs out of a total of 665 tons dropped on Germany in 162 raids. Some 450 aircraft in all were lost but the number of German civilian casualties remains unknown.

Below: German bombing raids led to an increased demand for fighters. Here British workers are building their wing sections.

Below: This extensive damage to a building in Paris was caused by a German bombing raid.

Heavy Bombers

Heavy bombers made their debut during World War I. They were mostly deployed to undertake long-range strategic raids against military installation and industrial targets but they were also responsible for the deaths of many civilians.

Russia's Army Air Service had the most reliable heavy bomber at the outbreak of the war. It was based on Igor Sikorsky's civilian "Le Grand" from 1913, the world's first four-engined aircraft, and a military version, the Sikorsky IM (Ilya Mourometz), was ordered by the service in August 1914. It was a biplane design with an enclosed cabin, and a crew of six. It had a top speed of 96kph (60mph), a pair of machine-guns for defence and could carry some 535kg (1,180lb) of bombs. The IMs began operating against targets in eastern Poland in February 1915 and these raids were gradually extended to take in targets in Austria-Hungary and Germany. Some 400 sorties were launched by 73 bombers during 1914–17 and they proved highly successful and largely invulnerable. Only one was shot down, after itself destroying three of a group of attacking fighters, and just two others succumbed to various mechanical problems.

Below: The Russian-built Sikorsky IM (Ilya Mourometz) was one of the world's first successful heavy bombers and had a six-man crew.

Italian Designs

Italy's fledgling air service, the Corpo Aeronautico Militare (CAM), was woefully prepared for war in 1915 but it did have a long-range bomber in the Caproni. CAM had focused on such aircraft because of the local conditions – the likely battle-field was mountainous, making tactical bombing in support of ground operations problematic, but there were tempting long-range targets in both Austria-Hungary and the Balkans. Four types of Capronis (designated Ca2 to Ca5) were developed and around 750 were built in all. They came in several forms: some were biplanes while others were triplanes but they all had three engines. The Ca5 four-man biplane, introduced in

GOTHA G-IV

The Gotha was the mainstay of Germany's heavy-bomber force during the war, and five variants were built in all. The most successful version, with 230 built, was the G-IV, which began operating in early 1917. Gothas were, however, fragile machines and clumsy to fly.

Engine: 3 x 260hp Mercedes DIV
Crew: 3
Ceiling: 6,500m (21,325ft)
Top speed: 140kph (87mph)
Armament: 3 x 7.92mm (0.312in) machine-guns, 500kg (1,100lb) bombs

early 1918, was ultimately the mainstay of the Italian strategic bombing force with a total of 280 being built.

The Gotha Menace

The mainstay of the German Army Air Service's heavy bomber force was the Gotha G-series of twin-engined biplanes (designated G-I to G-V) that first entered service in 1915. These launched the first sustained strategic bombing offensive against London from bases around Ghent from June 1917. The most numerous type was the three-man G-IV which had a speed of around 140kph (87mph) and a range of 480km (300 miles). It was protected by three machine-guns and had a bomb load of some 500kg (1,100lb). The Germans also developed an even larger bomber, the Riesenflugzeug ("giant aircraft"), based on Sikorsky's IM type, that first entered full service in late 1916. Various companies built these advanced biplane bombers and there was no fully standardized design. The best was made by the Zeppelin-Staaken company. Its four-engined RVI first appeared in mid-1917. It had a seven-man crew, four machine-guns for defence, and carried up to 18 bombs.

Britain's Reply

Britain's main heavy bombers were the twin-engined Handley Page O/100 (46 built) and O/400 (550 built). The former began operating in November 1916. Heavy O/100 losses during daylight raids led them to adopt night flying. The O/400 was a similar machine and went into full production in late 1917. It was expected to be the mainstay of the Independent Air Force's strategic bombing campaign against Germany in 1919, a role until then carried out by smaller bombers. Britain was also developing other heavy bombers, chiefly the four-engined Handley Page V/1500 and the twin-engined Vickers Vimy, but none saw action.

CAPRONI Ca5

The Caproni range of Italian heavy bombers made their debut during 1911 and launched their first bombing raid of World War I in August 1915. Four variants of the design were built and served with the Italian Army and Navy and the US Army Air Service.

Engine: 3 x 300hp Fiat
Crew: 2–4
Ceiling: 4,550m (14,900ft)
Top speed: 160km/h (100mph)
Armament: 2 x 6.5mm (0.256in) machine-guns, 910kg (2,000lb) bombs

HANDLEY PAGE O/400

The HP O/400 entered service in the spring of 1918. A number were used in the bombing offensive against Germany. Although they carried a sizeable bomb load, they were also prone to accidents. Some 550 were built in Britain and a further 107 in the United States before the war's end.

Engine: 2 x 275hp Sunbeam or 2 x 375hp Rolls-Royce
Crew: 4
Ceiling: 2,590m (8,500ft)
Top speed: 160kph (100mph)
Armament: 3–5 x 0.303in (7.7mm) machine-guns, 820kg (1,800lb) bombs

The First Day of the Somme Volunteers for Britain's New Army, who fought on the Somme.

Russia Aids its Allies Poor roads gave Russia many supply difficulties on the Eastern Front.

Battle of Jutland HMS *Queen Mary* blows up after being struck by German shells.

1916 – THE YEAR OF ATTRITION

The Allies focused their main efforts in Europe during 1916 and planned to launch simultaneous offensives on the Western, Eastern and Italian Fronts. These efforts were pre-empted by the Germans, who had opted to hold fast in the east and look for victory in the west. The Germans initiated the longest battle of the war, Verdun, in February and came close to defeating the French in the first few months. The fast-deteriorating situation there led the other Allies to bring forward their own offensives. These helped relieve the pressure on the recovering French but failed to knock Germany out of the war.

All of these attacks fostered great expectations of a decisive breakthrough – yet these hopes soon proved illusory. The German attack at Verdun stalled with fast-growing casualties on all sides by the middle of the year, the British offensive on the Somme suffered a severe setback on its very first day, and the Russian Brusilov Offensive made considerable progress in its first weeks but thereafter degenerated into stalemate. The Italians made no progress against the Austro-Hungarians. Even the war at sea seemed stalemated with neither the British nor German navies able to deliver a knockout blow against each other at Jutland, the largest naval battle of the war.

Stalemate on the Italian Front Austro-Hungarian troops with a captured Italian heavy howitzer.

Machine-guns A French Hotchkiss machine-gun team in position in a reserve trench.

Operations in Salonika 1916–17 A newly arrived French unit moves up to the front.

Verdun – The German Attack

The German Army Chief of Staff, General Erich von Falkenhayn, made the fateful decision to decimate the French Army at the fortress town of Verdun in 1916 but his plan backfired as his own forces suffered equally horrendous casualties.

Germany's generals had been preoccupied with events on the Eastern Front in 1915 but returned to the attack on the Western Front in 1916. France became the preferred target as General von Falkenhayn knew that the French would hold their ground whatever the cost in lives and were willing to expend more blood in retaking what they had lost. Falkenhayn believed that the French would ultimately sue for peace if their losses became unsustainable. With France defeated Britain would have to seek an end to the war.

KEY FACTS

Date: 21 February – 18 December 1916

Place: Verdun, eastern France

Outcome: Stalemated battle with very heavy French and German casualties.

THE BATTLE OF VERDUN
As with many other of World War I's great battles, the struggle for Verdun took place in a small area, only some 40km (25 miles) across.

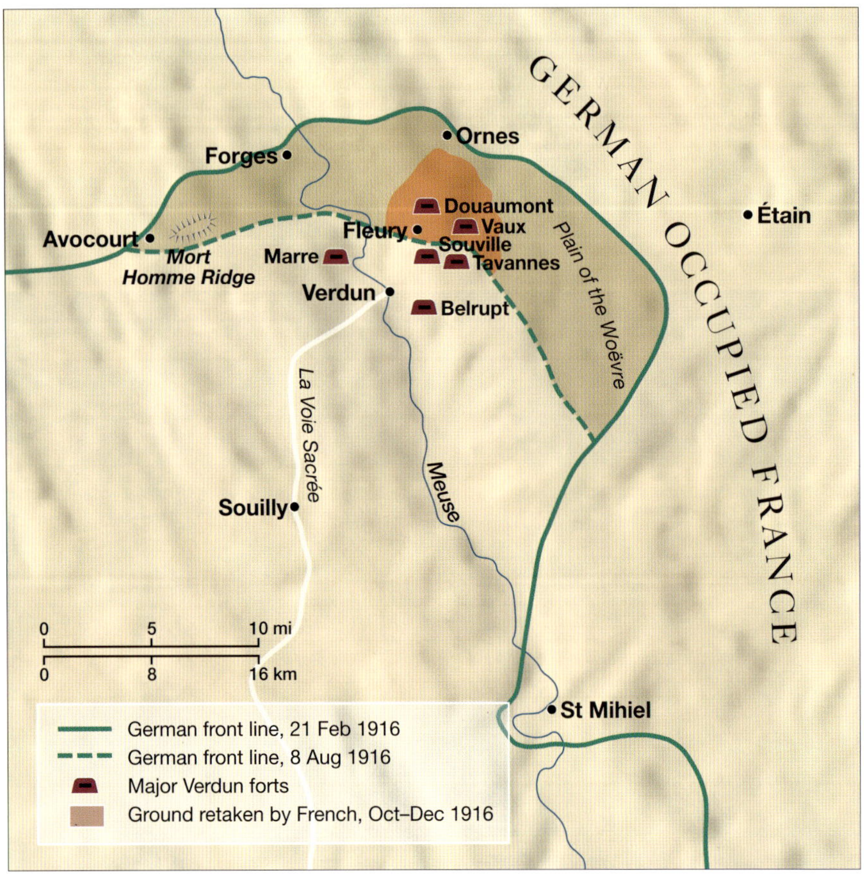

Falkenhayn choose Verdun on the River Meuse for his battle of attrition. The town was surrounded by forts but was close to a German-controlled railhead that would permit a steady flow of men and supplies to the front. Its garrison had been pared to the bone and many of the forts stripped of artillery. The German operation was codenamed Gericht, meaning "judgement" or even "place of execution". The attack was to be made on a narrow front by Crown Prince Wilhelm's Fifth Army, which was supported by some 1,200 artillery pieces and 3 million shells which had been stockpiled in secrecy.

The Killing Begins

Gericht was scheduled to begin on 12 February but snow and rain delayed the preparations and prevented accurate artillery fire. The weather cleared after eight days and the attack began on the 21st. The artillery bombardment created a lunar landscape of almost overlapping shell craters, and set the tone for the remainder of the battle. Some 100,000 shells fell in the first hour alone and 1 million rounds fell on the French before the first German assault units moved out into No Man's Land. Remarkably, some French troops survived the opening inferno and fought back with unexpected stubbornness but the German divisions mostly made steady progress. Fort

Above: French forward artillery observers seek out a suitable target on the skyline.

Douaumont was captured on the 25th, while other units took high ground overlooking the Meuse and inflicted heavy casualties on the numerous French counter-attacks.

Falkenhayn's brutal strategy seemed to be working but there were some ominous developments for the Germans, not least the loss of 25,000 men in just the first week of the battle. The German capture of Fort Douaumont – which might have been seen as a possible breaking point – actually caused a wave of national fervour in France.

Field Marshal Joffre, the French Commander-in-Chief, reacted to the crisis with great calmness. He asked the British on the River Somme to take over the sector of the front held there by the French Tenth Army, thereby freeing up some reinforcements for Verdun. He sent General Noël de Castelnau to Verdun to take temporary charge of the garrison until these reinforcements arrived and a new general, Henri-Philippe Pétain, was in place to direct the defence. He also asked the Russians to bring forward their Lake Naroch offensive to draw German troops eastward.

Continuing Attacks

Pétain arrived on the 27th and ordered his artillery to concentrate more on the German assault troops. German losses rose rapidly. They switched their attack to the north and north-west of the town on 6 March but they were stopped in front of the high ground around La Morte Homme ridge by early April. They now extended their front east as well and, after two months of intense combat, took La Morte Homme on 29 May. Fort Vaux fell on 7 June after a long siege. However, it was clear that both sides were now suffering equally in Falkenhayn's battle of attrition that had been intended to bleed just the French garrison white.

Below: The remains of Fort Vaux. Note the innumerable shell craters and trenches around the position.

SHELLSHOCK

Shellshock in World War I was akin to what is now generally referred to as post-traumatic stress disorder but was then little understood as military psychiatry was still in its infancy. Many senior figures, military, political and civil, simply refused to admit it existed, preferring to believe sufferers were cowards or, in a phrase commonly used, were "lacking moral fibre". Shellshock became manifest in many ways, from comparatively mild if regular panic attacks to the severest forms in which men were reduced to twitching wrecks or ended up in a catatonic state.

The First Day of the Somme

The officers and men of the much-enlarged British Expeditionary Force had high hopes of winning a decisive victory on the Somme but thoughts of triumph were dashed in a few hours on the first day of what was to become a prolonged battle.

When Britain went to war in August 1914 it had a tiny army by European standards and this had been largely destroyed by the year's end. The country was unable to launch any major attacks in 1915 but all that changed the following year. By then the volunteers making up the New Armies were trained and eager to take their place in the line. The aim for the planned offensive was to attack in Picardy north of the River Somme between Amiens and Péronne, break through the German line and then exploit the gap with cavalry. The battle was to be a joint Anglo-French affair but in the event many French troops had to be withdrawn to reinforce Verdun so leaving the British to take over the greater burden.

KEY FACTS

Date: 1 July 1916

Place: Around the River Somme, northern France

Outcome: Some British and French successes but no decisive breakthrough and heavy losses.

Above: Evacuating British wounded from No Man's Land while under German artillery fire.

THE BATTLE OF THE SOMME
The high hopes of the first day were soon replaced by a grinding attrition.

British Aims

General Haig planned a meticulous operation involving some 750,000 men. General Henry Rawlinson's Fourth Army was to make the main effort while the right wing of General Edmund Allenby's First Army to the north would carry out supporting

Left: British civilians answer the call for more volunteer recruits for the New Armies.

operations. British confidence was high, particularly among the New Army recruits going into battle for the first time.

The attack began after an eight-day bombardment. The heavily laden British troops moved off across No Man's Land at a steady pace at 07.30 hours on 1 July. Many were very soon hit by machine-gun fire or high-explosive shells as they walked up the gentle chalk slopes leading to the German line. Advances soon stalled in front of intact wire and trenches or broke down before the ruins of heavily defended villages. General Marie Fayolle's French Sixth Army did well in the south but the overall loss of life was appalling. The British recorded 57,470 casualties, including 19,240 dead. German losses are estimated at 4,000 killed or wounded and 2,000 captured.

Reasons for Failure

Why had the battle gone so badly wrong? The bombardment was inadequate; there were too few artillery pieces for the length of front, and most guns were too light to damage the German defences. Most of the shells were of the shrapnel type when high-explosive rounds were needed to cut wire and cave in trenches; many of both types also turned out to be duds. The delay between the barrage ending and the attack starting gave the untouched Germans time to emerge from their deep concrete dugouts and man their positions.

Haig had no alternative plan for 1 July. This was because he did not believe his untested troops were flexible enough to cope with anything other than the step-by-step approach that had been drummed into them before the battle. He knew that the primitive state of communications meant that any intelligence he did receive from the front would be out of date by the time it reached him as would be his new orders when they reached the front.

The first day of the Somme was the worst in the history of the British Army.

FIELD MARSHAL DOUGLAS HAIG

Douglas Haig (1861–1928) commanded the British Expeditionary Force from late 1915 but later became a much-maligned figure, one of the "donkeys" who led "lions". The truth was more complex, however. He was open to new ideas and weaponry, did care for the well-being of his troops and also had to carry on offensives long after the likelihood of a breakthrough had evaporated, largely to help the weakening French. He was undoubtedly in error in continuing to attack during the Battle of Passchendaele in 1917 but this lapse should be balanced by the fact that he went on to preside over the most militarily successful period in the British Army's history between August and November 1918.

Above: A formal portrait of Field Marshal Sir Douglas Haig.

Machine-guns

Machine-guns, which were used both defensively and offensively, were among the most effective weapons of the whole conflict. There were relatively small numbers in use in 1914 but all armies had many thousands by the end of the war.

Modern machine-guns were developed in the second half of the 19th century. They equipped all armies in 1914 and appeared in ever greater numbers as the war progressed. The reason was simple – a heavy machine-gun fired 400–600 rounds a minute and could effectively fulfil the tasks of 80 or more rifle-armed infantry. Heavy machine-guns were mostly associated with defensive roles, in which they would fire on attacking infantry from a fixed position in a trench but they were also used offensively. Gunners were trained to elevate their guns so that the bullets would fly over the heads of advancing infantry and then gravity would bring the rounds down on an enemy target.

The weapon usually came in three parts – a mounting tripod or sledge, the weapon itself and a reservoir of water in a can that fed into the "water jacket" that surrounded the barrel and stopped it overheating. Some guns, like the French 1914 Hotchkiss and the American Colt, were air-cooled but that system was the exception rather than the rule. Bullets were fed into a machine-gun by strips of 30 rounds or, more commonly, longer woven or metal belts.

Cumbersome in Action

Such bulky weapons were as difficult to manhandle as their name suggests. Most weighed 32–40kg (70–90lb), excluding the copious amounts of ammunition needed to keep the weapon firing. A British Vickers heavy machine-gun might have 16 250-round ammunition belts each weighing 10kg (22lb) available for immediate use and many more rounds in reserve.

MASCHINENGEWEHR 08

This weapon, introduced in 1908, was the mainstay of the German Army's heavy machine-gun detachments throughout the war in one form or another and was a very potent weapon indeed. Estimates suggest that it was responsible for around 90 per cent of the 60,000 or so casualties the British suffered on the first day of the Battle of the Somme in July 1916.

Calibre: 7.92mm (0.312in)
Rate of fire: 600rpm
Muzzle velocity: 823m/sec (2,700ft/sec)
Ammunition: 250-round belt
Weight with mount: 56kg (124lb)

Left: A Russian M1910 "Sokolov" Maxim machine-gun and crew. The gunshield protecting the firer was not a common design feature.

VICKERS MARK I

The Vickers was based on the 1884 Maxim, the world's first automatic machine-gun, and entered service with the British Army in 1912. It was lighter than the original Maxim and was known for its reliability.

Calibre: 0.303in (7.7mm)
Rate of fire: 500rpm
Muzzle velocity: 682m/sec (2,240ft/sec)
Ammunition: 250-round belt
Weight with mount: 33kg (73lb)

The average machine-gun needed two or three men to fire it, but most guns were operated by a team of four to six, the rest of whom carried ammunition. Soldiers often lugged heavy machine-guns around in battle but out of action they were broken down and transported by mules or placed on carts.

Light Machine-guns

The war also saw the development of an entirely new type of weapon, the man-portable light machine-gun that could be easily carried so that the user could keep up with attacking infantrymen. They generally weighed 10–14kg (22–30lb), most nearer the former figure than the latter, could fire 250–600 rounds per minute under ideal conditions and were air-cooled. Light machine-guns were either belt- or magazine-fed but magazines proved more practical in battle. Germany produced the Maschinengewehr 08/15, essentially a stripped down version of the Maschinengewehr 08 heavy machine-gun fitted with a pistol butt and bipod, while France had the Chauchat, which remained the French Army's standard light machine-gun throughout the conflict. Something like 250,000 of them were manufactured and they saw service with many Allied forces, including the US Army, which purchased some 34,000 in 1917. Although the Chauchat was very light it was notoriously unreliable due to frequently poor manufacturing standards.

The best light machine-gun of the war was the Lewis, a US design from 1911 which was manufactured in Belgium and Britain. It was quite a heavy weapon and was difficult to lug across a battlefield but it did become the most common infantry support gun in the Belgian and British Armies. It was also highly adaptable and was fitted to aircraft, armoured cars and tanks.

Right: The French Hotchkiss was introduced in 1900 and the first air-cooled version arrived in 1914. The original strip magazine held a mere 30 rounds and was replaced by a 249-round metal belt from 1915.

Verdun – The French Recovery

Although the French suffered horrendous losses in the first months of the battle, they slowly but surely took the initiative away from the Germans and in the final months of the fighting retook many of the most important positions.

The German attack on Verdun in February 1916 was supposed to bleed the French Army white but the plan for this battle of attrition went awry within a month or so of the battle opening. The French had suffered horrendous losses trying to hold their positions as General von Falkenhayn had intended but there was no sign that the lengthening toll of casualties was pushing them towards seeking peace. More worryingly, his own forces had been drawn deeper into the battle of attrition and were suffering losses at a similar rate. The pendulum, if anything, had swung in France's favour by early June.

Above: A French casualty is loaded into a Red Cross ambulance for evacuation from the battle.

Below: French cavalry escort a column of German prisoners captured during the bitter Verdun fighting. Around 17,500 Germans were taken prisoner during several months of combat.

New French Tactics

There were many reasons for this, not least the calibre of the new French commander at Verdun. General Pétain arrived on 26 February to command the Second Army and set about retrieving the situation. Rather than have units stay at the front until they were destroyed, he used a rotation system so that they could recover behind the lines while fresh replacements took their turn in the trenches. The French Army had 330 infantry regiments in 1916 and 259 of them fought in the battle. There was a better supply of artillery, improved food and replacement clothing, and the troops were ordered to hold their ground and avoid major counter-attacks.

Supplying Verdun

Pétain knew that the garrison needed supplies on a vast scale even though the main road and rail links had been severed, leaving a 64km (40 mile) secondary road to Bar-le-Duc as the only means of entering or leaving Verdun. Despite being under almost constant German artillery fire in places, the road, christened *La Voie Sacrée* ("The Sacred Way"), was extended and maintained by thousands of engineers. Trucks working round the clock brought huge quantities of ammunition to the battlefield every week as well as thousands of troops.

Pétain was promoted to army group commander in April and was replaced by General Robert Nivelle, who set about building on his predecessor's groundwork. He was aided in this by the Russians, who began their Brusilov Offensive on 4 June and then by the British, who opened the Battle of the Somme on 1 July. Both diverted German troops away from Verdun – some 15 divisions alone went to the East. The battle had become stalemated by late summer and Falkenhayn paid the price of failure. He was sacked on 29 August and replaced by Field Marshal Paul von Hindenburg and General Erich Ludendorff. They decided to close the battle down.

The initiative had passed to the French by autumn and they began to launch major counter-attacks. General Charles Mangin's Third Army took the lead on 24 October. Fort Douaumont, taken by the Germans on 25 February, was recaptured on the first day of his attack, while Fort Vaux, lost on 7 June, was retaken on 2 November. The battle finally ebbed away in mid-December, leaving the Germans still holding a little of the territory they had captured at the start.

Verdun was the longest battle of the war and both sides suffered roughly equally. The French recorded some 542,000 casualties and the Germans around 434,000. Some 50 per cent of the total were dead.

Left: A grim example of the cost of the battle. These are German dead, probably victims of artillery fire, but the French suffered in more or less equal measure.

GENERAL HENRI-PHILIPPE PÉTAIN

Philippe Pétain (1856–1951) was a mere colonel in August 1914 but gained rapid promotion and by July 1915 he was commanding the French Second Army. He was put in charge of the forces at Verdun in February and won popular acclaim for revitalizing its defences. Pétain was then made head of a group of armies in May 1916 and a year later was promoted to Commander-in-Chief of the whole French Army. He dealt with the ongoing mutiny in a firm but fair manner but was subsequently sidelined when Marshal Ferdinand Foch became the Allied supreme commander.

Above: General, later Field Marshal, Philippe Pétain was hailed a French national hero for his part in the battle.

Trench Warfare Weapons

Trench warfare demanded a whole new range of both fighting skills and specialist weaponry and the latter were often types that could be used at close quarters, not least hand grenades and the very earliest sub-machine-guns.

The need to clear trenches led to the development of specialist equipment. Troops required weapons that were less cumbersome and more lethal at close quarters than rifles and bayonets. Aside from improvised weapons, such as the coshes, clubs, knuckle-dusters and broad-bladed knives used in night-time trench raids, other weapons were developed through official channels.

Grenades were important in trench fighting as they allowed the thrower to attack an enemy without exposing himself to their fire. Yet, with the notable exception of Germany, many nations were slow to introduce them. The British authorities proved especially lax and soldiers at the front improvised grenades out of tin cans, bits of metal for shrapnel, some form of explosive charge and a fuse. There was eventually a plethora of official designs but the most successful mass-produced types were the hand-thrown German Stielhandgranate (stick grenade) and more common "pineapple" design, such as the British Mills bomb, which found favour with both the Allies and Germany. Grenades could also be fired from a rifle with a cup adaptor slipped into its barrel.

Above: A late war German stormtrooper throws a standard Stielhandgranate (stick grenade) towards an enemy outpost while his colleagues take cover.

Below: Although the Germans were mostly associated with the stick grenade, the early years saw a great deal of improvisation until standard designs entered service.

FLAMETHROWERS

Germany also developed two wholly new weapons. The flamethrower was first tested in

ANTI-TANK TACTICS

When the first British tanks appeared in 1916, they terrified the German troops they attacked, many of whom simply fled. However, the Germans soon developed techniques and weapons to counter the armoured threat. Trenches were made wider, thereby becoming effective anti-tank ditches. In 1918 the Germans also introduced "tank forts", which consisted of two field guns located in a forward position protected by several machine-guns and infantry. These weapons – artillery was the biggest tank killer – could take on tanks at close range as could flamethrowers, as illustrated here. The Germans also developed specialist anti-tank rifles and a special type of bullet that could penetrate a tank's armoured plate.

Germany in 1901 and during World War I it came in both portable and non-portable versions. The latter was effectively static and solely of use defending trenches but the former was more practicable for clearing enemy positions. Both types used an oil and petrol mix projected out of a pipe by a gas such as nitrogen. Fuel and propellant were stored in a cylinder and ignited by a burning taper attached to the pipe's nozzle.

There were two types of German flamethrower. The Kleif (Kleinflammenwerfer – "small flamethrower") was a cumbersome device needing a crew of two, one of whom carried a fuel container the size of a milk churn on his back and the other who aimed and fired the weapon. The more readily manageable Wex was operated by one man who carried the fuel in a lifebelt-like container on his back. The Kleif had a range of some 25m (27yds) and the Wex about 20m (22yds).

The French developed the Schilt, which was named after its creator, a captain in the Paris fire service. It had more fuel than its German counterparts so it could fire up to 10 bursts of flame out to 30m (32yd). The British devised two types of portable flamethrower, the Norris-Menchen and Lawrence, but they were never used in action save for a small version during the raid on Zeebrugge in 1918.

Flamethrowers were actually more of a psychological than a practical weapon and were very vulnerable when used offensively. Because of their short range they had to get very close to their objective, which was no easy feat as their carriers were invariably targeted before they got to close quarters.

Sub-Machine-Guns

The Germans also used the world's first sub-machine-gun – the 9mm (0.345in) Bergmann Maschinenpistole 18/1 – a type of weapon that was ideal for trench fighting. Production began in early 1918 but did not really get into its stride until the middle of the year by which time the Germans were totally incapable of major offensive operations. Nevertheless, it was a basically sound design, light enough to be used in attack, but its 32-round magazine did have teething troubles. It certainly worried the Allies – they put a clause in the Treaty of Versailles prohibiting its manufacture.

Above: British soldiers improvising grenades using tin cans filled with gun cotton, scrap and a basic fuse.

Attrition on the Somme

Although the first day of the attack had dashed many high hopes, the British battled away on the Somme for some 140 days, launching a string of offensives that ground down the opposing German units, which lost many combat veterans.

Despite the appalling losses suffered by the British forces on the Somme during 1 July 1916, there was no question of ending the offensive, not least because of the need to aid the French at Verdun. The fighting lasted until winter but the Battle of the Somme, the name usually given to the whole struggle from early July to late November, was in reality a succession of attacks. The offensive actually began with the Battle of Albert (1–13 July) and ended with the Battle of the Ancre (13–18 November), though the British did not again undertake a mass assault like that of 1 July. Subsequent pushes were smaller and their objectives less ambitious, but nearly every BEF division in France fought on the Somme and many more than once.

Britain's losses mounted as the Battle of Albert gave way to, among others, the battles of Pozières (23 July – 3 September), Thiepval (26–28 September) and the Ancre Heights (1–11 October). Most of these attacks came on either side of the Albert–Bapaume road. They generally nibbled away at the German line but the British did make some progress at the Battle of Flers-Courcelette fought from 15–22 September. That attack marked the debut of the tank. Only a handful took part and most very quickly succumbed to mechanical failure or enemy fire but they so unnerved the German infantry that many troops ran away, allowing British troops to occupy their positions.

Effects of the Battle

By the British Army's reckoning the fighting officially ended on 14 November, some 140 days after the first British troops had gone over the top. The number of men on all sides who were killed, wounded or missing totalled more than 1.3 million, including over 400,000 British casualties. Thus, the battle that had been supposed to win the war for the Allies on that distant July day had become one of attrition in which the BEF's New Army divisions were largely bled white. In five months or so the Anglo-French forces had pushed forward some 10km (6 miles) but the British in the north were still 6.5km (4 miles) short of Bapaume at the end, an objective that was supposed to have fallen on the first day. Yet the effort had not been for nothing as the German Chief of Staff, General Erich

Above left: A Mark I tank with a damaged rear steering wheel. Only a few tanks were deployed at first on the Somme, thereby lessening their impact.

Left: Canadian wounded are ferried away from the fighting around the village of Flers in September 1916.

von Falkenhayn, started to divert troops away from Verdun the day the battle began.

The fighting also had disastrous results for the German Army. It lost around 650,000 men and many generals felt that its fighting edge had been lost. Its veteran non-commissioned officers were the army's backbone and they had suffered greatly. Germany was also facing increasingly acute manpower shortages after the exertions on the Somme and at Verdun and this led its High Command to take an extraordinary step that reflected the growing crisis.

New German Ideas

Falkenhayn was replaced by the Third Supreme Command of Field Marshal Hindenburg and General Ludendorff in August. They decided to build a new defence system some 32km (20 miles) behind the existing lines on the northern and central sections of the Western Front. The aim was simply to shorten their front so that it could be held with fewer men. Work on what the Allies soon called the Hindenburg Line began in September. Its construction signified that Germany was struggling to wage war on two fronts and, as the strategic situation stood, was incapable of making a major offensive effort in the west.

Above: British troops drag a 6in (15cm) howitzer into position on the Somme battlefield. Its wheels have been fitted with "girdles" to spread the load over soft ground and to prevent ruts forming when the gun recoils on firing.

Below: A British soldier gives out water to a group of German prisoners captured near Pozières, the scene of bitter fighting between late July and early September 1916.

PALS BATTALIONS

The outbreak of war in 1914 saw a huge rush to volunteer in Britain. Many recruits from the same towns or working in the same business or industry who joined up together were allowed to serve in the same units, which became known as pals battalions. These new soldiers had excellent morale but suffered badly in their first major offensive, the Battle of the Somme. When a pals battalion took heavy casualties the simultaneous loss of so many men from a particular town often had a devastating impact on local feeling.

British Tanks

The British developed the first truly viable tank at the beginning of 1916 and, while they did score some noteworthy successes, they were generally too underpowered and overly prone to mechanical failure to reach their full potential.

The first tanks, tracked armoured vehicles fitted with some form of armament, were developed in Britain but the concept only emerged slowly and involved many different agencies and individuals. Although the gestation period was prolonged, the design moved swiftly from prototype to production to battle. The prototype, nicknamed Mother, first ran in January 1916 and was rhomboid in shape with two side-mounted "turrets", commonly known as sponsons. Production of the Tank Mark I began in April and they went into action on 15 September during the Battle of the Somme.

Their attack initially went well, literally scaring the Germans out of their trenches, but thereafter their effectiveness diminished rapidly. Due to the appalling conditions inside their armoured cabs, crews were soon left sick and disorientated; many tanks also broke down due to mechanical failure and others simply bogged down in muddy trenches and shell craters. Nevertheless, they had done sufficiently well for more to be ordered.

Males and Females

Tanks became available with different combinations of weapons. "Males" carried a pair of light artillery guns and four machine-guns and "Females" were armed with six machine-guns. The most widely used tank of the war was the Mark IV. The first of these arrived at the front in April 1917. There were 595 Female Mark IVs and 420

NAMING THE TANK

It may seem curious but the tank's complex development was partly the responsibility of the Royal Navy, mostly because First Lord of the Admiralty Winston Churchill was a backer of the project. Thus, the first tanks were actually known as His Majesty's Landships. It soon became apparent that the name potentially gave an enemy with a vivid enough imagination the opportunity to guess the nature of the top secret weapon. A less obvious codename was needed and various suggestions were made, each reflecting its shape. Cistern, container and reservoir were all suggested but tank quickly became the preferred option.

Below: The Mark A Whippet was, as its name suggests, an attempt to create a fast-moving medium tank to exploit any breakthrough but its top speed was still only 13kph (8mph).

Left: Mark V tanks, here fitted with trench-crossing cribs, made their debut in July 1918. They had slightly thicker armour and more powerful engines than earlier types.

Males, but a number of the former were converted into "Hermaphrodites" by replacing the right-hand sponson with a Male sponson with its mix of machine-guns and a light gun.

As the capabilities and limitations of tanks became better understood, they underwent various modifications and improvements. So that they could cross the wider trenches the Germans had dug in part as tank traps, "Tadpole Tails", extensions to the rear of the tank, were tried but proved to be too flimsy so designers much more successfully turned to extending the main body itself. It was, however, more common for tanks to carry fascines on their roofs that could simply be rolled into a trench, thereby making a bridge for them to cross. Early versions were bundles of logs and brushwood held together by chains, but later ones consisted of a steel crib. Tanks were often thwarted by the mud and shell craters of No Man's Land so they were given "ditching gear", essentially a wooden beam that could be drawn under the tracks to give greater purchase, or their tracks' width was extended with plates to spread the load.

Faster Designs

As the value of tanks became clear, the British developed a faster light tank that was supposed to work with cavalry and exploit any breakthrough made by the heavier tanks. The first Medium Mark A, more commonly known as the Whippet, was built in October 1917 and they went into action for the first time on 26 March 1918.

Tanks were neither as good as their exponents believed or as bad as their detractors argued. They made significant advances in the first days of the tank-led Battle of Cambrai in late 1917 but had performed woefully amid the mud of Passchendaele. However, they were never able to make a decisive breakthrough and then keep the momentum of the attack going. This was largely due to their mechanical unreliability.

TANK MARK I

The Mark I was the first tank to go into action. Some 49 were deployed and enjoyed a degree of local success but most were soon knocked out by enemy fire or broke down.

Weight: 28.5 tonnes
Crew: 8
Max. speed: 6.5kph (4mph)
Max. armour: 12mm (0.47in)
Armament: 2 x 6pdr (57mm) and 4 machine-guns (Male)

Russia Aids its Allies

Like the British on the Somme, the Russians launched their own major offensive to ease the pressure on the French at Verdun during 1916 and the attack, which was masterminded by General Alexei Brusilov, was initially a major success.

The Russians agreed to launch a summer offensive in 1916 to support the Anglo-French effort in the west but Verdun forced the French to ask for an immediate attack. The Russian Chief of Staff, General Mikhail Alexeev, chose to attack north of the Pripet Marshes to the east of Vilna where two of his army groups massed for the Battle of Lake Naroch. The main effort was against Field Marshal von Eichhorn's German Tenth Army and was spearheaded by the Second Army of General Alexei Evert's Western Army Group.

The Second Army advanced on 18 March but the troops were met by a withering fire from the German trenches. By late April, when the fighting ebbed away, the Russians had suffered 100,000 casualties and failed to divert any German troops away from Verdun; Eichhorn lost 20,000 men.

Brusilov's New Plan

The second Russian attack had its origins in Italy where an Austrian onslaught in mid-May led the Italians to request

THE BRUSILOV OFFENSIVE
The first successful large-scale attack by the Russian Army in WWI.

Left: German artillery officers observe the accuracy of their fire. Note how much more temporary the position looks in comparison with those on the Western Front.

Left: A Russian supply column. The generally poor road network on the Eastern Front caused problems for both sides, especially during the spring thaw and heavy autumn rains.

urgent help. The Russian high command were uncertain where to strike. Alexeev favoured another offensive in the north but the idea met with little enthusiasm – and preparations would take two months. Instead, General Alexei Brusilov outlined a radical plan that could be put into action in weeks.

He believed that a breakthrough on a narrow front was unlikely to succeed and suggested a broad-front approach. Brusilov also offered solutions that would regain the element of surprise. He suggested that his armies of the South-west Army Group should take the lead despite the fact they did not outnumber their opponents significantly. These plans were greeted with something close to incredulity by his peers as they believed that an attack on a broad front without huge superiority was bound to fail. The arguments continued into late May until the worsening situation in Italy forced Alexeev's hand and Brusilov was given permission to attack.

The targets of the offensive were five largely Austro-Hungarian armies strung out between the Pripet Marshes and the Romanian border. The attacks opened on 4 June and were almost wholly successful, pushing the Austro-Hungarians back along most of the front. The offensive marked the high point of Russia's involvement in World War I. In just two weeks Brusilov's troops captured some 200,000 prisoners. The greatest victory was in the south, where the Austro-Hungarian Seventh Army was pushed all the way back to the Carpathians.

Casualty Count

The battle ended in autumn. Although the later stages could not match the triumphs of the first days, the offensive had reaped dividends. Brusilov had inflicted 350,000 casualties on the German Army and perhaps 1 million on the Austro-Hungarians. They had to call off their offensive against Italy and the Germans had to transfer troops from the West. Yet Russia had paid a very high price for this victory. Around 1 million of its troops had been killed, wounded or taken prisoner and the morale of the survivors was at a low ebb.

GENERAL ALEXEI BRUSILOV

Brusilov (1853–1926) came from an aristocratic background and is widely thought of as the finest Russian general of the war. He began the conflict as an army commander and was known as an able and meticulous planner. His reputation was such that he took command of an army group in March 1916 and then planned and launched the highly successful Brusilov Offensive. He supported the Provisional Government of March 1917 and was made its Commander-in-Chief. He took part in the short-lived Kerensky Offensive but was replaced on 1 August.

Above: Brusilov studies a map while planning his offensive.

The Romanian Campaign

Romania sided with the Allies in 1916 in the hope of gaining Austro-Hungarian territory but it suffered the wrath of the Central Powers, who invaded the country rapidly and overran much of it in a matter of just a few months.

Pre-war Romania had a mostly unmodernized army of some 550,000 men but a declaration of war in support of either the Allies or Central Powers by Bucharest during 1916 would have given either a significant psychological boost. Romania had been courted by both warring camps, not least Germany as it relied on Romanian grain and oil and used its rail system to maintain contact with Turkey. The Romanian government had swayed first one way and then another depending on the fortunes of war of its various suitors. The royal family itself was divided as King Ferdinand was a cousin of Kaiser Wilhelm, while his wife, Princess Marie, was a granddaughter of Britain's Queen Victoria.

Above: Romanian troops guard one of the several key passes through the Carpathians that led to Austro-Hungarian territory.

Romania Picks Sides

The pendulum finally swung decisively in mid-1916 when Russia's Brusilov Offensive clearly weakened the Austro-Hungarian forces on the Eastern Front and brought the Russians close to the Romanian border. Germany acted immediately, informing the Romanian government that any attack into Austria-Hungary would lead to the commitment of German troops. Turkey and Bulgaria followed suit. Contingency plans to invade Romania by all four were drawn up in secret but no one expected a Romanian war declaration until September after the harvest had been gathered. The Central Powers did not realize just how extensive the Allies' diplomatic charm offensive had been and their promises of new lands once Austria-Hungary had been defeated tipped the balance. Romania signed a military agreement in mid-August and declared war on the 27th.

The announcement sealed Falkenhayn's fate. His failure at Verdun, his mistaken belief that Russia was incapable of serious offensive action in 1916, and a

THE DEFEAT OF ROMANIA
The Central Powers crushed Romania in a campaign that lasted from August 1916 to January 1917.

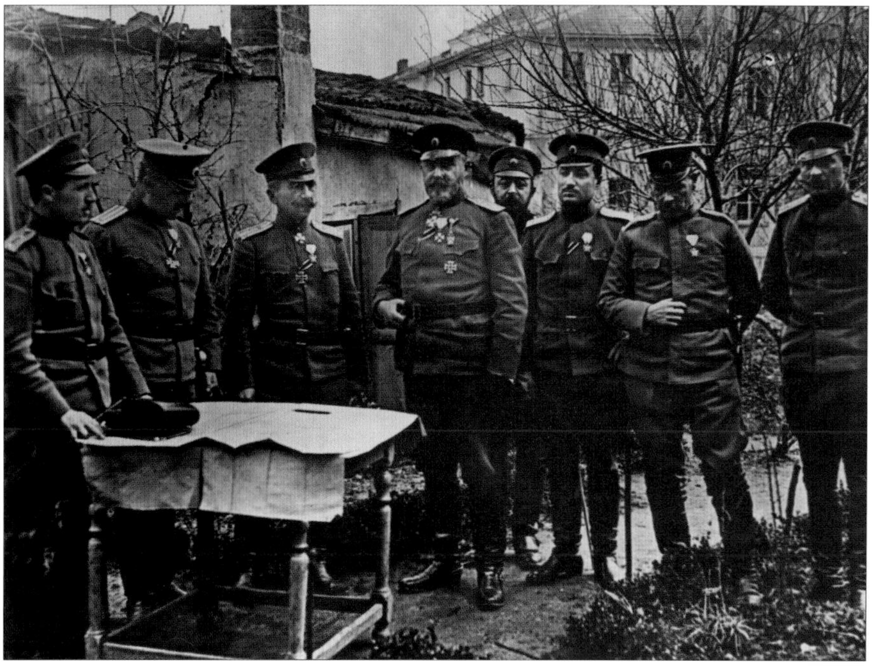

Left: A group of Bulgarian officers pose for the camera. Despite its comparatively small population, the country had a very large army and fielded some 850,000 men by 1918.

prolonged whispering campaign against him by other ambitious generals and senior politicians made his position untenable. He tendered his resignation on 29 August. Henceforth, Germany's war would be directed by the two top officers from the Eastern Front, who had led the anti-Falkenhayn faction, Field Marshal Paul von Hindenburg, who became Chief of Staff, and General Erich Ludendorff, who styled himself First Quartermaster-General. Collectively, they and their staffs were titled the Third Supreme Command.

Hindenburg and Ludendorff moved swiftly to deal with Romania. The Romanian First and Second Armies had made a half-hearted attack northward into Transylvania, Austro-Hungarian territory but home to three million ethnic Romanians. The attackers made sluggish advances through the four main passes across the Transylvanian Alps but were soon facing a battle for survival. Falkenhayn, now in charge of the German Ninth Army, struck and pushed them back through the passes into the province of Wallachia, while Field Marshal August von Mackensen at the head of the Bulgarian–German Danube Army moved up from the Salonika front and invaded the Romanian province of Dobrudja from the south.

Romania Defeated

The decisive clash came in early December 1916 at the four-day Battle of the River Arges during which the Romanians were crushed. Bucharest fell on the 6th and what was left of the Romanian Army headed northward towards the Russians. By the year's end the Romanians were only able to hold on to their province of Moldavia and the government and royal family had settled in the province's capital, Jassy (Iasi). The campaign had cost the Romanians upwards of 300,000 casualties and the invaders around 120,000 men. A British politician, John Norton-Griffiths, who had been sent to Romania to gather intelligence, had the presence of mind to sabotage much of the country's oil-producing facilities and destroy large quantities of stored grain, but there was no disguising the fact that these measures would only hinder Germany temporarily.

Right: Romanian troops cross a makeshift footbridge as they retreat to the north-east of their country.

Camouflage

Because of the real danger of being spotted either by reconnaissance aircraft or tethered balloons and then brought under artillery fire, all sides practised the art of camouflage to protect vital equipment and other military supplies.

Camouflage is essentially a form of visible deception and has always been used in warfare. However, it became even more important during World War I, despite the static nature of the fighting on many fronts. What made camouflage ever more necessary was the advent of reconnaissance aircraft. Previously, observers had been limited to spotting targets that were within their line of sight, so simply positioning troops behind a piece of high ground or beyond normal visual range would be sufficient to hide them from view. Static balloons like those deployed in the American Civil War (1861–65) and the Franco-Prussian War (1870–71) made this a much more difficult proposition but even their observers could reach only as far as their eyes and binoculars could see. Aircraft, however, could range deep behind enemy lines and cover large swathes of territory in a single sortie. These simple truths meant that camouflage became even more essential.

Above: A somewhat half-hearted attempt to camouflage a British tank. They were usually hidden in woods before moving up to attack.

Above: A German artillery observer in a lightly camouflaged position looks through a pair of stereoscopic sights in search of a target.

Concealing Plans

World War I was a war of supply as much as anything else. Rear areas were often filled with huge supply dumps that would grow ever bigger as a major offensive loomed. These were obvious, tempting targets for enemy aircraft and artillery and thus would be hidden in forests or covered in netting. Similarly, the British used to create large marshalling areas for tanks before they were committed to battle and to try to maintain the

Right: A British howitzer crew in action near Ypres. Camouflage netting partially hides their location from enemy counter-battery fire.

element of surprise these were usually hidden away in forests from which the undergrowth was cleared to make movement less difficult when the order to advance was given. It was also not uncommon for flights of aircraft to fly over German lines in a type of aural camouflage to hide the sound of the tanks turning over their engines as they prepared to move out of the rear base and go into action.

Closer to the front, in areas that were under direct enemy observation, vulnerable sections of road were often hidden by lengths of camouflage netting, something akin to washing drying on a line, so that any traffic moving down them would enjoy a measure of invisibility.

Observation Posts

Camouflage was also practised right at the front line and there were several ingenious ruses, mostly developed by the British, to confuse an enemy. Observation of enemy activity was dangerous in daylight and putting a head above a trench parapet foolhardy, so the British in particular developed a series of observation posts that looked like shell-blasted tree stumps so that they blended more easily into the surroundings.

The best camouflage of all was, of course, darkness and much activity took place at night. Men moved off into No Man's Land to dig saps, repair barbed wire cut by artillery fire, launch trench raids and conduct listening operations. If the conditions were wintry and snow lay on the ground, some troops had access to white oversuits. Behind the lines movement could usually be undertaken without being observed but it was always stressed that any supplies and troops moving up to the front needed to be brought forward with as little noise as possible.

DAZZLE CAMOUFLAGE

This form of maritime deception used both extreme colour variations and linear patterns in black, grey and white to obscure features of a ship, such as its waterline, deck or bridge, that a U-boat commander would use to estimate a ship's course, speed and distance. Without accurate information, it was difficult to score a torpedo hit. Dazzle camouflage was applied to over 4,400 Allied merchant and naval vessels but just how effective it was is debatable.

Right: HMS *Revenge* in dazzle paint late in the war.

Stalemate on the Italian Front

The Austro-Hungarians launched their first major offensive on the Italian Front during late spring 1916 but their early gains were soon lost, while the Italians continued to batter away with similarly little success along the River Isonzo.

The Italian Army planned a summer offensive along the River Isonzo once again in 1916, but the fighting at Verdun forced the French to ask them to attack in early spring. The Italian Chief of Staff, General Luigi Cadorna, really lacked the means for a major operation but agreed to aid his ally. The Fifth Battle of the Isonzo opened on 11 March but bad weather intervened and the inconclusive fighting ended on the 29th.

Mountain Battles

Although the Isonzo battles usually dominated the whole Italian campaign, the Austro-Hungarians briefly opened another battle area. This was the mountainous Trentino region of the South Tyrol, an area with a sizeable Italian-speaking population that had been occupied by the Italians during 1915. The main thrust by the Austro-Hungarian forces was directed southward towards the town of Asiago and the aim was to cut off the bulk of the Italian troops along the Isonzo line to the east from the rest of their homeland.

Above: Prisoners march away from the Isonzo fighting. The difficult terrain was typical of the region.

Below: Austro-Hungarian troops push forward as a flamethrower deals with an Italian position.

Despite his request for German aid being rebuffed because of events at Verdun, the Austro-Hungarian Chief of Staff, Field Marshal Conrad von Hötzendorf, felt able to attack in late spring. He had the Third Army under General Kövess von Kövesshàza and General Victor Dankl von Krasnik's Eleventh Army available. They were supported by around 2,000 artillery pieces and outnumbered their opponents, the 100,000-strong Italian First Army under General Roberto Brusati, by a margin of four-to-one. Command for the Asiago Offensive was given to Archduke Eugene but Conrad was the real driving force.

Austrian Progress

The Austro-Hungarians moved forward on a 72km (45 mile) front on 15 May and Conrad's forces made some early progress, pushing the Italians out of Asiago on the 29th before running out of steam. This was due to difficult terrain and the speed with which Cadorna used his homeland's railway system to rush around 400,000 troops to reinforce Brusati. Conrad had

Above: Austro-Hungarian troops surround an Italian heavy howitzer abandoned during the Asiago Offensive.

driven a salient into the Italian line but even this was soon given up as Italian pressure told.

The Eastern Front erupted on 4 June when Russia launched the Brusilov Offensive and Austro-Hungarian units had to be withdrawn from the Trentino a week or so later to shore up their crumbling front in the east. Italian counter-attacks continued and Eugene was finally given permission to withdraw to positions a mere 5km (3 miles) from his starting point. Losses were more or less even, around 150,000 men each, but the Austro-Hungarians had shot their bolt and would never again conduct offensive operations against Italy without German help.

The Asiago Offensive did not prevent Cadorna from renewing his efforts along the Isonzo. He transferred large numbers of troops away from the Trentino and launched them against the depleted Austro-Hungarian forces on 6 August. Although there was no breakthrough, Gorizia was finally taken at a cost of roughly 50,000 casualties. Austro-Hungarian losses had reached 40,000 men by the time the fighting ended on the 17th. A new Italian government felt emboldened enough to declare war on Germany on 28 August, making it likely that the latter would commit troops to the Italian Front.

There were three more Isonzo battles in 1916 – Seventh (14–26 September), Eighth (10–12 October) and Ninth (1–14 November). They made little progress beyond inflicting a further 65,000 or so casualties at a cost of 75,000 Italians killed, wounded or captured.

GENERAL LUIGI CADORNA

Luigi Cadorna (1850–1928) became the Italian Army's Chief of Staff in July 1914. He proved an able organizer but was a strategist of limited originality. Although his efforts were admittedly constrained by mountainous terrain, he conducted a series of highly costly offensives along the River Isonzo between June 1915 and September 1917. His downfall came after his forces largely collapsed in the face of the German-led Caporetto Offensive later in 1917. He lost the support of his own government and the Allied High Command and was sacked in December.

Right: Italian troops move up to the front line in preparation for one of the Isonzo offensives in 1916.

Seaplane Tenders and Aircraft Carriers

Naval aviation was very much in its infancy at the outbreak of the war in 1914 but over the following years the British in particular began to experiment with a variety of warships capable of carrying aircraft into battle.

Attempts to deploy aircraft from warships in World War I were largely advanced by Britain's Royal Naval Air Service. Its first seaplane tender was an old converted cruiser, *Hermes*, sunk by a torpedo in October 1914, but the first true aircraft carrier was *Ark Royal*, an ex-collier that entered service in December 1914. The Royal Navy also transformed several cross-Channel ferries into lightly armed seaplane tenders from 1914 onwards. The ferries' relatively high speed was important because it allowed them to maintain pace with the more conventional warships of the main battlefleet.

First Battles

Three, *Engadine*, *Empress* and *Riviera*, were converted that autumn and, while they could in theory at least fly wheeled aircraft from their decks, they invariably winched seaplanes fitted with floats into and out of the water. Nevertheless, they proved their worth by making the first-ever naval aviation raid when they launched seven aircraft against the Zeppelin sheds near Cuxhaven on 25 December 1914. *Engadine* later served in the North Sea and was present at the Battle of Jutland in 1916.

The three other conversions were the larger *Ben-My-Chree*, *Manxman* and *Videx*. A milestone in naval aviation was achieved by the last in November 1915 when a Bristol Scout C aircraft became the first-ever land-based aircraft to achieve take-off at sea. *Ben-My-Chree* went to the Dardanelles in the summer of 1915 and one of its Short 184 seaplanes made the first successful aerial torpedo attack that August. There was a final group of seaplane tenders that entered service in 1915–17, including the ex-liners *Campania*, *Nairana*

HMS *FURIOUS*

The forward flight deck on the ex-battle-cruiser HMS *Furious* allowed aircraft to take off but they could not land at sea. As first converted, *Furious* could carry 3 Short 184 seaplanes and 5 Sopwith Pup fighters.

Displacement: 22,000 tons
Crew: 737
Speed: 32.5 knots
Main armament: 10 x 4in (101.6mm) guns

Below: A fast cross-Channel ferry was converted into the seaplane tender HMS *Engadine* in 1914 and took part in a raid on the German airship base at Cuxhaven on 25 December.

Right: HMS *Argus* was the first flush-deck carrier from which aircraft could take off and land but did not enter service until October 1918.

and *Pegasus*, although their performance was generally no better or worse than their predecessors'. *Campania* saw little service before being lost in a storm in late 1918, while *Nairana* and *Pegasus* served in the North Sea before sailing for the Mediterranean during the same year.

France and Russia also developed tenders. The former began by converting a torpedo-boat depot ship, *Foudre*, so that by 1913 it had sufficient hangar space to carry a number of seaplanes. The French built just four more. The ex-passenger liner *Campinas* was converted in 1915 and again served in the eastern Mediterranean. Three cross-Channel ferries were also converted – *Rouen* acted as a convoy escort in the Mediterranean, while *Nord* and *Pas-de-Calais* operated in the Channel. Russia deployed six seaplane tenders with its Black Sea Fleet.

Aircraft Carriers

The use of wheeled aircraft on tenders and carriers was advanced by the arrival in 1916 of more powerful aircraft, notably Sopwith's Strutter and Pup, that could take off from short decks. However, they could not be landed and pilots had to ditch into the sea after a mission. The British tried to resolve this problem by further modifying *Furious*, a former light battle-cruiser, in late 1917. By March 1918 it had two flight decks and extensive hangar space but turbulence from the central superstructure still made landing at sea very hazardous. Conversion work on the first true flush-deck aircraft carrier, the former liner *Argus*, had begun in late 1916 but both it and the first purpose-built carrier, *Hermes*, did not see action before the war's end.

HMS *CAMPANIA*

The ex-liner *Campania* entered service as an aircraft carrier in May 1915. It could carry ten seaplanes but the sloping forward flight deck was too short for aircraft to take off safely.

Laid down: 1893
Displacement: 18,000 tons
Crew: 600
Speed: 22 knots
Main armament: 6 x 4.7in (119mm) guns

THE TONDERN RAID

This British attack against a Zeppelin base on the German–Dutch border on 18 July 1918 was the only occasion in the war when aircraft were launched from an aircraft carrier. Seven Sopwith Camels carrying bombs flew off the deck of *Furious* at dawn; six attacked the target and two airships, *L.54* and *L.60*, were destroyed. Two aircraft made it to neutral Denmark, while three others ditched in the sea. The fate of the sixth aircraft remains unknown but five pilots and one aircraft survived from the attacking force.

Operations in Salonika 1916–17

The Allies poured vast amounts of men and equipment into the Greek province of Salonika intending to open a new front against the Central Powers but instead they remained largely inactive, suffering greatly from various debilitating diseases.

The build-up of Allied forces in Salonika had begun in late 1915 after Greece became aware of the Central Powers' preparations to invade Serbia and requested urgent military aid. This request was soon withdrawn but the influx of Allied troops continued into 1916, most notably with the arrival of large numbers of Serbians who had been evacuated from their homeland during January. They landed on Corfu and were re-equipped by the Allies before then embarking for mainland Greece. Some 120,000 had arrived by July and they, like the other Allied forces, manned a fortified line that stretched across the neck of the peninsula.

Above: The build-up of Allied strength in Salonika continues – British troops unload a horse.

Allied Problems

The Allied effort was plagued by many problems, not least local conditions that produced crippling levels of sickness, chiefly malaria. The mountainous terrain also greatly favoured defensive rather than offensive action. There were also unresolved political issues. The French and British forces did not have a unified command structure and their commanders – General Maurice Sarrail and General Bryan Mahon respectively – often went their own way even though the former was supposedly in charge. Many British and French leaders, both civil and military, felt that Salonika was a sideshow and it was therefore often starved of the necessary military resources.

Below: Troops march off to the front in Salonika, a small part of one of the most diverse Allied forces in the war.

First Battles

Allied plans for the summer of 1916 centred on a push up the River Vardar in the direction of Uskub (Skopje) in southern Serbia but were pre-empted by a Bulgarian-led advance from south-west Serbia into northern Greece supported by a leavening of German units. These troops inflicted a defeat on the Allies at the Battle of Florina (17–27 August). Sarrail ordered a counter-attack the following month to retake the lost ground. Florina was recaptured on the 18th and, despite bickering between Sarrail and his generals, the advance continued.

The Allies crossed over into Serbia and, after a four-day battle, occupied Monastir (Bitola) on 19 November. The recent fighting had cost around

50,000 Allied casualties while the Germans and Bulgarians recorded some 10,000 more. The Balkans saw one final campaign during 1916, although it was largely conducted in isolation. An Italian corps in southern Albania defeated a similarly sized Austro-Hungarian force in November and linked up with Sarrail's command around Lake Ochrida (Ohrid).

The campaigning of 1916 established a front line across northern Greece and a small part of southern Serbia that would remain mostly unchanged until September 1918. Sarrail did try to break the stalemate in 1917 but had just 100,000 men, one-sixth of his command, actually fit for action. Two major battles were fought in the first half of the year, at Lake Prespa (11–17 March) and along the River Vardar (5–19 May), but to little effect. The Allies made no further attacks in 1917. A new French government sacked Sarrail and replaced him with the very able General Adolphe Marie Guillaumat on 10 December.

Above: Malaria was a major problem in Salonika and these men are receiving their compulsory daily dose of quinine.

The Allies had imposed themselves on Greece, an officially neutral state whose political leadership was divided over the war. Greece's King Constantine I, German Emperor Wilhelm II's brother-in-law, leaned towards the Central Powers, while his sometime prime minister, Eleutherios Venizelos, generally favoured the Allies. Matters were settled after the Allies put considerable military and diplomatic pressure on the Greeks over several months. Constantine finally abdicated his throne on 12 June 1917 and the new monarch, Alexander, then re-appointed Venizelos as prime minister on the 26th. Greece issued a war declaration against the Central Powers on 2 July.

Left: Resting British troops look on as a column of freshly arrived French soldiers moves up to the front line.

War in East Africa 1914–18

The campaign in East Africa was the longest of the war in large part due to the tenacity of the local German commander, General Paul von Lettow-Vorbeck, who only surrendered some days after the signing of the Armistice in November 1918.

There were four German colonies in Africa in August 1914 but three had fallen to the Allies by early 1916. The fourth, German East Africa (Rwanda, Burundi and Tanzania), was a much tougher prospect and its garrison did not finally surrender until two weeks after the Armistice. The campaign was a remarkable feat of arms because East Africa was initially defended by just 3,000 Europeans and 4,600 local troops (*askaris*) and police led by General Paul von Lettow-Vorbeck and was surrounded by British-controlled or neutral colonies. Even more remarkably, Lettow-Vorbeck received virtually no aid from Germany throughout the war, and had to rely on what his troops could capture, scrounge or manufacture locally to maintain the war effort.

PAUL VON LETTOW-VORBECK

Lettow-Vorbeck (1870–1964) was a true career soldier who was appointed commander in German East Africa in February 1914. He never had more than a few thousand, mainly local, troops and received virtually no aid from Germany but tied up many times larger Allied forces throughout the entire war.

Above: Lettow-Vorbeck became a national hero in his homeland.

Early Battles

The British ordered an immediate attack on Lettow-Vorbeck with some 12,000 untried Indian troops but these were roundly defeated during 3–5 November 1914. The major battle was at Tanga, German East Africa's main port. Some 8,000 Indian troops were beaten by Lettow-Vorbeck's 1,000 men and suffered 360 dead and 487 wounded, while he recorded 148 casualties. The British also abandoned 16 machine-guns, several hundred rifles and 600,000 rounds of ammunition. There was no major fighting in 1915 with both sides content to launch cross-border raids. Lettow-Vorbeck was able to build up his strength to 3,000 European and 11,300 local troops during the year and also recovered ten 10.5cm (4.1in) artillery pieces from the light cruiser *Königsberg*, which was destroyed by the British in the River Rufiji's delta on 11 July.

South African General Jan Christiaan Smuts became the new British Commander in February 1916, and he launched a new offensive into northern East Africa between March and September but failed to catch Lettow-Vorbeck and had to withdraw through exhaustion.

Below: A British soldier stands watch over a large artillery piece somewhere in East Africa.

There were two subsidiary expeditions into East Africa – an Anglo-Belgian force halted after taking Tabora in the north-west in September while an advance into the south-west from Northern Rhodesia (Zambia) was halted by the Germans at Iringa in late October. The various expeditions had overrun huge swathes of East Africa but something like 12,000 white troops had been evacuated through sickness and Lettow-Vorbeck's main force was still at large in the south-east.

Above: Trumpeters for a British-officered Nigerian regiment pictured on a troopship bound for East Africa.

Closing In

The British spent much of 1917 repairing damage done by Lettow-Vorbeck's hit-and-run raids, receiving reinforcements and dealing with the so-called Wintgens–Naumann Expedition, an unauthorized campaign by two German officers and just 700 *askaris* that caused havoc in much of occupied northern East Africa. The British did launch attacks against Lettow-Vorbeck in September but these were halted at Mahiwa and he was able to escape into Portuguese East Africa (Mozambique). He now led his remaining 2,200 men on a gruelling 2,000km (1,250 mile) trek that finally brought them back into East Africa on 12 September 1918.

With strong British forces converging on him, Lettow-Vorbeck took his command into Northern Rhodesia and fought a final skirmish at Kamasa on 12 November. He heard of the Armistice the next day and, after negotiations with the British, his small force had been interned in Abercorn by the 25th. His isolated and prolonged campaign had tied down some 160,000 Allied troops as well as many thousands of local labourers. Total British military casualties were around 10,000 but if local porters and labourers are included the figure rises to around 100,000.

THE CURSE OF MALARIA

Malaria, usually a debilitating rather than fatal disease, took a heavy toll of personnel in several theatres of war, notably Salonika and Africa. In the latter case there was something of a myth that locals, many of whom acted as porters, were immune but the figures suggest otherwise. In East Africa, for example, African soldiers fighting for the British suffered 1,377 combat casualties but 2,923 men were admitted to hospital with disease. Malaria was a very real threat to all. Some 50,000 British troops in East Africa were treated for the disease between June and December 1916 alone.

Above: British troops and local porters move through a swamp, an ideal breeding ground for malarial mosquitoes.

The Battle of Jutland

Although the British lost more warships and men in what was by far the largest naval action of the war, they gained an undoubted strategic victory over the German High Seas Fleet, which never left port in such strength again.

The only major fleet action between the German High Seas Fleet and the British Grand Fleet rather came about by accident. Both sides hoped to draw elements of the other into an unequal action in 1916 but the Germans took the initiative and sailed from their home ports during the early afternoon of 30 May. What they did not know was that the British were aware of the plan and their own fleet was already at sea.

KEY FACTS

DATE: 31 May – 1 June 1916

PLACE: Eastern and south-eastern North Sea

OUTCOME: The German High Seas Fleet was forced to retreat after sinking several major British warships.

Above: The dreadnought SMS *Ostfriesland* was holed by a mine as it sailed home after Jutland.

Opposing Fleets

The British force comprised the main fleet under Admiral John Jellicoe supported by Admiral David Beatty's battle-cruisers. Opposing them was the High Seas Fleet under Admiral Reinhard Scheer and Admiral Franz von Hipper's battle-cruisers. The British had a total of 151 warships available, led by 28 dreadnoughts and 9 battle-cruisers, while the Germans deployed 16 dreadnoughts, 6 pre-dreadnoughts and 5 battle-cruisers. The rest of the warships on both sides were mostly smaller cruisers and destroyers.

Below: The loss of the battle-cruiser HMS *Indefatigable*, a victim of accurate German gunnery, poor design and poorly observed damage-control procedures.

First Blood

Jutland opened at 14.15 hours on the 31st with a clash between smaller cruisers and destroyers, whose radio messages alerted the rival battle-cruisers. The action between these opened some 95 minutes later. Beatty's warships suffered terribly. His own flagship, *Lion*, was badly damaged by shells from *Lützow* but two other British battle-cruisers fared far worse. *Indefatigable* was targeted by *Von der Tann* and was ripped apart by a huge explosion and *Queen Mary* met a similar fate a little later after taking several hits from *Derfflinger*.

Beatty now withdrew and headed towards Jellicoe pursued by Hipper and by Scheer's main fleet. The German admirals did not know of Jellicoe's presence. He manoeuvred his dreadnoughts into an advantageous position in which all their firepower could be directed against the leading German warships as they sailed northward.

The main action began with a new clash between the battle-cruisers and the British lost *Invincible* to another huge explosion while Hipper's flagship, *Lützow*, was badly hit. The rival dreadnoughts finally came in range of each other at around 18.30. Hipper immediately recognized the danger that Scheer was in and used his battle-cruisers to draw the British fire. Scheer managed to turn about and retreat into the gathering darkness. Jellicoe feared torpedo attacks from German destroyers and did not follow closely.

Thereafter, there were periodic clashes through the night but the main action was over. The Germans returned home and Jellicoe ordered his forces to do the same at 11.00 on 1 June. Germany could boast that the British had lost 6,784 men and 14 warships while their losses totalled 3,039 men and 11 generally smaller and older vessels. In reality, these losses did not greatly inconvenience the larger British Grand Fleet and it was quickly back on its battle stations. The Germans knew that they had come close to losing much of the High Seas Fleet and with it probably the war. Germany's warships never set sail again in such numbers to look for a decisive victory and most remained at anchor in their various harbours until the Armistice in 1918. Jutland was a strategic victory for the British.

Below: The British battle-cruiser *Queen Mary* succumbs to an internal explosion – just eight men survived.

ADMIRAL JOHN JELLICOE

Jellicoe (1859–1935) was Commander of the Grand Fleet, the Royal Navy's main strike force, from 4 August 1914. His main task was to impose a naval blockade on Germany and not be drawn into a major battle in which he might lose his fleet. Jellicoe was criticized for excessive caution even though his strategy was correct, but his performance at Jutland in 1916 was deemed too lukewarm. He was promoted to First Sea Lord the same year but his tenure was deemed mixed – he introduced some better anti-submarine measures but opposed convoys. He was sacked on 24 December 1917.

Above: Admiral Jellicoe was criticized for his caution at Jutland.

Dreadnoughts

HMS Dreadnought, *the first modern battleship, was such a revolutionary design when it was launched that it instantly made all previous battleships obsolete and sparked a dangerous naval arms race between Britain and Germany.*

At the outbreak of the war naval commanders believed that the war at sea would be decided by a single titanic clash between surface fleets. This view was especially prevalent among the officers of Britain's Grand Fleet and Germany's High Seas Fleet, two powerful forces of warships that fully expected to clash somewhere in the North Sea. This view was based on key moments in naval history – most recently when the Imperial Japanese Navy had crushed Russia's Baltic Fleet during the Battle of Tsushima in 1905.

Naval engagements had usually been decided by the largest warships of both sides – battleships – taking each other on, and no one believed that World War I naval battles would be any different. Up to the early 1900s all navies had battleships that were generally similar in design but that all changed when HMS *Dreadnought* appeared. This revolutionary British warship was built in a never-matched 14 months and completed in December 1906. The driving force behind the project was the country's First Sea Lord, Admiral John Fisher, arguably the most dynamic and far-sighted naval officer of his generation. *Dreadnought* was a quantum leap in warship design. It quite simply made every other existing battleship outdated at a stroke.

Above: HMS *Dreadnought* is launched in 1906. It served throughout the war, only being decommissioned in 1919.

Below: HMS *Dreadnought*. It sank one warship during the conflict, *U-29* in 1915.

Guns and Turbines

Dreadnought was the first "all big gun" warship and it mounted ten powerful 12in (305mm) guns. By comparison the Royal Navy's latest pre-dreadnought battleships carried just four

Right: Evidence of the growing naval arms race. German Nassau-class dreadnoughts on manoeuvres, September 1911.

12in guns, while Germany's equivalents had four 28cm (11in) guns. Thus, the new design could fire a far greater weight of shells. Fire control was also improved by doing away with the medium guns carried by pre-dreadnoughts.

The extra weight of the big guns, coupled with armour that matched that of existing battleships, made *Dreadnought* much larger than its antecedents, yet its performance was superior. It had a top speed of 22 knots, at least 2 knots better than most pre-dreadnoughts, and a 30 per cent longer range, due to the use, for the first time in a battleship, of steam turbines.

Battleship Building

It was hardly surprising that the appearance of *Dreadnought* soon sparked a naval arms race between Britain and Germany. The Royal Navy launched an additional 23 dreadnoughts between 1909 and 1914 (with a further 11 during the war) while the Germans completed 17 in the same period and a further 2 during the conflict. Other major naval powers undertook similar building programmes – France laid down 7 in 1912–14, Italy 6 in 1912–15 and the United States 12 in 1909–15. Later types were even more powerful than the original and were known as super-dreadnoughts.

Clashes between rival fleets of dreadnoughts were rare with the Battle of Jutland in 1916 being the only example. Sinkings were also few and far between. Germany did not lose any to enemy action. Britain lost two: *Audacious* sank after hitting a German mine in October 1914 and *Vanguard* succumbed to an internal explosion at Scapa Flow in 1917.

Above: The aft 15in (380mm) guns of HMS *Queen Elizabeth*. The Queen Elizabeth class were the most effective British dreadnoughts of the war.

ADMIRAL JOHN FISHER

Fisher (1841–1920) is rightly regarded as one of the towering figures in the history of the Royal Navy. He was made First Sea Lord in 1903 and set in train a vast modernization programme that included such new technologies as aircraft and submarines. His main focus was on surface warships, however. Here Fisher created two entirely new classes – the dreadnought battleship and the battle-cruiser. He did much to prepare the Royal Navy for war with Germany. He retired in 1910, returned as First Sea Lord in 1914 but then resigned the following year after quarrelling with Churchill over the Gallipoli campaign.

The Rise of the U-boats

Germany initially relied on various surface warships to sever Britain's maritime trading links but these were increasingly superseded by the far deadlier U-boats that proved highly elusive and difficult to destroy in the first years of the war.

As most of its surface commerce raiders were swept from the high seas during 1914–15, the Imperial German Navy henceforth had to rely almost entirely on its submarines to attack Britain's maritime trade. U-boats had achieved little in 1914 but they were credited with sinking 396 of the 468 Allied or neutral ships lost the following year. Many senior German officers had been sceptical about their value but such results proved their worth. There were more and more coming off the slipways of Germany's naval yards so their campaign could undoubtedly be intensified in 1916.

Yet the senior figures in Germany's military and political circles were engaged in a struggle over naval strategy, chiefly whether U-boats should be allowed to "sink on sight" any ships they encountered, combatant or not. Some, mainly senior admirals, favoured a return to the strategy of unrestricted submarine warfare, which had been practised for seven months or so in 1915, hoping it would bring Britain to its knees quickly before the British naval blockade did the same to Germany. Others, mostly civilian politicians and diplomats, were more cautious, fearing that a renewal of such a campaign would ultimately bring the United States into the war on the side of the Allies.

U-BOAT ACES

Although underwater warfare was in its infancy in World War I, some U-boat commanders were able to sink a considerable tonnage of Allied ships. Five captains sank more than 210,000 tons of merchant ships and warships but one of them stands head and shoulders above the rest and remains the most successful submarine ace of all time. Lothar von Arnauld de la Périère, captain first of *U-35* and later *U-139*, sank 196 ships of 456,216 tons, almost all of them by gunfire not torpedoes, around a sixth of the total sunk in the war by the whole U-boat force.

Below: A U-boat closes in on one of its victims – a British merchant ship, probably sunk by gunfire.

New Plans

A compromise of sorts was reached. It was decided that only enemy freighters inside the war zone around the British Isles would be sunk without notice and such ships spotted outside the zone would only be sunk without warning if they were armed. Passenger liners would not be touched in either case. The compromise strategy was announced to the wider world on 11 February 1916 and came into operation on the 29th. The controversial decision proved too much for the head of the Imperial Navy, Admiral Alfred von Tirpitz, and he resigned on 29 March.

The new regulations were soon found wanting. *U-29* spotted the British *Sussex* as it was crossing the English Channel on 24 March and, mistaking the passenger steamer for a troopship, sank it. Three US citizens were among the 50 dead and the

United States forcefully demanded that Germany end its "present method of submarine warfare" or face a total break in diplomatic relations. The U-boats were ordered to halt their modified unrestricted campaign on 24 April but the sinkings of other targets continued. They scored a notable success on 5 June when the British armoured cruiser HMS *Hampshire* struck a mine laid by a submarine off the Orkneys. The warship sank within minutes, taking with it the country's Minister of War, Field Marshal Horatio Kitchener, who was setting out on a mission to Russia.

Above: HMS *Hampshire* was sunk by a mine laid by *U-75*. Only 12 of those aboard survived.

Yet More Sinkings

Despite the debate over unrestricted warfare, the U-boats had undoubtedly proved themselves in 1916 and the number of their successes had risen enormously. Some 1,157 Allied and neutral ships, including 396 British vessels, had been sunk and 964 of them were directly attributable to German submarines. Mines, some if not quite all laid by U-boats, accounted for a further 161, while surface warships managed just 32 sinkings. Twenty-two boats had been lost but 108 had been commissioned during the year and there were 149 available for action at the beginning of 1917. The clamour for a full return to unrestricted warfare had also been growing. Field Marshal Paul von Hindenburg and his deputy, General Erich Ludendorff, the senior officers who were effectively running Germany's war effort, had demanded as much on 31 August during a meeting with Emperor Wilhelm II.

LT-CDR LOTHAR VON ARNAULD DE LA PÉRIÈRE

German U-boat captain de la Périère remains the most successful submarine captain of all time. He led two submarines into action during the war, *U-35* and *U-139*, and in a total of ten cruises in the Mediterranean sank a staggering 194 merchant vessels and 2 warships. *U-35* was also the top-scoring boat of the war with a grand total of 224 sinkings to its credit.

Above: De la Périère's *U-35* (nearer) makes a rendezvous with another German submarine, *U-42*.

Left: An Allied steamer begins its final plunge to the bottom after a torpedo strike.

Destroyers

Small, fast destroyers were the workhorses of the rival fleets during the war and were arguably the most important surface warships to see service during the war, protecting battlefleets and merchant ships against submarine and surface attacks.

Scores of destroyers were available to all the major navies in 1914, but they were often in short supply once hostilities had begun. Britain had around 300 and Germany 144, but even a lesser navy like that of Austria-Hungary could call on 25. The various navies had major building programmes in the war – Germany managed to construct 107 but this figure was dwarfed by the 329 completed by the British. They served in a variety of roles but had originally been designed to protect larger warships from attacks by torpedo-boats and were therefore often referred to as "torpedo-boat destroyers" in the early days. They continued this task during 1914–18 but anti-submarine operations gradually became their main priority.

GERMAN DESTROYERS

The German Navy, like its rivals, used destroyers for a whole range of missions, not least as the eyes of the main battlefleet. Several classes were built in the pre-war period and rather than being given names they had letter and numerical designations, the letter reflecting the maker. Thus G was the Germania shipyard, S Schichau and V Vulcan, for example.

Type: G40 destroyer
Laid down: 1914
Displacement: 1,050 tons
Crew: 87
Speed: 34.5 knots
Main armament: 3 x 8.5cm (3.3in) guns; 6 x 50.8cm (20in) torpedo tubes

Below: The end of the road for the German destroyer flotillas – interned in Scapa Flow in 1918.

Destroyer Designs

There were two main types of destroyer in service at the outbreak of war. All generally had a top speed of 25–35 knots. A sizeable number were designed for deep-water operations with the main fleets and so sacrificed some speed for endurance. These types largely equipped the British and German navies. Several powers, such as Austria-Hungary and Italy, built smaller destroyers for short-range work in the calmer and more confined waters of the Mediterranean. For example, the Italian Navy's *Astore*, launched in 1907, had a cruising range of 3,335km (1,800 nautical miles) while the British *Gadfly*, commissioned a year earlier and twice as large, had an endurance of 4,075km (2,200 nautical miles).

Whatever the case, destroyers were generally small enough to be built in quantity by the major navies and inexpensive enough to be bought or constructed by second-rank navies. There were many types of destroyer classes in service but most displaced 500–1,200 tons, had crews of between 80 and 150 and carried a mixture of guns and torpedo-launchers.

Roles in Action

They generally operated in groups of between 4 and 10 but some flotillas had as many as 20 destroyers. Those flotillas attached to the main fleet were usually commanded from a

Right: A flotilla of British destroyers sailing in line ahead, part of the Harwich Force that was active in the southern North Sea.

larger warship, such as a light cruiser, and had several roles. They acted as fast scouts, prevented enemy surface ships or submarines from launching torpedo attacks against larger warships, and used their own torpedoes if the opportunity presented itself. Destroyers were indispensable and no main fleet would go to sea without their protective screen. The British committed 73 destroyers to the Battle of Jutland in 1916 while Germany had 61 present.

Destroyers did not just operate with the main fleets and had two main roles when acting independently. First there was coastal defence, stopping raids by rival destroyers against inshore maritime trade routes and ports. Second, and more importantly for the Allies, destroyers were the cornerstone of the anti-submarine warfare campaign against Germany's U-boats. These operations required types with greater range and endurance and later Allied destroyers were something like twice the size of earlier classes. Britain's W class, which appeared in 1917–18, had a displacement of 1,529 tons and an endurance of 6,430km (3,470 nautical miles).

Much of the destroyers' everyday work went unsung but because of their general ubiquity they also suffered considerably. The Allies lost 112 to all causes of which more than 50 per cent were British as the Royal Navy bore the brunt of the anti-submarine campaign. The Central Powers lost 62 destroyers in total of which 53 were German.

Left: HMS *Windsor*, like other British V and W class destroyers, was armed with 4 x 4in (101mm) guns and served on into WWII.

Naval War in the Mediterranean 1914–16

Controlling the Mediterranean was crucial to the Allies. Thanks to the Suez Canal it was part of the shortest route between Britain and India and, potentially, a means of supplying Russia with military aid.

The Mediterranean was vital to many countries during World War I. Some 75 per cent of Britain's trade passed through the Suez Canal and Straits of Gibraltar, and France and Italy both needed access to their North African colonies. Austria-Hungary's only maritime link with the wider world was through the Adriatic, while Turkey controlled the Dardanelles that led to the Black Sea. The rival naval strategies revolved around maintaining or breaking these links.

Above: The former German battle-cruiser *Goeben* in Turkish service as *Yavuz Sultan Selim*. *Breslau* became the *Medjilli*.

ESCAPE OF THE *GOEBEN*

The first major incident occurred on 4 August 1914. Two German warships, *Goeben* and *Breslau*, under Vice-Admiral Wilhelm Souchon, shelled Bône (Annaba) and Philippeville (Skikda) in French Algeria and then made for Turkey. Souchon passed two British battle-cruisers but no fire was exchanged as the two countries were not yet at war. Once the midnight dead-line had passed, Britain sent a squadron after him. Contact was made to the south-west of Greece but Souchon escaped and reached Turkey on the 10th. Both ships were transferred to the Turkish Navy, helping persuade Turkey to enter the war on Germany's side on 29 October. *Goeben* survived

Below: A British submarine returns to its base after a successful cruise in the eastern Mediterranean.

Above: *Goeben* and *Breslau* were mostly based at Constantinople, as shown here, so they could reach the Black Sea or the Mediterranean.

Above: Japan had an excellent naval tradition and it deployed a destroyer flotilla to the Mediterranean for escort duties.

the war but was badly damaged by mines in early 1918 while *Breslau* was lost.

With the exception of the Anglo-French attempt to force the Dardanelles in early 1915, large fleets saw little action. Britain's remained in northern waters, while the French and Italian Navies were merely kept ready to block any mass break-out by the Austro-Hungarian Navy, but such an event never occurred. Much of the Mediterranean naval campaign was fought by smaller craft.

Submarine Attacks

The British waged a successful submarine campaign in the Dardanelles and the Sea of Marmara between May and September 1915. They sank half of the local Turkish merchant fleet and several of the Turkish Navy's major warships. One submarine, *E-11*, despatched 27 steamers, 58 smaller vessels, 3 cruisers and the battleship *Hairedden Barberosse* in just three missions.

The greatest Central Powers' threat came from the submarines operating from Cattaro (Kotor) in the Adriatic and Constantinople. These laid numerous minefields that proved highly effective at times. The Italian battleship *Regina Margherita* succumbed to a mine off Albania on 11 December 1916, for example. U-boats operating against the main sea routes were even more effective – they sank 900 Allied merchant ships in 1917 alone – and remained so until the latter part of the war. Things began to change in early 1916 when the various navies were allocated specific patrol zones but it was the institution of the convoy system in spring 1918 that dealt the decisive blow.

There were also frequent clashes in the confined waters of the Adriatic. The Allies attempted to seal off the sea by building the Otranto mine barrage between Italy and Albania. It was not wholly effective but it was sufficiently inconvenient for the Austro-Hungarians to attack it in force on the night of 14–15 May 1917 and sink 14 trawlers. Yet the Italian Navy's smallest craft scored the greater successes. Two torpedo-boats sailed into Muggia Bay near Trieste on 9 December 1917 and one sank the battleship *Wien*. Another pair attacked the dreadnought *Szent István* on 10 June 1918 and torpedoes from one sent it to the bottom.

GOEBEN AND *BRESLAU*

Goeben, a battle-cruiser, and *Breslau*, a light cruiser, were German warships handed over to Turkey along with their crews in August 1914. They both opened the war for Turkey by bombarding Russian ports in the Black Sea and mostly remained there until 1917. They transferred to the Mediterranean in January 1918. Both launched a raid on the British base at Mudros but ran into a minefield on the 20th. *Breslau* was sunk and *Goeben* badly damaged, remaining under repair for the remainder of the war.

Torpedo-boats

Torpedoes were deadly weapons that allowed small, fast warships to pack a considerable punch. Torpedo-boats' main targets were meant to be the enemy fleets of old battleships and more modern dreadnoughts.

These light and speedy boats were the first warships to be armed with torpedoes, a weapon that was developed in the late 19th century. Torpedo-boats caused alarm in some naval circles when they first appeared, mainly because they gave the smallest navy a chance to sink the biggest battleships for little financial outlay. As the boats were so relatively cheap to produce, a country with a small defence budget could buy or build dozens of them.

Most navies had flotillas of torpedo-boats at the outbreak of World War I and they came in two main categories. Some boats were smaller, with only a limited range and were used in coastal waters, while other types were built for longer patrols and more distant operations. The latter were increasingly being superseded by destroyers, bigger and faster warships that also carried torpedoes.

The coastal boats tended to be armed solely with torpedoes, although some were fitted with machine-guns. Speed rather than defensive armament was usually their best chance of survival. If they were sent on longer-range missions, coastal torpedo-boats were usually towed to their target area but some were also deployed from the decks of a class of support vessels generally known as torpedo depot ships.

Above: Ships of France's Arquebuse class in port at Toulon.

Below: Sleek German torpedo boats pictured at anchor in the Kiel Canal in January 1914.

MAS Boats in Action

The Italian Navy operated the most successful coastal torpedo-boats and was the acknowledged world leader in their design at the start of the war. One of the leading producers was the Società Veneziana Automobili Nautiche (SVAN). Their 16-ton MAS (Motobarca Armata SVAN) boats waged a highly effective hit-and-run campaign across the Adriatic Sea during 1915–18. The boats became so successful and renowned for their exploits that the nationalist writer Gabriele d'Annunzio gave them a slogan which translates as "One against a hundred – Attack!"

The MAS boats often operated at night and their most spectacular feat of arms came on 10 June 1918, when a pair of them attacked the Austro-Hungarian dreadnought *Szent István* off Premuda Island in the northern Adriatic at around 03.00 hours and one of them, *MAS 15* captained by Commander Luigi Rizzo, scored a fatal torpedo hit. The dreadnought sank some three hours later and its loss was so psychologically damaging that the main Austro-Hungarian fleet never put to sea again. The attack was Rizzo's second major success of the war as his *MAS 9* had sunk the old Austro-Hungarian battleship *Wien* in Muggia Bay near Trieste on 9 December the previous year.

Baltic Operations

The other major actions involving coastal motor boats (CMBs) actually came some months after the end of the war, when British forces stationed in Russia became embroiled in the ongoing civil war. British torpedo-boats were based on the coast of newly independent Finland and they undertook two highly successful raids against Bolshevik targets. The three-man *CMB4*, commanded by Lieutenant Augustine Agar, sank the cruiser *Oleg* in Kronstadt harbour on 17 June 1919. Their greatest exploit came early on the morning of 19 August, when seven CMBs led by Commander Claude Dobson again broke into the heavily defended harbour at Kronstadt. For the loss of three of his small boats, Dobson's flotilla sank the armoured cruiser *Pamiat Azova* and the dreadnought *Petropavlovsk*, and badly damaged the battleship *Andrei Pervozvanni.*

BRITISH *CMB65A*

Britain developed a number of Coastal Motor Boats, mostly designed by the Thornycroft firm. They came in three types, ranging in length from 12–21m (40–70ft). The torpedoes were fired backwards out of the boat from troughs and the boats had to swerve away quickly to avoid being hit.

Displacement: 10 tons
Length: 16.7m (55ft)
Engine: 350hp Thornycroft Y type
Top speed: 35 knots+
Crew: 3
Armament: 1 or 2 x 18in (457mm) torpedo tubes; 2–4 machine-guns

Right: Destroyers originally evolved to take on smaller torpedo-boats like these French types seen docked at Le Havre in 1913.

Allied Submarines

Although the German U-boat fleet grabbed the headlines during World War I, the Allied navies also deployed their own flotillas of submarines and, even if they were not so spectacularly successful, they played their own part in the final victory.

All the main Allied nations deployed submarines during World War I. In 1914 France had the biggest fleet of all, 123 boats. Italy had 25 mostly short-range types in service and Russia had 41. Few boats were built during the war, just 25 in France, 46 in Italy and 40 in Russia. France's existing types were old and unreliable, Italy's were beset by logistical problems, and Russian submarines were outdated, although they did operate in the Baltic and Black Seas. French, Italian and Russian losses totalled 12, 8 and 20 respectively.

Right: British submarine crewmen stand watch protected from the elements by nothing more than a canvas screen.

BRITISH K-CLASS SUBMARINES

These large submarines (the conning tower and some crew members of *K-6* are shown) were designed to operate with the main surface warships of the Royal Navy but the general concept was flawed, not least because they took an age to submerge as the funnels for their steam turbines had to be made watertight. Collisions with large vessels and even their own kind were not uncommon and 5 of the 17 built before 1919 were lost in accidents.

DISPLACEMENT: 2,140 tons (surface)
CREW: 50–60
RANGE: 5,555km (3,000nm)
ARMAMENT: 10 x 21in (533mm) torpedo tubes; 3 x 4in (102mm) guns

Although the British did not have the world's largest fleet of submarines in 1914, they had its largest and most successful one by the Armistice. Some 17 D- and E-class boats were available in August 1914 and these were backed by 40 B- and C-class types that were considered fit only for coastal operations. By the Armistice the numbers had swelled to 137 on active service with a further 78 under construction; 54 were lost during the conflict.

British Actions

The British produced a number of different types but the mainstay were the E-class boats that were active particularly in the Baltic Sea and Dardanelles. Fifty-eight were built from 1913–17 and 22 were lost. The first pair sailed for the Baltic during October 1914, largely to help the Russians as their modern submarines were being crippled by a lack of (German-built) engines. A further four E-class boats reached the Baltic in 1915 and were joined by four C-class types that had been taken apart, carried by ship to Archangel and then transported by rail and barge to the Gulf of Finland where they were then reassembled.

The British submarines sank a number of warships but their greatest contribution to the war effort was to hunt down German freighters transporting Swedish iron ore down the Gulf of Bothnia. This campaign ended with the signing of the Treaty of Brest-Litovsk in March 1918. Under its terms the Germans demanded that the Bolsheviks give up the British submarines. Rather than surrender, the final seven sailed from Helsingfors (Helsinki) on 8 April and their crews scuttled them in deep water.

In the Mediterranean

The Dardanelles campaign in 1915 again involved a number of E-class boats. They crippled the Turkish merchant fleet plying the Sea of Marmara, bombarded various shore installations, and even reached Constantinople. One boat, *E-11* captained by Lieutenant-Commander Martin Nasmith, was particularly successful, sinking 27 steamers and 58 other vessels in three patrols. The campaign netted 2 battleships, 1 destroyer, 5 gunboats, 7 supply ships, 9 troop transports, 35 steamers and 188 other vessels. Four boats were sunk while trying to pass through the Dardanelles; 9 reached the Sea of Marmara and 3 were lost in action there.

The E class was a reliable design but the British also experimented with one of the worst submarines of the war, the steam-driven K class. These were huge boats developed to serve with the Grand Fleet rather than operate as lone hunters. Friendly warships had difficulty in detecting them on the surface in anything but dead calm conditions and the submarines themselves took an age to dive. Collisions and accidents were inevitable, as became clear during an exercise off the Scottish coast on the night of 31 January 1918. *K-4* was sunk by *K-6* and *K-17* was despatched by a British cruiser in the so-called "Battle of May Island".

HMS *E-11*

The British submarine *E-11*, seen here after sailing through the Turkish-controlled Dardanelles, served with great distinction in the Sea of Marmara in 1915, even sinking a Turkish vessel at anchor in Constantinople's Golden Horn on 23 May. In all, 58 E-class boats were built and these also served in the North Sea and Baltic; 22 were lost.

Displacement: 667 tons
Crew: 30
Range: 6,655km (3,600nm)
Armament: 5 x 18in (457mm) torpedo tubes; 1 x 12pdr (76mm) gun

Below: The French submarine *Diane* was lost to an unexplained internal explosion in March 1918.

The Mesopotamian Campaign 1917–18 Indian labourers at work on a railway line.

The "February Revolution" Disillusioned Russian soldiers surrender en masse to the Germans.

The Battle of Passchendaele British stretcher bearers struggle through the mud with a casualty.

1917 – EUROPE'S YEAR OF TRIAL

1917 was the year in which war-weariness took a firm hold on the peoples of all of the combatant nations. No one now believed the war would be over quickly or that it was in any way glorious; rather it was exacting a fearful butcher's bill. The Allies took the military initiative and focused on the Western Front, launching two huge attacks – the Nivelle Offensive and the Battle of Passchendaele – that led to 1.38 million men killed, wounded or captured and German casualties of around 884,000. However, with the notable exception of the French Army, morale at the front did not collapse and many soldiers appeared psychologically prepared to see the war through to a conclusion.

Both sides could point to successes by the year's end. Germany no longer faced a war on two fronts thanks to the collapse of Russia. However, its unrestricted submarine campaign was failing as the Allies had belatedly introduced the convoy system, and the blockade of Germany was biting ever harder. France and Britain placed their faith in the United States, which declared war on Germany in April, but their relief at having a new ally was tempered with the knowledge that the Americans would not be able to make any worthwhile military contribution to the fight in Europe until well into 1918.

Coastal, Fortress and Railway Artillery A French 155mm rail gun in action.

The Battle of Caporetto Italian troops on the retreat after the German-led attack.

Final Battles in the Caucasus 1917–18 A field gun in action against the Turks.

The Battle of Arras

The first major attack by the BEF in 1917 began well, especially for the Canadian troops who captured the supposedly impregnable Vimy Ridge, but then it was stopped in its tracks by the formidable defences of the Hindenburg Line.

Marshal Joseph Joffre, the French Commander-in-Chief, had been much criticized for the string of costly offensives he ordered in 1915 and 1916 and was replaced by General Robert Nivelle in December 1916. The ebullient Nivelle devised an Anglo-French strategy to break through the German line in early 1917 but Nivelle's plans were thrown into confusion when the Germans withdrew some 32km (20 miles) to a new and much stronger position, the Hindenburg Line, between Arras and Soissons during late February to early April. They left behind a wasteland of flattened villages, ruined bridges and smashed roads in the area where Nivelle had hoped to attack.

KEY FACTS

Date: 9 April – 15 May 1917

Place: Artois east of Arras

Outcome: Early British gains did not lead to a decisive, war-winning victory.

Despite this delay, Nivelle persisted with his plans for the offensive, having convinced his political masters – if not all his fellow generals – that he had found a new method of attack that would win the war. Field Marshal Douglas Haig's BEF launched the opening gambit of Nivelle's offensive in Artois on 9 April. Two British armies were to spearhead the attack – the First under General Henry Horne and General Edmund Allenby's Third. They were arrayed a little to the east of Arras on either side of the River Scarpe and faced the German Sixth Army under General Ludwig von Falkenhausen. Haig was no great believer in Nivelle and also resented the BEF being temporarily placed under the latter's command. Britain's new prime minister, David Lloyd George, had in fact forced the decision upon him.

Below: Canadian troops moving supplies by light railway look on as German prisoners are escorted to the rear near Vimy Ridge.

Bloody April

The Royal Flying Corps made a major effort to aid the offensive but in "Bloody April" its outclassed machines suffered severe losses to win only temporary air superiority, despite enjoying a large numerical advantage. The preliminary bombardment lasted five days and involved some 2,500 guns but alerted the Germans to the attack. The first day went well, particularly north of Arras, as Allenby's troops pushed forward more than 3km (2 miles) in places and Canadian troops serving under Horne's command stormed the supposedly impregnable Vimy Ridge. The news was less promising south of the Scarpe where troops faced a complete section of the Hindenburg Line and struggled to take the fortified village of Monchy-le-Preux, which eventually fell on the 11th after bitter fighting.

Haig lengthened the line of his attack the same day by unleashing General Hubert

Above: A British gun crew re-lays a field gun on a new target after it has been fired during the Battle of Arras.

Gough's Fifth Army in the south against another section of the Hindenburg Line. The mismanaged attack stalled almost immediately, especially around the village of Bullecourt, and Gough's Australian troops suffered their worst-ever losses on the Western Front. Haig halted the battle on the 15th to await news of Nivelle's major offensive, which was to open the next day. The French attack was a complete disaster and Haig was therefore forced to renew his battle around Arras on the 23rd to take some of the pressure off his ally. Some ground was gained during the next two days but the impetus was soon lost, although the tired British troops battered away until late May.

Continuing Attacks

Haig was roundly criticized by some politicians for his battle tactics but Arras was seen as a success in military circles, not least because of the capture of Vimy Ridge. The British suffered some 150,000 casualties, a lower rate of attrition among an attacking force than was the norm, while the Germans lost 100,000. With the French Army in total disarray, the BEF would now have to shoulder the greater part of the Anglo-French effort on the Western Front for the rest of the year and into 1918. Haig would have to attack again but this time in Flanders, on ground of his own choosing.

Below: British troops gather round a tank during the Battle of the Scarpe, part of the Arras fighting in April.

CANADA AT WAR

Canada made a major contribution to the Allied war effort. Some 418,000 men fought overseas in the Canadian Expeditionary Force and a further 21,000 served in other capacities, including 13,000 in Britain s air services. Roughly 210,000 men became casualties of whom 56,500 were killed. Canada's war effort went further. It produced large amounts of food for the Allies; its shipyards built 1,000 vessels and by 1917 its factories were producing more than half of Britain's shrapnel as well as huge amounts of heavy shells.

Right: Canadian troops buy oranges from local French civilians outside Arras.

Light Bombers

Largely developed to operate over or immediately beyond the battlefield to attack a wide variety of targets, light bombers later increasingly operated in direct support of attacks to destroy enemy positions that were holding up friendly forces.

Aircraft of this type gradually evolved during World War I as new designs with more powerful engines became available. Unlike the first under-powered aircraft that struggled to get a pilot off the ground, these could carry a practical if modest bomb load and were primarily used against targets in or near the front line. Some also flew longer-range missions but that was the exception rather than the norm. Most light bombers that saw service were two-seater, single-engined biplanes, although there were exceptions like the German AEG G-series that first appeared in 1916, which had three engines and a crew of three or four.

Although some countries, notably Britain and France, produced dedicated light bombers, both they and other combatants used fighters or multi-purpose aircraft in the light-bomber role. There was some sense in this as fighters stood a better chance of survival if attacked, although they generally carried smaller bomb loads, while multi-purpose reconnaissance/light-bomber types could easily fulfil two roles. Light bombers often needed fighter escorts anyway as they were slower and less well armed.

The Royal Aircraft Factory's BE-2 of 1912 was one of the first British aircraft to fly bombing

Above: The British Airco DH-4 day bomber was both manoeuvrable and versatile and entered service from March 1917.

VOISIN 3

France deployed the Voisin 3 pusher biplane, the only aircraft in any air force then to be fitted with a machine-gun as standard, from late 1914. Thanks to its steel airframe, it was a sturdy machine. It proved successful in short-range support missions but was also used as a strategic bomber, notably when 18 attacked two German poison-gas factories on 27 May 1915. Some were also sold to Russia.

Engine: 120hp Salmson 9M
Crew: 2
Ceiling: 3,350m (11,000ft)
Top speed: 105kph (65mph)
Armament: 100kg (220lb) bombs; 1 x 8mm (0.315in) machine-gun

missions but its two-man crew could only throw small bombs at a target and had only a rifle or pistol to defend themselves. Its replacement, the RE-7, arrived at the front from late 1915 and was soon found to be under-powered and under-armed, but it was at least given a machine-gun for protection and could carry 155kg (340lb) of bombs. Other British aircraft used in the light-bomber role included Airco's single-engined DH-4, which also saw considerable service with the American forces, and the company's less successful twin-engined DH-9.

French Designs

The development of French light bombers followed a similar pattern. Voisin was perhaps the major manufacturer and its two-seater Voisin 3 was the first aircraft to carry a machine-gun when it began to appear in late 1914. Although its bomb load was limited to just 100kg (220lb), some 800 were built. New models were gradually introduced with better characteristics. The Voisin 8 entered service in late 1916 and could carry some 80 per cent more bombs by weight but sacrificed so much speed and agility that heavy losses relegated it to night-time missions. The Voisin 10 of early 1918 had a better engine and nearly three times the bomb load of the Voisin 3. Other aircraft used in the light-bombing role were the successful multi-purpose Breguet B2 and B4, which saw service in 1915–18, and the Salmson 2, which appeared over the Western Front in early 1918.

German Responses

Germany did not develop many light bombers, although the two-seater LVG C-II was deployed in this role during 1915–17. The German Army Air Service used fighters for light bombing but preferred to develop ground-attack or multi-purpose aircraft to undertake similar operations. LVG's C-V, for example, entered service in mid-1917 and performed reconnaissance, light-bombing and ground-attack missions successfully until the Armistice.

BE-2

The BE-2 was designed by Geoffrey de Havilland before the outbreak of the war and continued in service until 1916. One was the first British aircraft to land in France in 1914, while another was flown by the first officer to win a Victoria Cross in aerial warfare.

Engine: 70hp Renault
Crew: 2
Ceiling: 3,000m (10,000ft)
Top speed: 112kph (70mph)
Armament: hand-thrown bombs; sidearms or rifle

Below: The French Breguet Type XIV B2 light bomber entered service in the summer of 1917.

The Nivelle Offensive

General Robert Nivelle won support for a massive offensive because he convinced the Allied governments that he could achieve a major breakthrough but his attack soon stalled, produced heavy losses and provoked a widespread mutiny.

The major French offensive on the Western Front in April 1917 is sometimes called the Second Battle of the Aisne and a simultaneous subsidiary attack is referred to as the Third Battle of Champagne. However, both are more commonly known as the Nivelle Offensive after their instigator, General Robert Nivelle, French Commander-in-Chief from December 1916. Nivelle was a highly persuasive orator and had convinced his political masters that an offensive along the Chemin des Dames, a road between Soissons and Craonne that ran over a series of wooden ridges, would produce the decisive breakthrough that had eluded the Allies since 1914. Nivelle's boast that he would win the war "in 48 hours" was less well received by both his own generals and those of the British.

Nivelle's plan of attack was not significantly different from what had been tried before but it was on a much bigger scale. The French Reserve Army Group, four armies totalling 1.2 million men and 7,000 guns, was assembled on a 64km (40 mile) front between Soissons and Reims. The two opposing German armies, the Seventh under General Max von Boehn and General Fritz von Below's First, were outnumbered but they had two vital advantages. They were holding strong defences based on the ridges that ran across Nivelle's line of advance and they knew when he was going to attack because they had captured the plans for the battle.

KEY FACTS

Date: 16 April – 9 May 1917

Place: Along the River Aisne

Outcome: Heavy French losses for very little territorial gain were followed by the outbreak of military indiscipline.

Opening Attacks

The much-delayed offensive began on 16 April after a ten-day preliminary bombardment. The main effort along the Chemin des Dames was made by General Olivier Mazel's Fifth Army and General Charles Mangin's Sixth Army but they made little progress at a very high cost. Boehn's troops inflicted some 40,000 casualties on the French on the first day alone and knocked out 150 of their new tanks. The subsidiary attack launched against Below by General François Anthoine's Fourth Army to the east of Reims began the next day and rapidly met a similar fate.

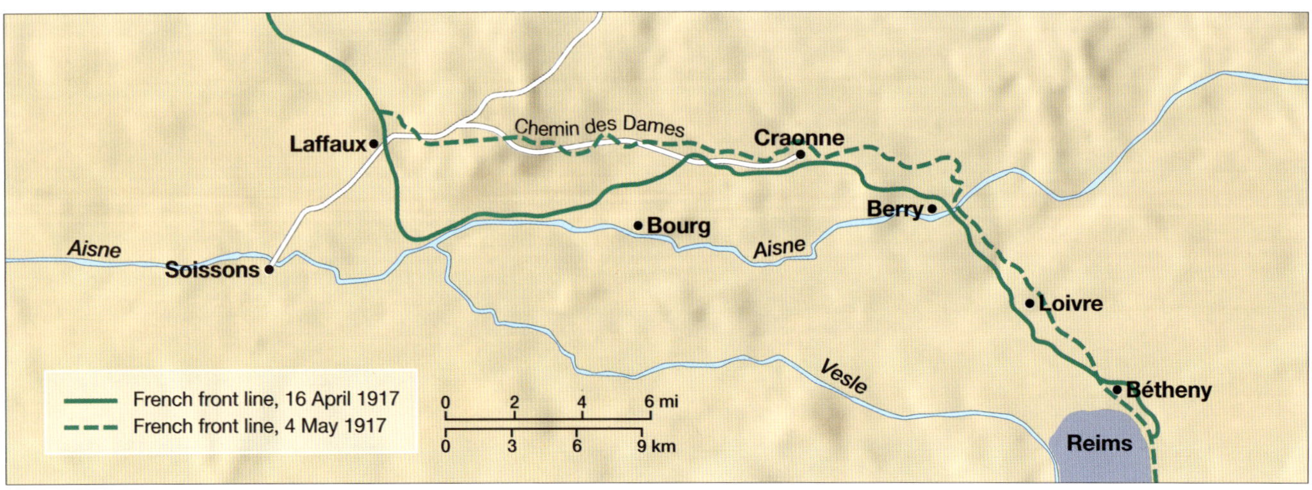

THE NIVELLE OFFENSIVE
The major attacks of the offensive took place from 16–20 April but the battle lasted for another few weeks.

Left: French dead lie scattered in a sunken road, just a small part of the price paid to disprove Nivelle's excessive boasts.

Despite a patent lack of progress, Nivelle continued to grind away until the 20th but the breakthrough he had promised never materialized. The increasingly pointless attacks were soon scaled down and eventually ended on 9 May. The troops did finally manage to capture a small part of the Chemin des Dames ridges by 5 May but this was scant consolation for the loss of 187,000 men. Nivelle was replaced by General Philippe Pétain on the 15th and, in what was to become a decisive move for the Allies' future strategy, General Ferdinand Foch was made the French Army Chief of Staff at the same time.

Mutiny

Nivelle's failure shattered the morale of the long-suffering French Army and it was torn apart by mutiny, brought about not only by the recent heavy losses but also by poor rations, low pay and a lack of leave. The unrest broke out in the last week of April and lasted until mid-June. Many units were involved and there were some executions but the mutineers were mostly persuaded to return to duty. The French Army was not really fit for action until the autumn. The Germans did not capitalize on the unrest as the news blackout was so strict that they did not learn of the mutiny until it was over.

GENERAL ROBERT NIVELLE

Nivelle (1856–1924) was a mere colonel in 1914 but enjoyed rapid promotion, becoming Commander of the French Second Army at Verdun in April 1916. His defence of the embattled fortress town made him a public figure and this, combined with his charisma, ensured that he became French Commander-in-Chief in December. He planned a major attack that would end the war "in 48 hours" but the Nivelle Offensive in April 1917 was a disaster and provoked a widespread mutiny in the French Army. He was sacked from his post in May.

Above: Nivelle's tenure of high command was brief.

Left: A remarkable – but possibly fake – photograph of German troops repelling a French attack at the height of the Nivelle Offensive.

French and German Tanks

Both the French and Germans produced their own armoured fighting vehicles during the war. France put three types of tank into service but Germany built just one model and instead often relied on tanks captured from the British.

The French were the keenest supporters of armoured warfare after the British. There was no one driving force behind their programme and the two Allies' tank plans evolved along largely separate lines. French armoured cars had been of some military worth before the arrival of trench warfare and a few enlightened figures in the Ministry of War believed that vehicles that could operate off-road might break the stalemate on the Western Front. The key figure was a colonel of artillery, Jean-Baptiste Estienne, who proposed a tracked armoured fighting vehicle to the general responsible for weapons procurement in December 1915. Estienne's concept was suitably impressive and an order for 400 *chars d'assaut* (assault vehicles) was issued on 31 January 1916.

Above: A St Chamond tank is camouflaged in the factory before delivery to the French Army in 1917.

First French Designs

Schneider was the first company to be given a procurement order and soon came up with a box-like armoured superstructure mounted on a chassis developed from a US Holt tractor. The vehicle weighed some 13 tonnes and had a top speed of less than 6.5kph (4mph). There were endless delays in production, largely because of shortages of armour plate. The first Schneider reached the army on 8 September 1916 but only seven more had arrived by late November, the date when all 400 should have been built. As Schneider was clearly struggling to fill its order from an early stage, St Chamond, a design company, was asked to fulfil a second order for 400 tanks in April. Its prototype was not dissimilar to the Schneider but was nearly 70 per cent heavier.

Neither tank performed well in action. Their high profile made them vulnerable to

RENAULT FT-17

The French FT-17 was the first tank to have a revolving turret and was designed in 1917. It had an adequate cross-country performance and saw service with both the French and US forces on the Western Front throughout 1918.

Weight: 6.5 tons
Crew: 2
Max. speed: 10kph (6mph)
Max. armour: 16mm (0.63in)
Armament: 1 x 8mm (0.315in) machine-gun or 1 x 37mm (1.46in) gun

artillery fire, their engines were not overly reliable and, worst of all, their trench-crossing abilities were poor. Of the two, the St Chamond was the worse. Its greater weight meant that it was even more likely to sink into soft ground and its superstructure overhung the tracks substantially at the front, making it prone to getting stuck while crossing a trench.

Both types achieved little during their combat debut, the Nivelle Offensive in April 1917. A number remained in service for the rest of the war but they were largely superseded by a light tank, the Renault FT-17, from the end of 1917. This was a much lighter and smaller design used extensively during the later stages of the war by both the French Army and the American Expeditionary Force. The Renault had a good cross-country performance and its turret gave it an all-round field of fire but thin armour made it very vulnerable.

German Scepticism

The German High Command was not overly impressed with tanks, citing their high rate of mechanical failure and their vulnerability to anything from difficult terrain to artillery fire. A German-built type did reach the front from late 1917 onwards but production was limited due to the crippling shortage of raw materials.

The A7V Panzerkampfwagen was by some way the biggest tank of the war. It had a large box-like structure that housed a 16-man crew, while firepower was provided by a single forward-firing 57mm (2.24in) cannon and six heavy machine-guns. The A7V was ponderously slow, prone to mechanical failure and was so top heavy that it was likely to overturn if moved along a slope. Only a few dozen of them were ever built and they were easily outnumbered by the captured and refurbished British tanks that the Germans also used in the later stages of hostilities.

PANZERKAMPFWAGEN A7V

Germany's massive A7V entered service in late 1917 but had a high centre of gravity and inadequate engines that gave it a poor cross-country capability.

Weight: 32 tons
Crew: 16
Max. speed: 13kph (8mph)
Max. armour: 30mm (1.2in)
Armament: 1 x 57mm (2.24in) gun; 6 x 7.92mm (0.312in) machine-guns

Right: The Schneider tank had poor ventilation and thin armour but worst of all its internal petrol tanks lacked adequate protection.

The Battle of Messines

The mining and subsequent attack on Messines Ridge was probably the most rigidly planned and tightly managed operation of the whole war and led to the capture of a supposedly impregnable section of the German front line in a matter of hours.

With the French Army crippled by the Nivelle Offensive and the mutiny that it provoked, Field Marshal Haig's BEF became the principal Allied army on the Western Front from mid-1917 onward. Haig decided to launch a large and long-planned offensive around Ypres in Flanders to break through the German front line. Before he could undertake the main attack it was necessary to eradicate a small German-held salient on an area of high ground around the town of Messines to the immediate south of Ypres. The task of taking Messines Ridge was given to General Herbert Plumer's British Second Army, which also included a sizeable proportion of troops from Australia and New Zealand.

Preparing the Attack

Plumer was in many ways the ideal commander for the job. He had a well-deserved reputation as a thoughtful and meticulous commander and had served in Flanders since 1915 so he knew the area well. He had also been planning an assault on the ridge since mid-1916 and had ordered a number of mines be dug under the German trench lines. The immense efforts to create the shafts began in January 1917 and the dangerous work involved excavating some 8,000m (26,250ft) of tunnels and removing the spoil without alerting the enemy. One shaft was detected by the Germans but the other 21 were never discovered and the tunnellers packed them with hundreds of tons of high explosive.

Plumer also intended to make the best possible use of artillery, tanks and gas to minimize his losses during the opening stages of the attack. Local air superiority ensured that the aircraft of the German Army Air Service would be unable to intervene in the fighting.

The preliminary bombardment by around 2,300 heavy artillery pieces and 300 mortars began on 21 May and increased in intensity seven days later. After another week or so of

KEY FACTS

Date: 7 – 14 June 1917

Place: Messines Ridge, south-west Belgium

Outcome: A clear-cut British victory that led to the eradication of a major German salient.

Above: General Herbert Plumer (with cane), the mastermind behind the attack on Messines Ridge.

Below: A good indication of the devastation wrought on the German positions atop Messines Ridge.

Above: British troops advance towards the top of Messines Ridge – many of its German defenders were too dazed to offer much resistance.

artillery fire, 19 of the surviving mines were detonated at 03.10 hours on 7 June. The simultaneous blasts sent huge columns of debris high into the sky and killed an estimated 10,000 German troops. Nine of the Second Army's divisions then attacked on a 14.5km (9 mile) front behind a creeping barrage in which the artillery dropped shells just a little beyond the advancing infantry so that the Germans kept their heads down in their trenches. The surviving defenders were so dazed that Plumer's units pushed forward against little opposition and captured all of their objectives in the first three hours.

Results of the Battle

As was by now common practice, German units vigorously counterattacked the following day but they were beaten off everywhere. Their attempts to push the British off the ridge continued but with less ferocity until the 14th by which point the whole of the salient was securely in Plumer's hands.

Plumer's men had suffered around 17,000 casualties during the battle but, unusually for World War I, the defenders had actually recorded greater losses, some 25,000 men in all, including 7,500 prisoners. By the usual standards of the conflict, the Battle of Messines had been an overwhelming success for the BEF but it was only a limited offensive with limited objectives and the main event of Haig's Flanders offensive was yet to come.

Below: Messines Ridge pictured from the British side during the intense preliminary bombardment before the attack.

Mine Warfare

The detonation of huge caches of high-explosive under an enemy's front line was a common aspect of trench warfare and could be highly effective as the explosions not only destroyed defences but also often left any survivors too dazed to fight.

Early versions of modern land mines were developed during World War I but they were rather primitive devices. The Germans, for example, made extensive use of mortar bombs part buried in the ground as an early type of minefield to destroy tanks. Mine warfare usually had a rather different meaning during the conflict and referred to digging shafts under enemy trenches, filling them with high-explosive and then detonating the charges. It was dangerous work due to tunnel collapses, flooding, gas and the danger that the enemy might explode camouflets (counter-charges) to bury the tunnellers in their own shaft. Almost all the mine warfare of World War I took place on the Western Front as the static nature of the fighting gave tunnellers the time they needed to drive their shafts underground.

First Mines

The Germans actually set off the first underground explosion of the war on 20 December 1914, when 10 out of 11 mines were detonated immediately beneath a brigade of Indian troops near Festubert, some 16km (10 miles) south of the Franco-Belgian border. However, the British became the war's greatest exponents of tunnelling but had no specialist units in existence in 1914. They were actually the brainchild of a persistent member of parliament, John Norton Griffiths, who submitted the idea in December 1914. He had a contract to build sewers through the clay soil under a northern town and employed men known as "moles" who "clay kicked"

Above: A lone soldier gives some indication of the size of craters left by a mine detonation.

Below: A vast crater produced by the detonation of just one mine at the beginning of the Battle of the Somme in 1916.

Right: Whoever reached the lip of a crater first after the detonation had the upper hand in the subsequent fghting – in this case the Germans.

or "worked on the cross". They sat in the tunnel with their backs supported on a wooden backrest (cross) with their feet pointed at the tunnel face and used them to work a spade-like implement to dig out the clay, which was then passed back for disposal. Alternative methods using mining machines were rarely tried and not successful.

Formal approval for the creation of specialist mining units was finally issued on 12 February 1915 and the first units were designated 170 to 178 Tunnelling Companies, Royal Engineers. The first recruits were British miners of every sort but companies were later also raised in Australia, Canada and New Zealand.

British Attacks

The first British mines were exploded under Hill 60 near St Eloi on the evening of 17 April and thereafter the operations grew larger and more complex. The biggest mining operation in military history reached fruition in mid-1917 but the idea had first been mooted as far back as 6 January 1916.

The target was Messines, a German-held ridge a little to the south of Ypres. The tunnellers planned 21 explosions in all and the charges were placed in 12 main shafts, some with two or more galleries leading off them, along a 16km (10 mile) stretch of the ridge. The building of the mines was an immense effort – one was over 640m (2,100ft) long. Once completed they were mostly filled with Ammonal, the most powerful explosive then known. One particular mine contained more than 43 tonnes and the tunnellers placed close to 430 tonnes of explosives under the German lines.

Nineteen mines in total were exploded on 7 July 1917 (two failed to go off) and the devastation caused was immense. The largest crater, Lone Tree, was 12m (40ft) deep and 76m (250ft) across. No one knows how many German troops were killed by the simultaneous detonations, which were heard in London and beyond, but some 10,000 men were recorded as missing on the first day of the battle. A further 7,350 were taken prisoner, many in a wholly dazed condition.

Below: German officers prepare to detonate a mine under the enemy trenches in the early part of the war.

The Battle of Passchendaele

Passchendaele, or the Third Battle of Ypres, was planned in the expectation of crashing through the German defences but quickly degenerated into probably the most horrific battle of the war, largely due to the truly awful conditions.

The British victory at the Battle of Messines in June 1917 had captured part of a long ridge to the south and east of the Belgian town of Ypres but the northern section remained in German hands. Field Marshal Haig, commander of the BEF, had intended to launch a major attack in Flanders for some time, partly because he believed – and the success at Messines seemed to confirm – that the German Army was close to collapse. He also saw that a breakthrough at Ypres followed by a drive across Belgium would capture the ports from where German U-boats were decimating Britain's maritime trade.

KEY FACTS

Date: 31 July – 10 November 1917

Place: East of Ypres, south-west Belgium

Outcome: After a terrible struggle, the British captured Passchendaele village.

BATTLE OF PASSCHENDAELE
This map shows the battle's painfully slow progress over several months.

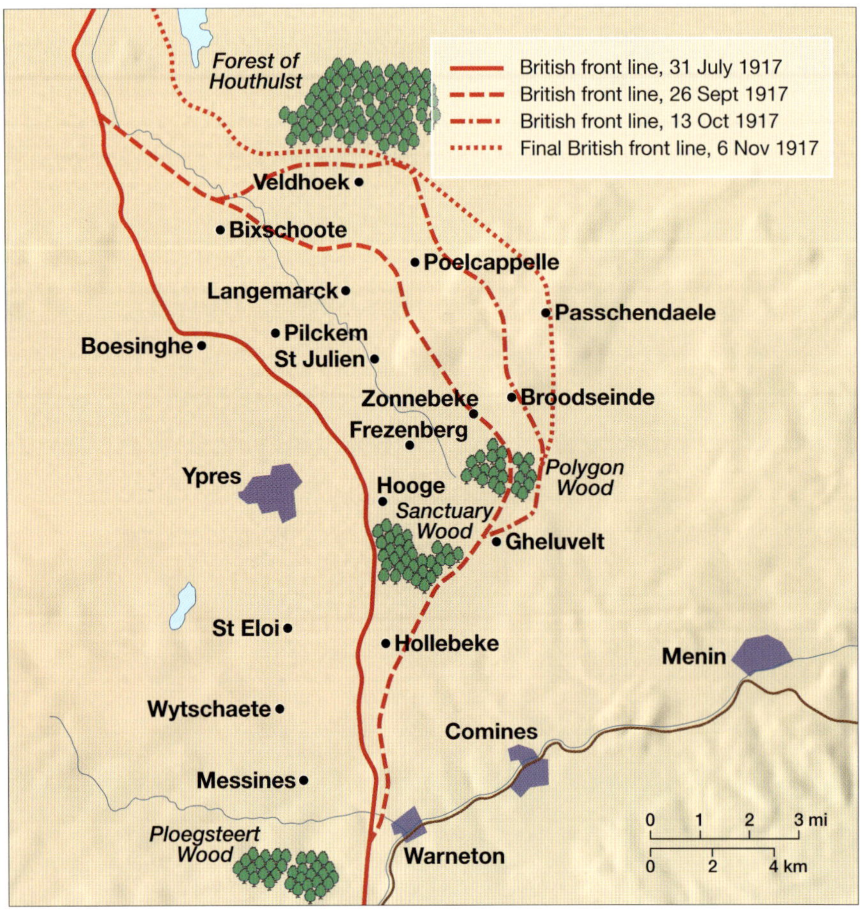

Gough's Attack

The main effort was to be by General Hubert Gough's British Fifth Army with support from the British Second Army under General Herbert Plumer to the south and General François Anthoine's French First Army to the north. There was a 10-day preliminary bombardment from some 3,000 guns before the main attack on an 18km (11 mile) front began at 03.50 hours on 31 July. The barrage had alerted the opposing German Fourth Army under General Sixt von Arnim and he had set about extending the already extensive defence system.

An attack down the Menin Road to the south-east of Ypres was blocked and there were

Below: British casualties, just a small fraction of some 300,000 men listed as killed, wounded, missing or taken prisoner. German losses totalled around 260,000.

Right: A British stretcher party struggles to make any progress through the thick mud that typified the Ypres battlefield.

small gains around Pilckem Ridge to the north-east where the main effort was made. The Battle of Pilckem ended on 2 August with the British having advanced just 2,750m (3,000yds) at a cost of some 32,000 casualties. The battlefield was also being turned into a quagmire due to unseasonable heavy rainfall and the damage inflicted on the land drains by the incessant shelling. Nevertheless, the fighting had to continue. The next major effort was the Battle of Langemarck (16–18 August) but the British attackers again made little progress.

Plumer Takes Over

Haig gave Plumer command of the floundering offensive in late August and the latter devised a new strategy that took into account the awful conditions. Plumer recognized that the idea of a decisive breakthrough was impractical, so he launched a succession of limited offensives that had relatively modest objectives. Rather than punch through the German line, Plumer was going to nibble away at it. What had begun as a war-winning offensive was thus transformed into a battle of attrition. Haig had little choice but to continue as the French were still recovering from the mutiny of May–June that had broken out after the disastrous Nivelle Offensive.

Plumer launched several attacks between 20 September and 10 November, beginning with the Battle of the Menin Road (20–25 September) in the south-east and culminating in the First and Second Battles of Passchendaele (12 October – 10 November) in the north-east. The BEF was finally left holding the greater part of the long ridge that had been mostly in German hands since 1914–15. The British had extended the salient around Ypres by some 8km (5 miles) but the cost had been very high. The British and Empire troops had suffered some 300,000 casualties while the Germans recorded 260,000.

TRENCH FOOT

Trench foot (or, in its more descriptive modern name, immersion foot) is a fungal infection caused by cold, wet and insanitary conditions. If not caught early, the infection can turn gangrenous and require amputation of the limb. The first cases among the British forces became apparent in late 1914 and some 20,000 cases were recorded over that winter. Improved conditions in the trenches, regular foot inspections by officers and changes of socks whenever possible reduced but never stopped the flow of cases. There were potential penalties for those who contracted trench foot, not least because some officers saw it as a type of self-inflicted wound.

Above: Australian troops undergo foot inspection, a necessary routine of trench life especially in cold and wet conditions.

Coastal, Fortress and Railway Artillery

Although most artillery weapons deployed during the war were mounted on wheeled carriages, other artillery pieces were either placed in fixed positions, such as fortresses, or, if especially large, on purpose-built railway mounts.

There was something of a mania across much of Europe for updating existing frontier fortresses or building modern versions of them in the decades before World War I. Austria-Hungary, Germany and Russia all built such fortresses but the greatest exponents were the French and Belgians. Theirs were generally built around strategic towns and cities, like Liège and Namur in Belgium or Verdun and Belfort in France, and comprised a number of outlying forts fitted with heavy artillery pieces and machine-guns. The artillery was positioned inside retractable steel domes in the most modern forts.

Above: The French, like the British and Germans, operated railway artillery. In this case, an improvised 155mm (6.1in) rail gun fires on a distant German position.

The frontier fortresses proved to be paper tigers as they could not withstand the newest and heaviest forms of artillery introduced before and during the war. After both supposedly impregnable Liège and Namur had fallen in a matter of a few days in August 1914, the French saw the writing on the wall and began to remove many of their fortress guns, mount them on field carriages or flatbed rail trucks and send them to the field army as it was especially short of heavier forms of artillery no matter how ancient.

BRITISH BL 12-INCH RAIL GUN

The British built just two of these large rail guns initially (the guns themselves were originally designed for naval service). They were in France by late 1915 and two more went into action during 1916.

WEIGHT: 170 tonnes (approx)
CALIBRE: 12in (305mm)
WEIGHT OF SHELL: 340kg (750lb)
MUZZLE VELOCITY: 813m/sec (2,666ft/sec)
MAX. RANGE: 30km (18.5 miles)

COAST DEFENCES

Coastal artillery received a major overhaul in the second half of the 19th century largely due to the development of the armoured warship. Generally, the guns were placed in brick and earth and later concrete emplacements to protect important sections of the coast or key harbours, although lighter types were more mobile and might be placed behind extemporized defences. They were usually supported by various other weapons, such as machine-guns, searchlights and anti-submarine barriers. However, coastal artillery actually saw little action during the war, aside from occasionally replying to long-range fire from distant enemy warships, as amphibious assaults were extremely rare.

The British did keep their coastal artillery largely intact to combat any invasion threat and the Germans also used such types to protect certain bases. The island of Heligoland was heavily defended not least because it protected the seaways leading to the home ports of the High Seas Fleet. The German Navy was also particularly anxious to protect the entrance to the canals at Zeebrugge and Ostend on the coast of occupied Belgium as they led inland to the U-boat base at Bruges. The coastal defences at Zeebrugge and Ostend were both tested by a British attack in April 1918 but they survived mostly unscathed.

Above: An armoured revolving artillery cupola in an Alpine redoubt, of the kind found in many fortresses of the era.

Rail Guns

The heaviest guns deployed in the ground war were usually moved about on rail mounts so that they could be easily transferred from firing position to firing position by locomotives. Such guns were overwhelmingly deployed on the Western Front where there were usually excellent rail links not far behind the static battle lines. The first experiments were carried out by the French, who put redundant coastal or fortress guns on flatbed rolling stock during late 1914. Purpose-built rail guns began to appear later. The chief drawback with these types was that they had limited left–right traverse and thus had often to be moved about on a section of curved track to acquire a new target. Smaller calibre railway guns were commonly mounted in such a way that they could be traversed through 360 degrees.

Left: A captured German coastal battery in Belgium. These concrete emplacements offered very little protection for their crews.

The Battle of Cambrai

The British offensive at Cambrai in late 1917 saw the first use of massed tanks in warfare but despite early morale-boosting successes much of the captured ground was soon retaken by the Germans, who were masters of the rapid counter-attack.

The first British tanks went into action in September 1916 during the later stages of the Battle of the Somme, but they had never really been given the chance to prove their true capabilities since their debut. The problem was that they had always been used in small numbers and had frequently been sent into battle across exceptionally difficult terrain, muddy and pitted with shell craters.

An ardent supporter of the tank, Colonel John Fuller, devised a plan to use tanks in a summertime raid against a quiet section of the Hindenburg Line to the south-east of Arras. The terrain there comprised dry ground still relatively undamaged by heavy shellfire.

KEY FACTS

Date: 20 November – 7 December 1917

Place: West of Cambrai, north-east France

Outcome: Early British gains were lost to German counter-attacks.

Below: Tanks were far from being immune to artillery fire as this comprehensively smashed example at Cambrai clearly shows.

Planning the Battle

Fuller's plan was approved by General Julian Byng, commander of the British Third Army, but it was rejected by Field Marshal Haig when it was first presented to him. Haig later relented when it became all too apparent that the Battle of Passchendaele was failing badly and he needed a morale-boosting victory to stem the growing tide of criticism being directed against his leadership. Fuller's idea for a raid soon developed into something very much grander – Byng ordered a full-scale breakthrough attack. His subordinate commanders were not overly impressed as the weather in late 1917 was likely to be bad, there were too few reserves to exploit any early gains and the tank crews had been given little time to practise their new battle tactics.

Into Action

Nevertheless, six infantry and two cavalry divisions backed by 1,000 guns were concentrated along a 10km (6 mile) front held by two divisions of General Georg von der Marwitz's German Second Army. The attack opened at around dawn on 20 November 1917 when 475 tanks moved forward without even the slightest preliminary bombardment. The front-line German troops were caught by surprise and in many instances either surrendered or fled.

The tanks and accompanying infantry had made 6km (4 miles) by mid-afternoon, creating a new salient in the line, and the only reverse had been around the village of Flesquières where the local British commander had ordered

Right: German prisoners help to bring British wounded out of an underground dressing station near Cambrai, 20 November 1917.

his infantry not to work closely with the tanks. Cambrai was in sight by the end of the day but then the Germans threw in local counter-attacks that blocked the way forward.

The tanks had done remarkably well on the first day, taking more ground than in the three-month-plus Third Battle of Ypres, but many were soon either destroyed or more commonly abandoned when they ditched or suffered some form of mechanical failure.

TANK TACTICS

The British developed special trench-clearing techniques for their tanks during the Battle of Cambrai in November 1917. They operated in groups of three. The first tank would turn left at the first trench, firing down into it, while the second would arrive at the trench, drop its fascine into it and cross over. It, too, would then turn left, firing into the trench. The third tank, would cross over the trench and push on to the next trench, where it would drop its fascine, cross over and turn left to engage the enemy. The first tank would now cross over the first two trenches, reach the third and drop its own fascine – and so the process would continue.

Above: A pair of British tanks lie abandoned near Cambrai. Many simply suffered mechanical failure rather than falling prey to enemy fire.

Haig ordered the battle to continue but there was no more progress and then the Germans counter-attacked in force on the 30th. The British managed to stop them in the north of the salient but were forced back in the south. When the fighting ended on 7 December the British had abandoned virtually all of the ground the tanks had helped to capture. The British had lost some 45,000 men and the Germans 50,000, including 11,000 prisoners. Only one-third of the tanks deployed on the first day survived the battle – and most of them were in need of a major overhaul.

Cambrai led the British commanders to conclude that an attack did not need a long preliminary bombardment and that the mass use of tanks was a battle winner. The Germans, in contrast, concluded that tanks were too unreliable to be truly useful. These findings would colour both sides' battle tactics in the final year of the war.

Aces and Fighter Tactics

Although the truly great aces were undoubtedly expert pilots and skilled marksmen, they had one particular trait that marked them out from all of their contemporaries – their absolute ruthlessness when in air-to-air combat.

While it is true that the tactics of air combat developed significantly during the war, most aircraft were not shot down after prolonged bouts of air combat, and mass dog-fights between dozens of fighters were virtually unknown until the later years of the conflict. The best way to down an opponent was to get behind and slightly below him at close range, preferably unseen in a faster, more manoeuvrable and better-armed aircraft. This last point cannot be overstressed as the air war in World War I was a technological struggle as much as anything else and the arrival of a better fighter frequently tipped the balance of power – at least until it was superseded by a better enemy aircraft.

Nevertheless, a handful of fighter pilots on all sides proved to be exceptionally skilled and were seen as aces. The French press invented the idea in 1915 to honour a pilot who had shot down five enemy aircraft and then the German Army Air Service required that a pilot score eight (later sixteen) kills before he could receive its highest decoration. The British authorities rather frowned on the idea of this type of personality cult, but set a benchmark in March 1918 announcing that a fighter pilot needed to score eight victories to win the Distinguished Flying Cross.

Above: US ace Edward "Eddie" Rickenbacker trained as a pilot in 1917, then joined and later led the elite 94th "Hat in the Ring" Squadron in 1918.

BILLY BISHOP

Canadian ace William "Billy" Bishop (1894–1956), seen here in front of his French-built Nieuport 17 Scout fighter, was one of the war's top-scoring pilots. He began flying fighters in March 1917 and scored his first victory on the 25th. He received a Victoria Cross in August for attacking a German aerodrome and destroying several enemy aircraft – all in a matter of just 37 minutes on 2 June. After the war, he rose to the rank of air marshal.

Top Aces

As air combat was most intense over the Western Front, it was there where most aces were to be found. Leading the pack was Germany's Baron Manfred von Richthofen with 80 confirmed kills between August 1916 and April 1918. No one else in the German forces came close to his score but the second most successful German ace of the war, Ernst Udet, managed to down 62 aircraft. Three Allied aces came nearer to matching Richthofen – France's René Fonck with a score of 75, English pilot Edward "Mick" Mannock with 73, and Canadian William "Billy" Bishop with 72. Despite their prowess in air combat, aces were far from invulnerable. Mannock was killed by ground fire and it is thought most likely that Richthofen suffered the same fate.

BARON MANFRED VON RICHTHOFEN

Richthofen (1892–1918) was a Prussian cavalry officer but transferred to the German Army Air Service in May 1915. He fought as an air observer on the Eastern Front, flew with bombers in Belgium and then undertook reconnaissance missions over Verdun. He thereafter began flying fighters and by April 1917 had shot down 52 aircraft, becoming a household name in the process. He commanded Jagdgeschwader 1 (Fighter Group 1), the renowned "Flying Circus", from June and his tally grew. He was killed by ground fire on 21 April 1918 with 80 kills to his credit.

Above: As Richthofen's fame grew he became a valuable propaganda tool for Germany but his loss was keenly felt.

ERNST UDET

Ernst Udet (1896–1941), seen here beside his Fokker D-VII fighter, was the highest-scoring German ace to survive the war, amassing 62 victories over the Western Front from the spring of 1918 onward. He was lucky, however, as in an early combat during 1917 he met the outstanding French ace Georges Guynemer. Udet's guns jammed as the fight began but Guynemer saw this and chivalrously flew off without attacking.

Elite Units

Most of the rival air forces also contained fighter squadrons that could boast outstanding combat records and in some cases they also were the focus of intense propaganda campaigns to boost morale on the home front. The most famous of course was Manfred von Richthofen's "Flying Circus", which was a group of four 12-aircraft squadrons formed in late June 1917 that gained its name because of the aircraft's garish colour schemes.

The French also had their fighter elite, the *Cigognes* ("Storks"). This unit originally included just a single squadron but two more were added in 1915 and four more joined at a later date to form Combat Group XII. Most of France's leading aces served with the Storks including both Georges Guynemer (54 kills) and Fonck.

The United States also had an elite squadron but it actually took to the skies before the country entered the war in April 1917. The Lafayette Squadron was founded in 1916, when it was known as the American Squadron, and was staffed by American pilots already serving with the French as volunteers. Its 38 pilots scored 38 confirmed victories before they transferred to the United States Army Air Service in February 1918. The most successful US ace of the war did not actually serve with the squadron but ex-racing driver Eddie Rickenbacker shot down 26 aircraft and balloons in a brief career that began in March 1918.

The "February Revolution"

Even before the war, Russia was a divided nation, largely between the wealthy few and the poor majority, and the strains of war, not least the ever-growing casualty list, brought matters to a head in the spring of 1917.

Ordinary Russians lived in a repressive, undemocratic state and various long-standing and divisive economic, political and social problems became even starker under wartime conditions. Russia had suffered something like 6.6 million men killed, wounded or captured on the Eastern Front by the end of 1916 and Tsar Nicholas II, who had made himself supreme commander in September 1915, had become personally identified with the mismanagement of the war. His domineering German-born wife, Alexandra, had been criticized for her links with the mystic and womanizer Grigori Rasputin, who, she believed, could help her haemophiliac son. While the royal family and nobility continued to live in luxury, the vast majority of people faced hardships that seemingly worsened every day.

The "February Revolution", which actually took place in March by the calendar in use in most of the world (Russia then used the Julian calendar), was spontaneous rather than planned. It was sparked by a series of mass strikes, mostly led by socialist and workers' organizations that began in the capital, Petrograd, on 22 January 1917 when 140,000 workers took to the streets. A further 85,000 struck again on 27 February and the unrest spread rapidly from early March onward. Workers were joined by others protesting about food shortages. Troops in the capital refused to fire on protesters on 11 March and calls for revolution grew shriller.

Tsar Nicholas's cabinet resigned to a man on the 13th and, having lost the backing of the army's senior generals, he abdicated on the 15th. His brother, Grand Duke Michael, then refused the throne, effectively ending the Romanov dynasty. Nicholas and his family hoped to live out their lives in foreign exile but they were eventually sent to the remote town of Ekaterinburg in Siberia later in the year. The royal family remained there under close house arrest until they were murdered by their Bolshevik guards in July 1918.

Below: Signs of the growing opposition to the 1917 Provisional Government – Bolshevik activists under fire in Petrograd.

A New Government

The power vacuum that followed the events of the first two weeks of March 1917 was immediately filled by the creation of the liberal Provisional Government under Prince Lvov on the day of Nicholas II's abdication, yet its authority was challenged from the outset by more radical elements of the political landscape. The most vehement opponents of the new government were the Bolsheviks, a small, rather insignificant group of revolutionary socialists within the broader church of Russian socialism. Their charismatic leader, Vladimir Lenin, was known for his fierce opposition

Above: Forces opposed to the Russian emperor man barricades in the capital, 12 March 1917.

to the war but he was living in exile in Switzerland when the revolution took place. He returned to Russia with German help in April and reached Petrograd on the 16th.

Power to the Soviets

Lenin addressed the Petrograd Soviet (workers' council) the very next day and his speech, the "April Thesis", demanded the transfer of power to the soviets, immediate peace with the Central Powers and the redistribution of wealth. His manifesto attracted some like-minded socialist radicals such as Leon Trotsky, but most moderates proved lukewarm to his agenda. Yet Lenin's April Thesis found support among ordinary Russians. This was in part because of deteriorating conditions on the home front but also because the Provisional Government's Minister of War, Alexander Kerensky, launched another disastrous large-scale offensive with the increasingly demoralized Russian Army in July. The attack broke down in a few days and rates of desertion and insubordination soared.

VLADIMIR ILYICH LENIN

Lenin (1878–1924) was a left-wing revolutionary who came to lead the Bolshevik Party. He fled Russia after the failed 1905 Revolution, first to Austria and then Switzerland but returned home with German help in early 1917. He arrived in Petrograd on 16 April but his attempt to undermine the authority of the Provisional Government failed, and he briefly went into exile in Finland. He returned to co-ordinate the successful October Revolution that brought the Bolsheviks to power. His immediate task was to secure a peace with Germany and then defeat anti-Bolshevik forces.

Above: Lenin was in exile during the first days of the February Revolution but returned home a little later.

Left: The Russian Army collapsed during the Kerensky Offensive, due to poor morale and political agitation for change by Bolshevik activists in the ranks. Here, disgruntled soldiers surrender willingly to the Germans.

The "October Revolution"

In the months after the "February Revolution" the Provisional Government lost its authority as Russia's economy and war effort disintegrated. In November the Bolsheviks felt strong enough to launch their own revolution to seize total power.

Russia descended into even greater chaos following the collapse of the Kerensky Offensive in mid-1917 and the authority of the Provisional Government was increasingly challenged by the Bolsheviks. Evidence of this came when there was an uprising by some troops in Petrograd, the capital, on 16 July that first spread to the naval base at Kronstadt and then to other towns and cities throughout all of Russia. The Bolsheviks joined the unrest, named the "July Days", and gained some kudos among the increasingly anti-war general public for their role but the weak Provisional Government was just able to restore order.

Above: Leon Trotsky, a leading figure in the Bolshevik movement and the main organizer of the "October Revolution".

Matters deteriorated over the following weeks, not least when a recently dismissed senior officer, General Lavrenti Kornilov, marched on Petrograd in September. He was met by local rail workers and forced to surrender on the 14th but the event heightened fears of a tsarist revival and pointed to the weakness of the government. Both factors played into the Bolsheviks' hands and by late October, their leaders, Vladimir Lenin and Leon Trotsky, were demanding that the soviets

Below: The Bolshevik delegation, Leon Trotsky among them, arrive at Brest-Litovsk to discuss peace terms with Germany.

(workers' councils) seize power, arrest members of the government and immediately sue for peace with the Central Powers.

Trotsky, head of the Military Revolutionary Committee (MRC) from 29 October, had effective control of the capital's disgruntled garrison and on 7 November (28 October in the Russian calendar, hence the name "October Revolution") the MRC declared that power had been transferred into the hands of the Petrograd Soviet. The next day saw the creation of a new government, the Soviet of People's Commissars, a wholly Bolshevik body, with Lenin taking office as chairman and Trotsky as foreign minister.

Peace Negotiations

Once in power the Bolsheviks had to consolidate their weak control over greater Russia, which would lead to a prolonged civil war (1917–20), and, more immediately, fulfil their promise to leave the war. Armistice negotiations began at Brest-Litovsk on 3 December and both sides agreed a ceasefire on the 16th. Talks on the substance of any treaty began six days later but the Russians began to prevaricate, largely in the hope that revolutions would break out in Austria-Hungary and Germany and this would obviate the need for any settlement. Germany's patience soon wore thin, not least because it wanted to speed up the transfer of forces to the Western Front for a spring offensive in 1918.

German Harshness

The Germans launched an attack, Operation Faustschlag, on 17 February to bring the Russians back to the table. Their troops advanced around 240km (150 miles) in two days and the Bolsheviks accepted the peace terms 48 hours later. The Treaty of Brest-Litovsk was signed on 3 March and it was exceptionally harsh. Russia lost a huge swathe of territory, including the Baltic States, Finland, Poland and the Ukraine, the last an important grain-producing region whose output eased Germany's acute food shortage.

The treaty had an adverse strategic impact on Germany as occupying these lands required keeping 1–1.5 million troops in the East – all at a time when the flow of American troops to France was turning into a flood. Most of the units remained inactive but the Baltic Division under General Rüdiger von der Goltz was sent to newly independent Finland after a civil war had broken out between pro- and anti-Bolshevik forces. Goltz arrived in April and remained until the Armistice.

Left: A posed photograph of Bolshevik troops with an armoured car during the November fighting.

TSAR NICHOLAS II

Nicholas II (1868–1918) was the last ruler of Russia's Romanov dynasty. Autocratic, rigid and not blessed with great intelligence, he was easily led by courtiers and his domineering wife, Alexandra. He made disastrous wartime decisions, mismanaged the economy and became more repressive as the conflict progressed. By 1916 his own advisers were warning him that revolution was in the air but he refused to make any concessions. He abdicated following the outbreak of the "February Revolution" and he and his family were held in internal exile until executed by the Bolsheviks in July 1918.

Above: Nicholas II photographed in captivity with some of his Bolshevik guards.

The Battle of Caporetto

Italian successes in the Eleventh Battle of the Isonzo prompted the weakening Austro-Hungarian Empire to request urgent German aid and the subsequent Battle of Caporetto almost brought about Italy's military collapse.

The Italian Chief-of-Staff, General Luigi Cadorna, met his French counterpart, General Ferdinand Foch, at Vicenza on 8 April 1917. Cadorna's great worry was that Germany would send troops to the Italian Front to aid the faltering Austro-Hungarian war effort and he wanted to develop a plan for British and French forces to be sent to Italy from the Western Front if the need arose. An agreement was reached and their staffs began to devise a practical scheme. Foch in turn reached an understanding with Cadorna that the Italian Army would launch an offensive to support the major Anglo-French effort on the Western Front that same April.

THE BATTLE OF CAPORETTO
The Italian defeat and the German-led advance to the River Piave.

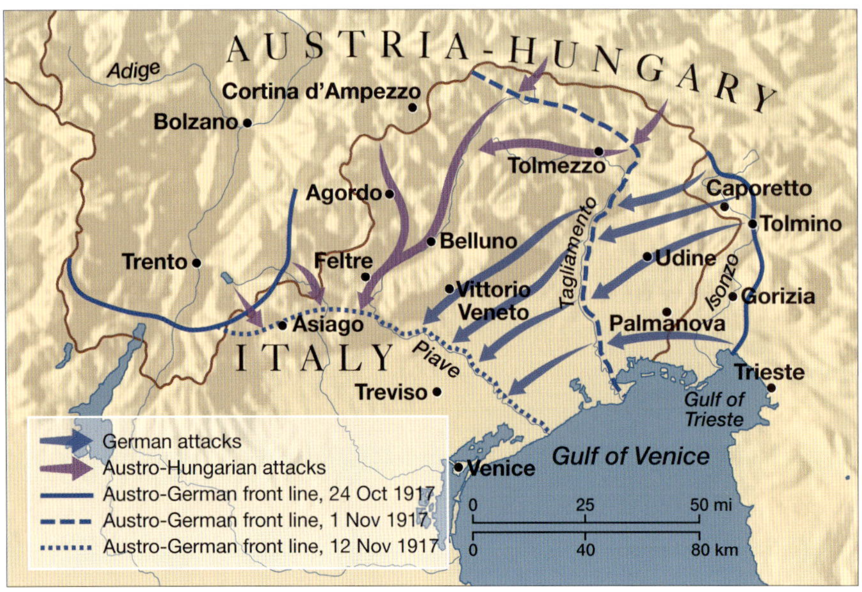

KEY FACTS

Date: 24 October – 12 November 1917

Place: Along the River Isonzo, north-east Italy

Outcome: The Italian forces came close to destruction but were in part saved by Allied reinforcements.

Both the French Nivelle Offensive and the British Battle of Arras had largely been concluded before Cadorna finally launched his attack, the Tenth Battle of the Isonzo, on 12 May. The fighting, which took place in difficult mountainous terrain, lasted 17 days but the Italians made little progress and Cadorna called off the fighting on 8 June after his men had suffered 157,000 casualties. The Austro-Hungarians lost 75,000.

Above: An Austro-Hungarian machine-gun detachment in action along the Isonzo.

Cadorna now regrouped and sent reinforcements to north-east Italy in preparation for the Eleventh Battle of the Isonzo. This time he unleashed two armies, the Second under General Luigi Capello and the Duke of Aosta's Third, against the Austro-Hungarians on 18 August. The Duke of Aosta's advance in the south between Gorizia and Trieste was soon halted but Capello's attack in the north made some significant progress by capturing the Bainsizza Plateau. Shortages of supplies forced the Italians to halt the battle on 15 September after they had suffered a further 148,000 casualties.

German Intervention

The Austro-Hungarians had lost some 55,000 men in the Eleventh Battle of the Isonzo

Right: Some of the German troops who helped spearhead the Caporetto offensive in late 1917.

and the surrender of the plateau and a near-collapse in morale now led them to ask for major German assistance. A new Fourteenth Army was created under the command of German General Otto von Below and it included seven well-trained divisions from his homeland. Below was outnumbered in terms of divisions but he concentrated his better-quality forces against the weakest part of the Italian line and attacked on a narrow front around Caporetto and Tolmino in the northern sector of the Isonzo.

The attack on 24 October was heralded by a huge artillery barrage from around 1,500 guns and mortars. The tough German divisions then advanced led by stormtroopers using infiltration tactics to bypass any points of resistance.

Below: Italian troops fall back towards Udine shortly after the beginning of the Battle of Caporetto.

Frantic Retreat

The Italian Second Army collapsed, sparking a wholesale westward retreat of the armies on its flanks. Italian attempts to hold the lines of the Tagliamento and Livenza rivers came to naught but Cadorna was just able to hang on to positions along the lower reaches of the River Piave when the battle ended on 12 November. A total disintegration had been avoided largely because Below's men had outrun their supply lines and the British and French had rushed 11 divisions under General Plumer to Italy in the nick of time. The Italians lost some 40,000 killed or wounded and a staggering 275,000 prisoners – the last a good indicator of a near-total collapse of morale. Austro-Hungarian and German losses reached around 40,000 men. The Battle of Caporetto sealed Cadorna's fate and he was replaced by the more cautious General Armando Diaz on 9 November.

THE RAPALLO CONFERENCE

Rapallo, a port in north-west Italy, was the scene of an emergency conference of the national leaders of Britain, France and Italy in November 1917 when the Italian forces had all but collapsed during the ongoing German-led Battle of Caporetto. Italy was promised economic aid, heavy artillery and reinforcements but the conference's most important decision was to create a committee, later known as the Supreme War Council, to co-ordinate Allied strategy. This would develop into a much-needed unified military command under General Ferdinand Foch.

Final Battles in the Caucasus 1917–18

The fighting in the Caucasus did not cease with the removal of Russia from the war in 1917 and Turkish, German and British forces struggled for dominance in the region until the very end of the war the following year.

The outbreak of the Russian Revolution in March 1917 effectively ended Russia's war effort against Turkey in the Caucasus and many Turkish troops were freed for operations elsewhere, chiefly Mesopotamia and Palestine. Yet the fighting in the region continued, drawing in not only Turkish and Russian revolutionary troops but also British and German units and local nationalists.

Above: A member of Britain's Dunsterforce pictured with an Armenian soldier near Baku.

Armenian Massacres

Christian Armenians suffered horribly at the hands of the Turkish authorities during the war and an estimated 600,000 died of hunger or lack of water during forced marches, or were simply massacred between mid-1916 and May 1918. Turkey had always denied the Armenians' nationalist aspirations but Russia was more supportive for purely pragmatic reasons as it saw them as a buffer against Turkey. After the February Revolution the Armenians met with representatives of Georgia and Azerbaijan, two neighbouring Russian provinces with similarly frustrated nationalist aspirations, to discuss the formation of a united homeland. The talks began in Tiflis (Tbilisi), Georgia, during August 1917 and, although the

Below: Armenian recruits are put through rifle drill to prepare them for action against the approaching Turkish forces.

three groups were mutually antagonistic, their representatives agreed to establish the Federal Republic of Transcaucasia on 17 September.

New Turkish Invasion

Armenia sought a measure of reconciliation with Turkey in the later part of 1917, but could not prevent Turkey from taking advantage of the Treaty of Brest-Litovsk between Germany and Russia on 3 March 1918. The treaty included a clause that reaffirmed Turkey's right to control the Caucasus provinces. Enver Pasha, the Minister of War, sent some 50,000 troops with a few German units into the Caucasus and northern Persia but general mismanagement of the invasion limited its effects. The Turks and Armenians agreed the Treaty of Batum (Batumi) on 26 May. Transcaucasia was broken up and Armenia proclaimed an independent state but Turkey still had ambitions in the Caucasus. The Turks had occupied Batum on Georgia's Black Sea coast on 15 April and more troops were sent eastward to capture oil-rich Baku on Azerbaijan's Caspian Sea coast.

Baku had been occupied by Russian revolutionary forces in early 1918 and then taken over by Georgian nationalists. They garrisoned the town with some 10,000 ill-equipped men but faced an advancing Turkish force of some 14,000 troops and called on the British for aid. Britain sent a small but highly mobile column, known as "Dunsterforce" after its commander, from Mesopotamia and it had reached Baku by 24 August. The Turks prepared to attack the port and Dunsterforce was withdrawn on the night of 15 September just as Baku fell.

The capture of Baku marked the end of major Turkish operations in the region and most of their forces gradually withdrew from both the Caucasus and northern Persia. An armistice was signed on 31 October 1918 and the British briefly returned to Baku before finally leaving in August 1919. The various parts of Transcaucasia did not remain independent for long – Russian forces occupied Baku in late April 1920, Russian and Turkish troops then took over Armenia the following September, and Georgia was incorporated back into the Russian republic during November 1919.

Above: Baku's oilfields go up in flames to prevent their capture by the Turks in 1918.

Right: Members of an artillery detachment attached to Dunsterforce open fire on Turkish positions aided by Armenian troops.

The Battle of Beersheba

The British effort in Palestine had previously been ponderous and hindered by several setbacks in the first years of the war but in mid-1917 a new commander transformed the fighting and Jerusalem had been captured by December.

General Archibald Murray, British commander in Palestine, began 1917 with the intention of ejecting all the remaining Turkish troops from their positions in the Sinai Peninsula. Murray launched the Battle of Magruntein (or Rafah) on 8 January and within 48 hours his opponents had been routed. The British lost some 500 men but took 1,000 prisoners and a number of artillery pieces. Murray was now authorized to push into Palestine but the manoeuvre was supposed to be limited in scope. The Turks had fallen back to a defensive line stretching inland some 40km (25 miles) from Gaza on the coast to Beersheba that covered the only two practical routes into Palestine.

One of Murray's deputies, General Charles Dobell, attacked on 26 March but the plan fell apart due to weak staff work and poor communications. Some 16,000 British troops were committed to the First Battle of Gaza against a roughly equal number of Turks and Dobell lost 4,000 men before withdrawing later in the day. Murray somehow passed off what was effectively a fiasco as an outright victory and was given permission to march on Jerusalem without further delay.

KEY FACTS

DATE: 31 October 1917

PLACE: Between Gaza and Beersheba, southern Palestine

OUTCOME: Deception plans helped the British to concentrate against a weak sector of the front and smash through Turkish lines.

Right: The ANZAC cavalrymen seen here spearheaded the main attack on Beersheba.

FAILURE AND DISMISSAL

Dobell launched the Second Battle of Gaza on 17 April and his troops made a near suicidal frontal attack against the main Turkish line of defence. The British recorded some 6,500 casualties to the Turks' 2,000 by the end of the fighting on the 19th. Dobell was dismissed by Murray who was in turn sacked by the War Office in London. His replacement was an experienced commander, General Edmund Allenby. His orders were to capture Jerusalem by Christmas but he flatly refused to advance until he had received reinforcements to bring his strength up to 200,000 men.

Allenby finally attacked with some 80,000 infantry and 12,000 cavalry on 31 October and was opposed by just 35,000 men of the Turkish Seventh and Eighth Armies. Allenby's imaginative

Left: British troops are moved up to the Beersheba–Gaza line by railway shortly before the battle.

plan called for a diversion against Gaza, which had been under artillery bombardment for six days, while the bulk of his force was flung against Beersheba. This was a risky option as his infantry and cavalry would need to capture the town's wells intact or face acute water shortages. Beersheba fell around dusk in part to a spirited charge into the town by Australian cavalry.

On to Jerusalem

Allenby was delayed for several days as the wells did not yield as much water as possible but the Turks did retreat from the rest of the Beersheba–Gaza line when their commanders mistook a small camel-mounted patrol towards Hebron for a major outflanking attack. The Eighth Army began to retreat along the coast while the Seventh Army fell back towards Jerusalem. The British hit the Eighth Army again on 13–14 November and sent it reeling farther along the coast after the Battle of Junction Station.

Above: General Allenby enters Jerusalem through the city's Jaffa Gate on 11 December 1917, marking the end of several weeks of campaigning.

Allenby now made his bid for Jerusalem but faced a new enemy commander, the former German Chief of Staff, General Erich von Falkenhayn, who established a new defensive line south-west of Jerusalem in the Judean Hills. Turkish reserves were also arriving and it took the British several weeks to overcome the defenders but Allenby entered Jerusalem on foot on 11 December. The campaign had cost Allenby's force 18,000 casualties while the Turks recorded 25,000 losses.

THE ARAB REVOLT

Some Arab nationalists living in the Arabian Peninsula greatly resented living under Turkish rule and, with British aid, rose against their overlords in June 1916. The uprising was led by Feisal ibn Hussein and he was aided by a British officer, T. E. Lawrence, better known as "Lawrence of Arabia". The Arabs conducted a series of wide-ranging guerrilla-style raids, many of which targeted the only railway line that ran through the region. The Arabs eventually took Damascus in early October 1918 but the British reneged on their promise to help the nationalists secure a homeland.

Above: Bedouin chieftains wait to meet Lawrence of Arabia and other Arab leaders.

The Mesopotamian Campaign 1917–18

The British effort in Mesopotamia had stalled in 1916 but from the next year onward greater military resources and manpower enabled them to push the Turkish garrison farther and farther northward to ensure ultimate victory in 1918.

Above: Locals look on as British troops manhandle a 6in (155mm) howitzer gun through the streets of Baghdad.

The British commander in Mesopotamia, General Frederick Maude, had launched a major offensive up both banks of the Tigris towards Baghdad with some 166,000 troops in mid-December 1916. By late February 1917 he was arrayed outside Kut, the site of a major British defeat in April 1916. The Second Battle of Kut was fought on 22–23 February and Maude was able to overwhelm the Turkish defenders after attacking their flanks and forcing them to withdraw northward towards Baghdad. The Turkish troops fought skilful rearguard actions and the British advance briefly faltered at Aziziyeh, some 72km (45 miles) from Baghdad, on the 27th. Maude then brushed aside the Turkish Sixth Army under Khalil Pasha and Baghdad fell on 11 March.

Maude was now forced to halt all large-scale operations mainly because of the intense heat, but he attacked again during the cool of early autumn. This time he sent his columns in three directions – from Samarrah up the Tigris, from Falluja along the Euphrates and east towards Persia. The main Turkish force in the region was stationed at Tikrit, some 48km (30 miles) north of Samarrah. The portion of Maude's troops advancing up the Euphrates, won the Battle of Ramadi on 27–28 September, while the two other drives also pushed the Turks back and captured Tikrit on 5 November.

Left: Indian troops and labourers were employed extensively during the Mesopotamian campaign. Here, they help build a railway.

Change of Command

Maude succumbed to cholera on 11 November and a new commander, General William Marshall, hoped to complete the campaign. Instead, Marshall was ordered to reduce his forces in early 1918 and was therefore unable to undertake much action, although there was a brief push along the Euphrates in March. Thereafter, the hot season intervened and the British ceased operations completely. When Marshall was ready to advance again in the autumn, the strategic situation in the Middle East had changed dramatically. This was chiefly because British forces advancing from Palestine into northern Syria had taken Aleppo (Halab) on 26 October, the same day that three Turkish envoys arrived at Mudros (Moudros) on the Aegean island of Limnos to discuss a possible armistice.

Turkish Retreat

The capture of Aleppo effectively cut off the Turkish forces in Mesopotamia from their homeland and made their further resistance pointless. Although the isolated Turkish garrison was unlikely to put up much of a fight, Marshall was ordered to undertake one last attack along the Tigris in October mainly to ensure British control of the local oilfields. The demoralized Turkish troops fell back steadily but the British had a stiff fight at the Battle of Sharqat before forcing some 11,000 of them to surrender on the 30th. An armistice was signed on a British warship in Mudros harbour the same day and British–Turkish hostilities ended officially on the 31st. In what was the final act of the offensive, a British flying column took Mosul, some 120km (75 miles) north of Tikrit, on 4 November.

The Mesopotamian campaign had begun as a small-scale affair in October 1914 and for the first two years it had been dogged by incompetence and muddled thinking. Ultimately, it took hundreds of thousands of troops from across the British Empire to win what many considered a sideshow. The British were left in control of the local oilfields as intended but they had suffered some 97,000 casualties, many succumbing to disease, while the number of Turkish casualties is unknown but certainly very much higher.

BRITISH RIVER GUNBOATS

The campaign in Mesopotamia was largely conducted along the banks of the country's two great rivers, the Tigris and Euphrates, which were also the area's most viable lines of communication for moving men and supplies between the front and the rear bases. As most of the fighting took place close to the river, the British opted to supplement their land artillery with a number of shallow-draught gunboats fitted with various types of guns and machine-guns. These provided valuable service in the latter part of the campaign.

Above: The Insect-class gunboat HMS *Ladybird* pictured at Port Said, Egypt, on its way to Mesopotamia, November 1917.

Left: The final week of the war saw the British capture Turkish troops in ever greater numbers.

Defeating the U-boats 1917–18

No one weapon or tactic sealed the fate of Germany's powerful fleet of U-boats but the tide most definitely turned with the much-delayed introduction of the convoy system in May 1917, shortly after the United States had entered the war.

Germany decided to recommence unrestricted submarine warfare on 9 January 1917 and announced that the new campaign would begin on 1 February. The consensus was that Britain could be brought to its knees in five months or so and that the sinking of neutral vessels and loss of neutral lives was an acceptable risk. The danger was that such a policy would inevitably lead to US entry into the war. President Woodrow Wilson had already broken off diplomatic relations with Germany after *U-53* sank the ship *Housatonic* off the Scilly Isles on 3 January. Nevertheless, Germany's policymakers convinced themselves that the United States would not be able to intervene to a significant extent either on land or at sea for two or more years after declaring war.

Above: President Woodrow Wilson addresses Congress requesting that those assembled back a declaration of war against Germany. There were few dissenters.

Below: A German U-boat stands off a sinking steamer in 1917.

U-Boats Unleashed

At the beginning of the year the Imperial German Navy had 105 U-boats in service, including 42 under repair, plus 51 on order from the manufacturers. Its submarines sank 180 ships in January and more than a third of these were from neutral nations, but losses soared after 1 February. Some 245 Allied vessels were sunk during that month, 310 in March and a record 373 in April. However, Germany's relations with the United States had noticeably worsened over the same period. The British liner *Laconia* was sunk by a U-boat on 25 February and 4 Americans were among the 12 dead. Further US ships were sunk thereafter leading the US State Department to announce on 12 March that all US merchant ships would be armed. The Department of

THE ZEEBRUGGE RAID

Some German U-boats were based at Bruges, an inland port in Belgium, and could only reach open waters by way of a canal that entered the North Sea at Zeebrugge. The British decided to block the entrance by sinking old warships in the channel and also to destroy various facilities by putting a landing party ashore. The amphibious assault took place on the night of 22 April 1918 and, though the attackers suffered heavy losses, it was portrayed in the media as a great victory. The reality was that the blockships had not been scuttled in the right place and U-boats were again using the canal within a few days.

Right: The cruiser HMS *Vindictive* showing battle damage from the Zeebrugge Raid.

the Navy authorized ships to take action against U-boats the next day.

America Goes to War

The turning point came on 1 March when the US government made public the Zimmermann Telegram, a note sent to the German ambassador to the USA, Count Bernstorff, by his foreign minister, Alfred Zimmermann, on 17 January. This was decoded and passed on by the British. It suggested that Bernstorff should secretly seek a German alliance with Mexico and that the Mexicans should be allowed to "reconquer the lost territory in Texas, New Mexico and Arizona". US public opinion now turned against Germany and President Woodrow Wilson was able to secure congressional approval for a declaration of war on 6 April. Although the US Army was not ready for war the Navy was and would play its part in the anti-submarine campaign.

In April the British calculated that they would run out of food and other vital materials by June if the U-boats were left unchecked. Attempts to destroy them had so far been largely unsuccessful, with just a handful sunk in the first months of the year. The decision was finally made to adopt the convoy system in which merchant ships sailed together with a protective umbrella of smaller warships and, later, a measure of air cover. The system began on 10 May and did not become fully effective until the last four months of the year – but the results were spectacular.

U-boats had sunk more than 881,000 tons of Allied ships (63 per cent British) in April 1917; by December the total had dropped to under half that and in October 1918, the last full month of the war, the Allies lost just 118,500 tons (50 per cent British) of shipping. U-boat losses had also risen in the final two years of the war. A mere 46 had been sunk between August 1914 and the end of 1916 but a further 132 were lost to all causes during 1917–18.

Below: A convoy escorted by the Royal Navy on its way across the North Atlantic in 1918.

Anti-submarine Weapons

In 1914 no weapons existed that could destroy a submerged submarine but the dangers posed by Germany's U-boats forced the Allies – and especially Britain – to develop a range of passive and aggressive techniques to combat this new menace.

Anti-submarine warfare was very much in its infancy at the outbreak of World War I as most navies had focused their energies on developing offensive surface technologies in previous years. The need to combat submarines became apparent in the first weeks of the conflict and was felt most acutely by the British as their crucial maritime trade and large merchant fleet bore the brunt of Germany's U-boat campaign.

Passive Defences

At first the best defence for vessels, both warships and freighters, was speed and zigzagging as U-boats were very slow both submerged and on the surface and found it difficult to hit targets that were changing course regularly. Ships sailing at night or ones that avoided busy sea lanes also stood a better chance of survival. Next came complex camouflage of the "dazzle" type that covered ships in geometrical patterns of paint to break up their outline. Warships at anchor were often protected by anti-submarine nets that were let down over their sides on booms to stop torpedoes but these were found too cumbersome and of little value. Larger anti-submarine barrages – combinations of nets, minefields and patrolling warships – were also devised to protect narrow stretches of sea and vulnerable routes, such as the English Channel, but they were far from impervious.

Above: One of the first successful depth-charge launchers stands ready for action.

Warships in 1914 could only sink surfaced submarines and then only by ramming or gunfire, while submerged U-boats were effectively invulnerable. For much of the war U-boat captains liked to use gunfire to sink unarmed targets rather than waste torpedoes, so the Allies responded by fitting weapons to merchant vessels. The British also created Q-ships, seemingly unarmed vessels that invited attack on the surface at close range but which actually carried an array of hidden weapons. These were not as successful as hoped and submariners became wary of approaching too close to any likely Q-ship.

The British also developed a system in which a potential target towed a friendly submerged submarine. If a U-boat attacked on the surface, the surface ship could telephone the submerged submarine by a line attached to the tow rope

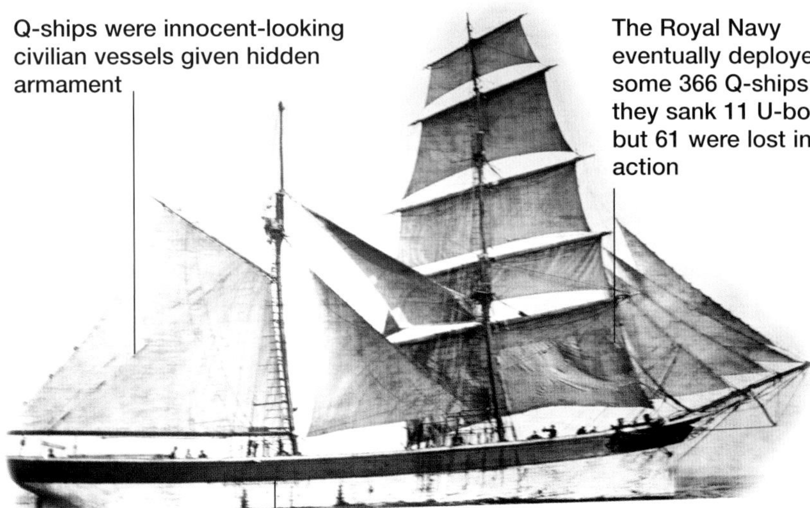

Q-ships were innocent-looking civilian vessels given hidden armament

The Royal Navy eventually deployed some 366 Q-ships; they sank 11 U-boats but 61 were lost in action

Sometimes their holds were filled with wood so that they would stay afloat longer if hit below the waterline

Right: Q-ships like this were a British invention designed to lure U-boats into a surface attack.

and its captain would then slip the rope and manoeuvre into a position to attack the U-boat.

New Weapons

There were other new means of attacking targets. British destroyers towed electronically detonated charges (sweeps) behind them but these needed very close contact to sink a submarine. Depth charges (bombs designed to explode under water) became available in late 1915 but only appeared in quantity from 1917 onward. Hydrophones, directional underwater microphones for listening to U-boat engines, were developed but submariners learned to outfox them by diving deep or by silent running. The first successful attack using both hydrophones and depth charges took place on 16 July 1916. Other means of locating submarines included intercepting their radio messages and using various aircraft and airships to find them on the surface.

Above: US troopships head for Europe. The convoy system was so successful that not one troopship carrying the US Army to France was lost to a U-boat attack.

Some 178 German U-boats were lost during 1914–18; 38 were sunk in accidents or for some other unknown reason. Of the remaining 140, 50 were sunk by mines, 29 by depth charges, 19 by gunfire, 19 by ramming, 18 by torpedo and 1 in an air attack. The most lethal areas were the waters immediately around the British Isles and the near North Atlantic, where 90 and 44 U-boats were lost, respectively. Most sinkings occurred after convoys were introduced in April 1917.

THE SPIDER'S WEB

Mathematical methods were used to develop a pattern of anti-submarine patrols to be conducted by British naval aircraft over the North Sea. A mixture of Curtiss H-12 and Felixstowe flying boats began flying an octagonal pattern of patrol lines from May 1917. and these were calculated to allow just four flying boats to cover some 10,000 sq km (3,860 sq miles) in a mere five hours. The patrols were over routes known to be taken by surfaced U-boats. The British claimed their first success on the 20th and several other kills were recorded. Though these were unconfirmed the web certainly made life more difficult for the U-boats and their crews.

Left: Part of an Allied convoy arrives at an unspecified port. Note the dazzle camouflage pattern.

Final Battles in Italy American troops throwing grenades at Austro-Hungarian positions.

Later Fighters The British Sopwith Camel, probably the leading Allied fighter aircraft of 1917–18.

The Battle of Megiddo Some of the many thousands of Turkish prisoners captured in October 1918.

1918 – TRIUMPH OF THE ALLIES

Both sides began 1918 with a measure of optimism. Germany was shackled to a number of failing allies and could see the United States looming in the near distance but it did have a chance to strike in the West with strength much increased by the end of the war in Russia. The Allies knew that their naval blockade was undermining Germany's war effort and hoped to hang on until sizeable US forces were committed to battle. The key, therefore, was the outcome of Germany's spring offensives – an actual breakthrough or something close to it might force Britain and France to sue for peace but defeat would throw away Germany's last reserves of manpower at a time when hundreds of thousands of US troops were landing in Europe every month.

In the event the Allied line buckled but did not break and Germany did indeed use up its last reserves. The Allies went over to the attack, but simultaneously up and down the Western Front and on a scale that Germany could never match. They did not expect a rapid victory and had begun plans for attacks in 1919, but the Central Powers suddenly collapsed. Armistices were agreed with Austria-Hungary, Bulgaria and Turkey in a matter of five weeks or so. Germany hung on for a few more days but its Armistice with the Allies came into force on 11 November.

Germany's Final Offensives
Indian and Senegalese troops of the British and French forces.

Breaking the Hindenburg Line
A German machine-gunner, unable to halt the Allied advance.

Germany's Naval Mutiny
Armed naval mutineers in the streets of Berlin in November 1918.

Operation Michael

Troops withdrawn from the Eastern Front gave the German High Command a numerical advantage on the Western Front in the spring of 1918 and allowed them to launch an all-or-nothing offensive before the Allies gained a decisive advantage.

During the winter of 1917–18 General Erich Ludendorff, the *de facto* head of the German Army, realized that time was fast running out for his country. The British naval blockade was biting as never before and US troops were arriving in Europe in ever greater numbers. He would have to strike early in 1918 if Germany was to win the war or at least secure a favourable negotiated peace. He placed his faith in troops released from the east after Russia's collapse and a new training regime that produced stormtrooper units, men able to conduct fast-moving operations to bypass points of resistance.

Ludendorff also believed that the French and British had different strategic priorities on the Western Front and that these would make it difficult for them to come to each other's aid if they were hit by a series of large offensives. He felt that the French were preoccupied with the defence of Paris, while the British were more concerned with protecting the Channel ports. He therefore opted to launch his first attack at the point where that part of the Western Front manned by the French gave way to that held by the British.

KEY FACTS

DATE: 21 March – 5 April 1918

PLACE: North-east France between Lens and La Fère

OUTCOME: Despite significant early gains, the German onslaught was eventually contained by the Allies.

Right: A handful of the 72,000 British troops taken prisoner during Operation Michael.

EARLY GAINS

The attack, code-named Operation Michael, was directed against a 96km (60 mile) section of the line between Arras and La Fère held by the British Fifth Army under General Hubert Gough and General Julian Byng's British Third Army. Michael opened on 21 March and was heralded by a five-hour artillery barrage of previously unseen complexity and ferocity. Then the stormtroopers from three German armies advanced under the cover of fog. Gough's army, spread thinly along some 40km (25 miles) of the front, collapsed but Byng's men to the north managed to limit the German gains thanks to their deeper line of defences. Field Marshal Haig committed all his reserves to plug the gap and some French troops were sent to his aid.

Left: German stormtroopers move across a battlefield after the Allied defenders have withdrawn.

Ludendorff ended Michael on 5 April. His troops had advanced up to 64km (40 miles) but there had been no decisive victory, not least because the Allies had reacted swiftly and deployed their formidable air power to help their ground units. The attack had also been hamstrung by three factors – the assault troops had run short of supplies despite capturing some Allied dumps; they had lacked the mobility to exploit their initial gains; and the artillery had been unable to keep up with the leading stormtroopers. The Germans had suffered some 240,000 casualties, roughly the same as the Allies, but whereas the latter's losses could be made good, Ludendorff's could not.

Foch in Command

Michael demonstrated that the Allies had effectively gained air superiority over the Western Front but it also prompted another equally significant event. For the greater part of the conflict the French and British had been waging almost separate wars but matters now changed. The Allied Supreme War Council appointed General Ferdinand Foch as co-ordinator for the Western Front on 26 March and he was made Commander-in-Chief of the Allied forces on 3 April. For political reasons the United States was not technically an ally, but rather an Associated Power; however, the American commander in France, General John Pershing, agreed to accept Foch's authority.

BRUCHMÜLLER'S BARRAGE

Colonel Georg Bruchmüller was a brilliant artillerist who was put in charge of the bombardment for Operation Michael. He brought together 6,500 guns and 3,500 trench mortars and planned to fire 1.6 million shells in just five hours. This whirlwind was broken down precisely into seven distinct phases lasting from two hours down to just five minutes. It proved highly successful and its creator was given a new nickname – *Durchbruch-Müller* ("Breakthrough Müller").

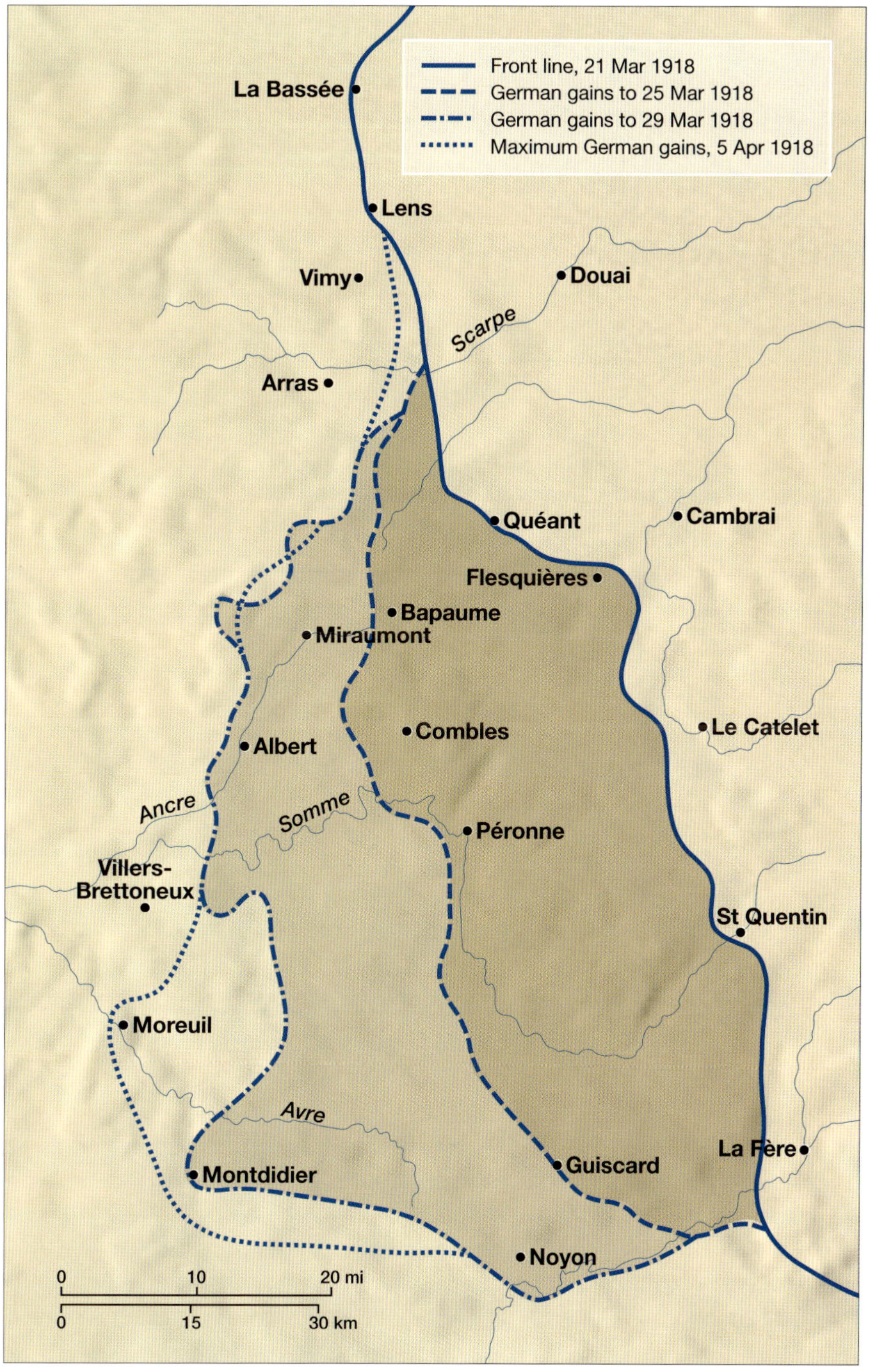

OPERATION MICHAEL

The attack deeply dented the British line but never made a breakthrough.

Later Fighters

The latter part of the war saw the emergence of highly specialized fighters that flew higher and faster than ever before and their emergence meant the battle in the air swayed first one way and then the other in a hard-fought technological struggle.

The fighters of the second half of World War I were far superior to their predecessors. All combatant nations were now able to fit forward-firing machine-guns to their fighters and the later machines were also usually far more streamlined and fitted with more powerful engines. They therefore had a better rate of climb, greater speed, and were much more manoeuvrable. Better fighters appeared on both sides at regular intervals and thus air superiority would switch back and forth between the sides – often in just a few months – as new arrivals outclassed their older opponents.

Above: US ace "Eddie" Rickenbacker pictured in his French-built Spad XIII fighter in June 1918.

Battles in 1917

This was demonstrated in the Battle of Arras in the spring of 1917. The British enjoyed a 3:1 advantage in aircraft over the Germans but were reliant on the Royal Aircraft Factory's two-seater BE-2s and RE-8s. These were no match for the Albatros D-types and, during what became known to the British as "Bloody April", they lost 151 aircraft and 316 crew compared to German figures of 66 and 119. Yet the D-types were soon outclassed by British SE-5s and France's Spad S-VIIs.

The fighters of 1917–18 were mostly biplanes, although there were a few notable three-winged designs, chiefly the British Sopwith Triplane and the famed Fokker Dr-1 as flown for a time by Baron Manfred von Richthofen. The Fokker was introduced in June 1917 but was withdrawn in the autumn after a number of accidents. It briefly re-emerged in 1918 but was obsolescent by the summer.

FOKKER DR-1

This legendary German fighter entered service in the summer of 1917 as a stop-gap design and was not particularly successful – it was not especially fast, though it was very manoeuvrable. Nevertheless, some 329 were built before the war ended.

Engine: 110hp Oberursel or Le Rhône
Crew: 1
Ceiling: 6,100m (20,000ft)
Top speed: 165kph (102mph)
Armament: 2 x 7.92mm (0.312in) machine-guns

SOPWITH F-1 CAMEL

The Sopwith Camel was one of the best fighters of the war and was the first British aircraft to be built with two synchronized machine-guns. It was agile and had a good rate of climb but was difficult to fly. Many less experienced pilots paid the price.

Engine: Various including 130hp Clerget
Crew: 1
Ceiling: 5,500m (18,000ft)
Top speed: 185kph (115mph)
Armament: 2 x 0.303in (7.7mm) machine-guns

The Sopwith Triplane had a similarly short combat history. It made its debut on the Western Front in April 1917 with the Royal Naval Air Service (RNAS) and it simply outflew and outmanoeuvred any of its German rivals, so much so that some units amassed a large number of kills. The Canadian pilots of B Flight of the RNAS's No. 10 Squadron, commonly referred to as the Black Flight as its aircraft had their upper fuselages painted black, were a case in point. The flight consisted of just five Sopwith Triplanes yet these downed 87 German aircraft without loss between May and September 1917. However, their heyday was soon over as the Germans introduced better performing fighters and the last Sopwith Triplane was withdrawn from the Western Front during November.

Biplanes

Triplanes were the exception and the single-seat biplane fighter fitted with two forward-firing machine-guns was the norm. All sides on the Western Front, where the most extensive air fighting took place, produced some outstanding designs. The French introduced their Spad S-XIII in the late summer of 1917, largely to replace the Spad S-VII, and it became the mainstay of the country's fighter strength as well as equipping Belgian, Italian and US squadrons. The British Sopwith Scout, which was nicknamed "Pup", appeared in numbers in late 1916 and was highly manoeuvrable, if underpowered and lightly armed. The Pup was superseded by the Sopwith F-1 Camel from July 1917 and it became Britain's leading fighter for the remainder of the war, shooting down some 1,300 enemy aircraft. Also in service in large numbers was the effective SE-5.

Germany's last notable biplane fighter was the Fokker D-VII, which was actually built by both Fokker and Albatros. It first saw action in May 1918 but despite its manoeuvrability, especially at high altitudes, the Allies would keep almost total air superiority due to some good aircraft but more importantly thanks to superior numbers.

FOKKER D-VIII

The Fokker D-VIII was one of the last German fighters to enter service on the Western Front and was basically a high-winged monoplane version of the previous D-VII biplane. It won a competition to find a new-generation fighter in April 1918 but it was soon plagued with problems – three of the first six to be delivered suffered catastrophic wing collapses. The problem was traced to some inflexible wing spars and these were replaced. The D-VIII was an extremely fast aircraft but, because of its early design flaws, only 85 ever reached the front.

Left: The Fokker D-VIII had a top speed of 200kph (124mph) and had two forward firing machine-guns but saw limited service.

Below: Australian troops with a captured Albatros D-III fighter, one of the most successful German fighters of the latter part of the war.

Anti-aircraft Guns

There were very few anti-aircraft guns in existence in 1914 but with the rapid development of aerial warfare they soon became an important weapon in the battle for air supremacy and were deployed in their thousands.

No one had given much thought to the threat posed by aircraft in the years before World War I and, therefore, no one had given much thought to developing anti-aircraft guns to knock them out of the sky. Germany was the first country to demonstrate such weapons in 1908–9 and these, which were known as "balloon guns" and built by either Krupp or Rheinmetall, merely consisted of a field gun converted to fire at a high angle from a truck or large automobile. At the time there was a belief that these would actually be able to keep up with the slow-flying aircraft of the day. Other types, usually those positioned to defend targets like major cities, were essentially guns taken from their original carriages and placed on static angled mounts that could be turned through 360 degrees.

As there were so few aircraft around both before and at the outbreak of the fighting in August 1914, there was very little incentive to spend large amounts of money developing dedicated anti-aircraft guns. The British, for example, had no more than a handful of guns on towed mounts, while the French, who were even less prepared, had just two armoured cars based on the De Dion Bouton automobile that each carried a field gun fitted to a special high-angled mount in the rear for anti-aircraft work. Nevertheless, these autocannon were subsequently used extensively by the French and were also sold to Britain to bolster London's air-defence network in 1915–16.

Mobile Guns

Anti-aircraft guns in the field tended to be a marriage of an existing light or medium field gun placed on a high-angled mount and fitted to a flatbed truck or to a purpose-built carriage that could be towed by another vehicle. Thus, in one case, the British adapted a light field gun, a weapon normally associated with horse artillery batteries that fought alongside cavalry units. It was put on the back of trucks with drop-down sides, chiefly the Peerless Motor Lorry or the Thornycroft J-type. These were usually fitted with stabilizers and screw jacks to prevent the recoil of the gun from overturning them. Guns could typically be elevated between 70 and 90 degrees and

BRITISH 13-POUNDER

This anti-aircraft weapon was a combination of a light field gun used by British horse artillery batteries and a Thornycroft J-type lorry, one of the most ubiquitous petrol-engined vehicles of the war. It first saw service in 1915. A standard gun section was two such weapons accompanied by two other lorries for the crew, range-finding equipment and ammunition.

Shell weight: 5.9kg (13lb)
Gun weight: 975kg (2,150lb)
Elevation: +80 degrees
Vertical range: 4,000m (13,100ft)
Muzzle velocity: 520m/sec (1,700ft/sec)

Left: The crew of a German anti-aircraft machine-gun await the order to open fire. Note the gun s very large ammunition drum.

their shells generally had a maximum altitude of around 4,000m (13,100ft), although some could reach higher.

Fire Control

The main problem for the anti-aircraft gunners was trying to hit a target that, although comparatively slow-moving, was effectively able to move in three dimensions. So if a gun was fired directly at the target then by the time the shell arrived at the right altitude, the target would have moved on. The gunners began dealing with the problem by fitting complex sights to their weapons but this was effectively a duplication of effort within a battery and it was found simpler to have what was known as a central post sight. This was positioned in the middle of a group of guns and, once its crew had worked out the necessary data of height, range and speed, the information was given to all of the guns.

In reality, the available anti-aircraft technology was very much in its infancy during the war and, while there are no firm figures of the number of aircraft downed by such batteries, it was overwhelmingly dwarfed by the number of aircraft shot down in combat by other aircraft. However, anti-aircraft fire could be of sufficient nuisance value to disrupt a reconnaissance or put a pilot off when making an attack.

FRENCH 75MM ANTI-AIRCRAFT GUN

The French made extensive use of their famed 75mm (2.95in) gun in the anti-aircraft role, largely because of its high rate of fire. The weapon's wheeled carriage was simply removed and the gun mounted on a De Dion car fitted with several stabilizers, one of which is shown here in front of the rear wheel. Note also the rangefinder on the right.

Shell weight: 7.16kg (15.8lb)
Gun weight: 4,000kg (8,800lb)
Elevation: +70 degrees
Vertical range: 4,725m (15,500ft)
Muzzle velocity: 530m/sec (1,740ft/sec)

Right: US troops man a French-built Hotchkiss heavy machine-gun deployed in the anti-aircraft role. This weapon's greatest weakness was the metal strip magazine that can be seen here as it held no more than 30 rounds and thus required frequent changing.

Germany's Final Offensives

Despite the failure of Operation Michael, the German High Command continued to launch major attacks along the Allied line on the Western Front between April and July 1918 but the attacking stormtroopers suffered severe and irreplaceable losses.

Germany's first major offensive in spring 1918 had come so near to breaking the Allied line that General Ludendorff resolved to try again as he knew time was fast running out. His second attack, the Lys Offensive or Operation Georgette, was once more against the British, this time between Ypres and La Bassée. The attack opened on 9 April and the Germans seemed so close to breaking through that Field Marshal Haig issued an order on the 12th that prohibited any more withdrawals. This did the trick. Resistance stiffened and the German advance was halted by the 17th but only after a 16km (10 mile) salient had been punched in the line. The British had suffered around 100,000 casualties but had prevented Ludendorff from reaching the vital Channel ports and had inflicted severe losses on his stormtrooper units.

Above: German stormtroopers push past a British barricade in the town of Bailleul on 15 April 1918.

Below: A worrying sight for the Germans – US troops arriving at the front in late May 1918.

Striking the French

Ludendorff now turned on the French along the Chemin des Dames. Operation Blücher–Yorck, or the Aisne Offensive, was actually a diversionary attack to mask preparations for another operation against the British forces in Flanders. Two German armies advanced on 27 May and carved out a deep salient some 48km (30 miles) wide and 32km (20 miles) deep. There was no breakthrough but Ludendorff was encouraged to launch another diversionary attack. Operation Gneisenau, the Noyon–Montdidier Offensive, opened on 9 June but the French had been forewarned by deserters and had strengthened their defences. Two German thrusts towards Compiègne, headquarters of the Allied supreme commander, General Foch, were halted by the 13th.

Ludendorff now persisted with targeting the French and launched his final attack, the Marne Offensive, to the west of Reims, on 15 July. His assault troops made no significant gains and he finally conceded defeat, ordering a withdrawal from the great salient his recent attacks

Above: Colonial forces, such as these Senegalese and Indian troops, were an important part of both the French and British war efforts.

PEACEFUL PENETRATION

Australian troops devised a new and imaginative offensive tactic and put it into practice for the first time on a large scale at Le Hamel in July 1918. The aim was to seize control of enemy territory not with infantry, who invariably suffered heavy losses in an assault, but by using fire-power from aircraft, artillery, machine-guns and tanks to overwhelm a section of the enemy line. Once the enemy defences were subdued, the infantry would advance against minimal opposition, hence the slightly misleading title "peaceful penetration".

had created between Soissons and Reims on the 17th. His forces had suffered some 500,000 casualties in five months and Ludendorff knew that US troops were now arriving at a rate of 300,000 per month, while he had virtually no reserves to call on. He was also aware that his troops' morale was faltering and that cases of indiscipline were rising.

ALLIED ATTACKS

There was to be no respite for the Germans as Foch unleashed a major counter-attack, the Second Battle of the Marne, on the 18th. After a series of hammer blows by the French and eight US divisions, the Soissons–Reims salient was eradicated by 5 August. Ludendorff finally gave up all hope of launching an offensive in Flanders, knowing full well that the initiative on the Western Front had wholly passed to the Allies. Foch, the architect of the Allied victory, was created Marshal of France on 6 August.

Ludendorff suffered yet another blow that August. Anglo-French forces launched the Amiens Offensive on the 8th and the attack, which brilliantly combined infantry, tanks, artillery and aircraft as never before, shattered the German line in hours. Some 15,000 German troops surrendered on the first day alone and many had put up absolutely no resistance. Ludendorff was shocked to the core and called it the "black day of the German Army". The battle ended on 4 September by which time Germany had lost some 100,000 casualties and the Allies just 42,000. The war now entered its final phase.

Below: A battery of US 155mm (6.1in) guns in mid-1918 as mobile warfare returned to the Western Front.

The Paris Gun

German troops pushed to within 160km (100 miles) of Paris in the spring of 1918 and this allowed them to deploy a pair of huge, technologically advanced artillery pieces to bring the French capital and its inhabitants under direct fire.

The Paris Gun was a huge artillery piece designed purely to fire on the French capital to undermine civilian morale at a time when the German Army was launching a series of offensives on the Western Front in March – August 1918. It was officially designated the Lange 21cm Kanone (Long 8.3-in Cannon) but was nicknamed "Wilhelm's Gun" in honour of the German emperor.

Below: Test firing the "Paris Gun". Each shot wore the barrel away significantly so succeeding shells had to be a little larger until, after 60 shots, the barrel had to be changed.

The idea of the gun was first mooted in spring 1916, a time when some sections of the Western Front were "just" 96km (60 miles) east of Paris.

Designing the Gun

The project was masterminded by Krupp and a body known as Artillery Direction, part of the Imperial German Navy. Their work was exceedingly difficult, not least because of the weapon's complex ballistics, and it was made doubly so when German troops withdrew to the Hindenburg Line from autumn 1916, thereby increasing the distance to Paris by a further 20km (12 miles) or so. Nevertheless, they pushed the project forward over the following months and finally conducted successful test firings of the weapon at their Mappen proving ground. The ultimate design could be broken down into sections, transported by rail on specially produced carriages and then reassembled at the required point – but all this was an immense effort.

Into Action

The bombardment of Paris was conducted from three positions to the north-east and east of the capital, all near various railway

Left: An interior view of one of the great Krupp armaments factories where the monstrous "Paris Gun" was produced in great secrecy before being deployed to the Western Front in March 1918.

lines running around Laon and Reims and all in the middle of a forest. The work on these positions began in November 1917 and carried on into January and February 1918. Each required much preparation work – new track was laid, emplacements were dug and huge volumes of concrete made to create foundations sound enough to take the weight of the reassembled gun. Great efforts were also made to camouflage the various firing positions. The first of these was located at Crépy-en-Laonnois and was used 23 March – 1 May when 183 rounds were fired; the Bois de Corbie was used on two occasions, 27 May – 11 June (104 rounds) and 5–9 August (66 rounds); while the third position was used only briefly 15–19 July (14 rounds) at the Bois de Bruyères.

Thus, 367 shells fell on or near Paris during the various attacks, killing 256 civilians and wounding a further 620, but there was no set routine. More shells might fall on one day than the next, and several days might pass without any landing at all. This might have been because the gun's barrel needed replacing after just 60 rounds had been fired or because the gun was being moved. One thing did become clear on the second day of the bombardment. The previous day's shells had landed some 20 minutes apart but on the morning of 24 March two struck just three minutes apart, meaning that there were at least two Paris Guns in action.

The Paris Guns proved largely invulnerable and neither was ever destroyed by the Allies. Their bombardment only ended following the successful Allied counter-attacks in August that pushed the German line back so that the French capital was beyond their range. Some of the guns' emplacements were overrun but there was no sign of the weapons themselves. Nor was any trace of them ever found. The most likely explanation is that they were cut up and the high-grade metal put to other uses.

Below: A crowd of curious onlookers examines a little of the damage done by a round from the "Paris Gun".

Ground-attack Aircraft

Close co-operation between ground and air units became a very important part of offensive operations during World War I but few dedicated aircraft were ever built and still fewer entered service before the later stages of the conflict.

Light bombers and fighters were commonly used for close-support missions during World War I infantry offensives but they were not as effective as dedicated ground-attack aircraft. Light bombers tended to drop their ordnance from medium altitude and would often be inaccurate, while fighters could strafe enemy positions with their machine-guns and drop small loads of bombs – but such low-level work was very dangerous and heartily detested by the majority of pilots. Both they and their unprotected aircraft were highly vulnerable to the huge volume of machine-gun and rifle fire that would greet them as they swooped down on a target. True ground-attack aircraft began to appear from 1917 onward and were usually, but not always, fitted with some form of armoured protection to improve the chances of their crews' surviving over the battlefield.

German Designs

Germany's AEG company produced one of the first ground-attack aircraft, the J-type. It was introduced in 1917 and based on the company's C-type, a two-seater reconnaissance aircraft with an armoured engine. The J-type was given a more powerful engine and two downward-firing forward machine-guns. This design was only intended as a stop-gap measure until dedicated ground-attack aircraft appeared but production problems with the latter led the J-type to be used until the end of the war by which time some 600 had been built.

Another of the major German producers was Albatros, who introduced a two-seater, also known as the J-type, on the Western Front from late 1917. It was essentially a replacement for the AEG J-type and was based on the earlier Albatros C-type, which was primarily a two-seater reconnaissance/light bomber series that was also used for ground-support work. The Albatros J-I was by no means fast and had a reputation for being difficult to fly but it had some useful attributes. The designers had added armoured protection for the two-man crew and fitted the aircraft with three machine-guns of which two were positioned to fire down through the fuselage. The J-I's chief weakness in action was that its designers had neglected

Left: A close-up view of the rear gun position of a German AEG C-IV, a multi-purpose aircraft that performed ground-attack missions.

to protect the engine. This oversight was remedied with the J-II, which was introduced in 1918, but few had reached the front before the end of the war.

Two of the leading aeronautical designers of the day, Hugo Junkers and Antony Fokker, developed the Junkers J-1 two-seater biplane as a ground-attack aircraft. It was based on an all-metal prototype but was modified so that its rear fuselage was made of wood. The J-1 first flew in late 1917 and participated in the great German offensives of spring 1918. Its greatest assets were that it was popular with pilots and the crew had a radio so that it could be easily directed to a target by ground units. The biggest drawback was that the J-1 was rather difficult to build and only 227 had entered service by November 1918.

SALMSON 2

This sturdy and agile aircraft entered service with the French in early 1918 and was also purchased by the United States Army Air Force. Despite the crew positions being rather far apart, which made communication difficult, it was a well-liked type and some 3,200 were built in total.

TYPE: Ground-attack, light bomber, reconnaissance
ENGINE: 260hp Canton-Unné
CREW: 2
CEILING: 5,000m (16,400ft)
TOP SPEED: 184kph (114mph)
RANGE: 500km (310 miles)
ARMAMENT: 3 x 0.303in (7.7mm) machine-guns, light bombs

JUNKERS J-1

The Junkers J-1 was an all-metal biplane designed by Hugo Junkers and it first entered service in early 1918. Some 227 were built jointly by the Fokker and Junkers companies before the end of the war. The aircraft was partially armoured and this extra weight necessitated longer take-offs and landings. It was also slow and clumsy in flight and somewhat difficult to handle but it was popular with its crews for its robustness – especially in action at low levels.

TYPE: Ground-attack, air–ground liaison
ENGINE: 200hp Benz Bz.IV
CREW: 2
CEILING: 4,000m (13,120ft)
TOP SPEED: 155kph (96mph)
ARMAMENT: 3–5 x 7.92mm (0.312in) machine-guns

ALLIED RESPONSES

The Allies tended not to build dedicated ground-attack aircraft but relied more on multipurpose types. The French, for example, introduced their Salmson 2 in early 1918 and it not only undertook ground-attack duties but also flew as a light bomber and conducted reconnaissance sorties.

Britain used its Sopwith F-1 Camel fighter for ground-support work but it suffered heavy losses because it lacked armoured protection and an attempt to produce the TF-1 (Trench Fighting 1) Camel came to nothing. The first true type was the Sopwith TF-2 Salamander, which went into mass production in May 1918 but saw little service.

Equipping the Americans

The United States had to build a mass army of hundreds of thousands from scratch but lacked an industrial base that was geared up for war production to equip its troops so largely relied on Britain and France for its weaponry.

Britain and France had well-developed war industries by mid-1917 but were increasingly short of manpower due to the heavy casualties they had suffered in the preceding years. The United States, in contrast, had huge reserves of untapped manpower but largely lacked the wartime industrial base needed to equip them. Rather than wait for the Americans to clothe and arm their own armed forces, a time-consuming business at a point when speed was of the essence, it was thought better for Britain and France to provide US land and air forces with the means to fight the war. The US Navy, the country's strongest service, was fit to go to war and required no help from either Britain or France.

This decision on supply also meant that the shipboard space that would have been used to carry vast quantities of arms and equipment overseas was left free to ferry greater numbers of US troops to Europe much more quickly. There was no doubt that this plan was a wise one as some two million US troops crossed the North Atlantic during 1917–18.

Above: US troops fighting in the Argonne make use of a French-built 37mm (1.46in) trench gun.

Uniforms and Rifles

US troops did largely go to war in their own uniforms and carrying home-produced small arms but there were exceptions even to this. The infantry mostly wore British steel helmets but troops serving with French formations, generally segregated African-American units, instead wore the French Adrian helmet.

CURTISS JN-4D "JENNY"

The Curtiss JN-4 was the most successful US aircraft of the war period but it was a trainer not a combat type. Nevertheless, this version, the first to be mass-produced, was used in large numbers and some 5,500 had been built by the end of 1918.

Engine: 90hp Curtiss OX-5
Crew: 2
Ceiling: 3,000m (9,850ft)
Top speed: 112kph (70mph)
Armament: none

American troops were equipped with US small arms, including the excellent 1903 Springfield Rifle and the Browning Automatic Rifle but they also used French and British weapons, including the Rifle M1917 (Enfield), derived from a British design, and the wholly French Chauchat light machine-gun. The African-American troops serving with the French were armed with the Lebel and Berthier rifles. The main heavy machine-gun deployed throughout the US Army was the US 1917 Browning.

ARTILLERY

However, when it came to heavy equipment the American Expeditionary Force (AEF) was overwhelmingly dependent on French and British designs. In the case of artillery the AEF relied mainly on the French 75mm (2.95in) field gun and 155mm (6.1in) howitzer. The British also supplied a number of 8in (203mm) howitzers. The AEF's armoured force mainly consisted of French Renault FT-17 light tanks and its few heavier tanks were all British. There were plans to mass produce an "Allied" or "Liberty" tank based on the British Mark VIII design fitted with a US aero-engine at a plant in France but the war ended before it came into service.

The pilots of the United States Army Air Service largely earned their wings on US-built aircraft like the Curtiss JN series but they went into combat flying British and French designs, many of which were built under licence in the United States and fitted with US aero-engines. Others were simply bought from Britain and France; they had delivered 4,881 and 259 aircraft, respectively, by the war's end. The chief fighters flown by US squadrons were the French Nieuport 28 and various Spad S-types, while by later in 1918 the bomber units were mostly equipped with French Breguet 14 and Salmson 2 machines supported by a significant number of American-built DH-4s.

Left: A US communications detachment with a field telephone. Line repair was a constant task.

Below: Most of the American Expeditionary Force was equipped with foreign-built artillery, including the famous French 75mm (2.95in) field gun seen here in action.

The First American Battles

The first US troops arrived in Europe during late May 1917 but they did not appear in combat in any numbers until the first months of 1918 and did not go into action on a significant scale until May to halt a major German offensive.

The United States declared war on Germany on 6 April 1917 but its 200,000-strong army was small by European standards and ill-prepared for battle. Congress agreed the Selective Service Act to introduce conscription on 19 May with the aim of having one million men serving overseas within a year. General John Pershing had been named commander of the American Expeditionary Force on the 10th and he arrived in France on 13 June. The first sizeable body of troops, some 14,000 in all, disembarked on the 28th but months passed before any saw action as they required schooling in the arts of trench warfare. Nevertheless, the first US troops went to the front in October and they suffered their first fatalities on 3 November.

KEY FACTS

Date: May – June 1918

Location: Various points on the Western Front

Outcome: The US forces helped to stem a major German offensive and retook some lost ground.

AMERICA'S BATTLES, 1918
US forces fought several minor actions and the St Mihiel and Meuse–Argonne Offensives in 1918.

First Engagements

It was not until late May 1918 that AEF units were committed to battle in any strength. The Germans had been hammering away at various parts of the Allied line on the Western Front since late March. On 28 May the US 1st Division under Major General Robert Bullard was ordered to attack Cantigny, which the Germans had captured and turned into a strongly fortified observation post. The village was retaken and then Bullard's men successfully beat off several counter-attacks over the next 48 hours.

Below: A Renault FT-17 tank operated by the AEF lies abandoned after failing to cross a trench.

Above: US troops leave their trench during an attack around Cantigny, 28 May 1918.

Battle of the Marne

The Germans opened their Aisne Offensive, between Reims and Montdidier on 27 May. Their forces had reached the River Marne by the next day and the French troops there were on the point of collapse. The US 2nd and 3rd Divisions were deployed to stem the tide from the 30th. The 3rd Division held vital bridges at Château-Thierry, threw back several German assaults and then counter-attacked with French units, driving the Germans back across the river. The 2nd Division was positioned to the west of Château-Thierry, between the villages of Belleau and Vaux, and was also able to stop the German advance. The Aisne Offensive ended on 4 June and the 2nd Division then successfully counter-attacked at several points, most notably Belleau Wood (6–25 June).

Although the AEF's commitment was larger than it might seem because US divisions were twice the size of those of the other Allies, the Battles of Cantigny, Château-Thierry and Belleau Wood were small-scale affairs by the usual standards of the Western Front. The next US attack was of an altogether different magnitude as on 24 July Pershing had finally been able to persuade General Foch, the Allied Commander-in-Chief since March, to assign the AEF a whole sector of the front, one immediately to the south-east of Verdun. The offensive, from 12–16 September, was conducted by the US First Army to nip out a salient around St Mihiel.

Pershing advanced on both the northern and southern flanks of the bulge after a four-hour barrage from some 2,970 guns. The troops made their attack supported by the biggest air armada ever seen. The two pincers had converged at Hattonchâtel by nightfall on the first day and the St Mihiel Offensive was effectively over by the 16th. The Germans had actually evacuated many of their troops before Pershing moved but the operation had been conducted with a great deal of skill, indicating that the AEF was now ready to play a full part in the war. Pershing immediately moved his entire army to the west of Verdun and ten days later launched the largest – and last – US offensive of the war.

GENERAL JOHN PERSHING

Pershing (1860–1948), who commanded the American Expeditionary Force on the Western Front, was a career soldier who had fought against Native Americans and the Spanish and conducted raids into Mexico in early 1917. Much to the chagrin of the British and French, Pershing refused to put his command under their direct control, although he did relent somewhat in times of crisis, but he mostly preferred to conduct his own offensives, notably at St Mihiel and in the Meuse–Argonne. He was promoted to become the first US General of the Armies in 1919.

Above: Pershing with Allied commanders Foch, Haig and Pétain (right to left).

Supply Transport

As befitted a highly industrialized war fought on a vast scale, World War I demanded the production of huge quantities of weapons and equipment and these were transported to the fronts by both long-established and much newer means.

The movement of men and equipment, indeed all types of military necessities up to the front, was a vital if unglamorous part of every country's military effort during World War I. Such items would be transported to the theatre of war by sea and rail, and then be moved by rail to stations usually some way behind the front where they would be unloaded and transported to large supply dumps. From these distribution points they would be sent forward to those who needed the particular supplies. The task of getting such quantities of supplies to the front was immense, virtually ceaseless and the rate of consumption often huge, especially during major battles and offensives.

Above: This shell dump gives a good indication of the huge quantities of all types of war material required to keep the armies fighting.

For example, on 5 September 1914, the first day of the Battle of the Marne, the French had 465,000 rounds of 75mm ammunition stockpiled; five days later they had just 33,000 shells left. The British hit similarly high levels of consumption in 1916 – they fired more rounds in the week before the opening of the Battle of the Somme than they had in the previous 12 months. The Germans stockpiled some 1.16 million shells for their March 1918 offensive and fired virtually all of them in just five hours on the 21st.

Foreign Labour

Several of the combatants scoured the world for workers to keep an existing supply system going or expand it. Both Britain and France used labour drawn from their overseas colonies. Britain alone used more than one million porters from its own

Below: A camel supply column, as used by the British forces during the campaign in Palestine.

and various other African colonies during the war in East Africa but even this was not enough as the average soldier there required three porters. Even in Europe where the war was far less mobile, the supply network required huge numbers of labourers. China was a major contributor and by 1918 some 100,000 Chinese workers, both skilled and unskilled, worked in British labour corps on the Western Front, roughly the same number served with the French and a further 6,000 with the AEF.

Animal Power

World War I was largely powered by the horse. The official establishment of a British infantry division in 1914 included 877 vehicles and close to 5,600 horses, but only 9 motor cars, and matters had not changed much by 1918. The very same division was allocated 822 horse-drawn vehicles and some 8,840 horses but just 11 motor cars, 3 lorries and 21 motor ambulances. The need for horses and other animals, such as mules, camels and even bullocks, was all but insatiable and produced a terrible death toll. Some 542,000 horses died in French service alone during 1914–18, for example, and the British lost close to 485,000 horses and other animals.

Despite these figures, there is little doubt that motor transport did play a growing role in the supply chain. Trucks and a small light railway largely fuelled the French resupply effort during the titanic Battle of Verdun in 1916 and by June some 12,000 vehicles, at times one every 14 seconds, had moved up and down the *Voie Sacrée*, the only available road into the town.

Many of the original motor vehicles were simply civilian types pressed into service. The British, for example, converted around 1,300 buses belonging to the London General Omnibus Corporation into B Type Motor Lorries. Increasingly, however, major vehicle manufacturers, including such companies as Dennis, Leyland and Wolseley, began to supply purpose-built designs. A similar pattern was followed by the French Army, which requisitioned 1,049 civilian buses, 2,500 cars and 6,000 lorries in the final months of 1914, but thereafter Renault, Schneider and others began to supply appropriate vehicles.

LIGHT RAILWAYS

The importance of narrow-gauge railways cannot be overemphasized. Their tracks were usually just 60cm (2ft) apart and this made them much faster to build. The British Army, for example, estimated that a mile of light railway took 1,760–2,400 man-days to build while standard gauge took 4,300. Light railways were used by all sides and were pivotal in supplying the front line with every necessity. Some were also used to bring troops to within easy distance of the trench line.

Left: A British light railway pictured beside the River Scarpe – itself used as a supply artery – during the Battle of Arras in 1917. Water transport was often used to take wounded men to hospital as it gave a smooth ride.

Above: Motor transport, like these French trucks, was little used in 1914 but had become commonplace by later in the war.

The Meuse–Argonne Offensive

The last weeks of the war saw a successful joint US–French effort designed to break through the Western Front in the direction of Sedan but, more importantly, this was the first prolonged major attack made by the American Expeditionary Force.

KEY FACTS

DATE: 26 September – 11 November 1918

PLACE: Argonne region of eastern France

OUTCOME: Despite stubborn German resistance US forces advanced to the River Meuse.

By late September 1918 Marshal Foch had finalized his plans to deliver a succession of hammer blows on the Western Front. He intended to launch two major offensives against the Germans, realizing that they had used up their strategic reserves during the bitter fighting of March–July and, if attacked simultaneously, there would be no quiet sector of the front from where troops could be sent to reinforce an area facing an attack. Foch aimed to launch French and US forces northward from west of Verdun towards the key rail junction of Mézières, some 48km (30 miles) behind the German line. The British were to attack eastward between Péronne and Lens and seize another key rail centre. He also organized two smaller assaults, one by Belgian, British and French troops stationed in Flanders and one between Péronne and La Fère by French and British units.

The Meuse–Argonne attack opened on 26 September and involved some 600,000 Allied troops, 5,000 guns, around 500 tanks and 500 aircraft. The French Fourth Army under General Henri Gouraud was positioned on the left of the line but General Hunter Liggett's US First Army, which was in position between the Rivers Aisne and Meuse, increasingly bore the brunt of the action as it tried to break through four heavily fortified lines that made great use of the difficult terrain found throughout the heavily wooded Argonne area. The US troops made some initial progress but their push on a narrow, congested front ground to a halt in both the Argonne and around the town of Montfaucon as the Germans rushed reinforcements to the area. By late September the US troops had cut through just the first two lines of defences, advancing 16km (10 miles) in all, but had been unable to make headway against the especially formidable third line.

Below: German troops withdrawing from France, abandoning territory captured in 1914.

Renewing the Battle

The US Commander-in-Chief, General Pershing, now paused to regroup and then flung some of his most experienced divisions against the third German line on 4 October. Progress was again costly and painfully slow in the Argonne but the US drive allowed the French Fourth Army to push towards the Aisne. Pershing now split his forces in two, creating the First and Second Armies on 12 October. The First Army continued to batter its way northward and by

Above: US-manned Renault FT-17 tanks move forward for the opening of the Meuse–Argonne Offensive.

the end of the month had at last pushed beyond the Argonne. As this was taking place the Second Army under General Robert Bullard was forming up to the east of Verdun.

The Final Assault

The last stage of the offensive began on 1 November. The First Army cut through the remaining German defences to the north and west of Buzancy. The capture of the town helped the French Fourth Army finally to cross the Aisne, while the First Army drove through open country along the Meuse Valley in the face of disintegrating opposition. The Meuse was reached a little below Sedan on the 6th and US artillery was able to open fire on Mézières. The US Second Army began its drive in the direction of Montmédy on the 10th and had made some progress before hostilities ended with the Armistice at 11.00 hours the next day. The US troops had shown considerable dash during the offensive but their relative inexperience had helped cost them some 117,000 casualties. The Germans lost 100,000 men, including 26,000 prisoners.

MARSHAL FERDINAND FOCH

Foch (1851–1929), a well-established military theorist, took on an active field command when war broke out in 1914 and by 28 August was in charge of the French Ninth Army. He was promoted to army group command in October but was sidelined when General Robert Nivelle became Commander-in-Chief in December 1916. Foch's career recovered in 1917 when he co-ordinated a unified Allied response to the German Caporetto Offensive in Italy and in 1918 he was made the Allied Supreme Commander, a position that required great tact. He was seen as the architect of the Allied victory and was made a marshal on 6 August 1918.

Above: Marshal Ferdinand Foch, effective head of the Allied forces in 1918.

Left: US engineers work to clear away German barbed wire during the final days of the war.

Communications

All generals were dogged by the particularly thorny problem of communicating effectively with their troops at the front and, although various means were tried to overcome the long-standing difficulties, none was wholly satisfactory.

One of the greatest problems faced by any commanding officer in World War I was the difficulty in receiving progress reports and sending orders once a battle had begun. In most previous wars a general had been able simply to roam the comparatively small battlefields at will, seeing for himself what was happening and issuing and revising orders as required, but this was clearly impossible when the 1914–18 battlefields stretched over many miles and might involve much bigger forces. Consequently, commanding officers planned their attacks down to the smallest detail and issued step-by-step timetables for offensives so that every unit knew what it was to do and when. The problem was that battles rarely went to plan and it was difficult to respond to events quickly because of communication problems.

Most belligerents used wireless telegraphy for Morse code transmissions during the hostilities (speech transmission was not yet available) but it suffered two great weaknesses. First it could be intercepted by the enemy and even if the message was in code it might still be read. The Allies were fortunate enough to capture two sets of German naval codes in August 1914 and in one case the Germans did not realize the codebook was in enemy hands until 1918. The second problem was the wireless sets – they were bulky, heavy and fragile. Underpowered early aircraft, for example, could not take off with a wireless on board, while the sets could not long withstand the rigours of front-line service on the ground. Lighter, smaller and more robust models did become available as the war progressed and were commonly found in reconnaissance aircraft and balloons, but other means of communication remained in place on the ground.

Telephone Systems

Once static warfare had developed the preferred method of communicating was either by voice or Morse code via telephone or buzzer but this had one major drawback – its vulnerability. Even though cables were often buried a metre or more below ground, they were repeatedly cut by artillery fire. Repairing such breaks was a difficult and dangerous occupation

Above: A German messenger dog captured in mid-air as it races to the rear to deliver a message.

Right: A US soldier mans a field telephone during the fighting in the Argonne in late 1918.

for the signallers whose duty it was to maintain the system. Matters were even worse once a battle had begun. Portable handsets existed but as their cables had to be laid on the surface of No Man's Land, an area undoubtedly under heavy artillery fire and often by both sides, there was a high probability that the cables would be cut.

Live Messengers

More often than not attacking soldiers had to rely on other methods of sending and receiving messages but each had weaknesses. Written or oral messages were often sent by runner. This was arguably the most dangerous occupation on a World War I battlefield with a high probability of death or injury so that the message might never get through. It was also obviously much slower than transmission by telephone, especially if the runner got lost as many did. Carrier pigeons fulfilled a similar role and, although also highly vulnerable, could be effective. One played a pivotal role in the defence of Fort Vaux during 1916's Battle of Verdun and was posthumously awarded France's top award for gallantry.

There were other means of transmitting information but they were generally even more haphazard. Signal rockets were widely used in emergencies, often to call down artillery fire on pre-arranged co-ordinates, and the British even sewed reflective metal triangles on their back packs during the opening stages of the Battle of the Somme in 1916 so that the sun would glint off them and give those in reserve some idea of the troops' progress.

Above: Most of the major combatants deployed carrier pigeon units on the Western Front and the birds were housed in specially built lofts such as this impressive example.

Below: A pigeon is released from the interior of a British tank during the summer of 1916. Some animals were given decorations for their war service.

Breaking the Hindenburg Line

The complex and in-depth defences of the German Hindenburg Line were by any measure exceptionally strong in many places yet the British were able to smash through them in a matter of days from late September 1918.

There were three Allied attacks on the northern Western Front in the final weeks of the war. In the north, between Armentières and the sea, Belgian, British and French divisions were ready by late September, while British, French and US divisions were positioned between La Fère and Épehy in the south. Twenty-seven divisions of the British First and Third Armies lined up in the centre between Épehy and Lens.

Above: British cavalry during the final weeks of the war when mobility returned to the Western Front.

Tough Defences

The main British effort in the central sector opened on 27 September. Field Marshal Haig expected a hard fight as his assault troops were facing the toughest part of the Hindenburg Line. Yet his fears were never fully realized. The whole of the Hindenburg Line had been taken by 9 October and Marshal Foch was able to issue orders for the final advances of the war. The Belgians were to march on Bruges, a key U-boat base, and the BEF was to push towards Maubeuge and Mons, the latter somewhat ironically where it had fought its very first battle of the war back in 1914.

Below: Although German morale was generally poor, some troops, especially machine-gun units as here, fought to the bitter end.

Advances in Belgium

The attack in Flanders had opened on 28 September. The Allied Flanders Group made good progress initially as it pushed east from around Ypres. The high ground was captured by 1 October but thereafter the offensive stalled due to the difficult going and the stubborn resistance offered by the troops of Crown Prince Rupprecht of Bavaria's opposing Army Group North. The key moments came in the middle of the month – Lille was captured by the British and the Belgians took Ostend on the 17th, while Belgian troops occupied Zeebrugge and Bruges two days later, thereby ending the U-boat menace from those ports. All of the Belgian coast up to the Dutch border was in Allied hands by the next day and thereafter the fighting switched to the south.

After breaking the Hindenburg Line, the BEF made for the Rivers Sambre and Scheldt. As a preliminary, the River Selle

FINAL ALLIED ATTACKS

The German Army was decisively defeated by the end of the war.

was crossed on 17–20 October. Next came a push into the Franco-Belgian border region on 1 November. The capture of Valenciennes the next day confirmed that German resistance was weakening. The Sambre Offensive was the BEF's last attack of the war. It began on 4 November and, aside from meeting occasional strong pockets of resistance, the troops moved forward with little difficulty. Canadian troops re-entered Mons on the 10th and the British advance was halted when the Armistice came into effect the next day.

The BEF had conducted a stunning series of offensives in the last hundred days, beginning with the victory at Amiens on 8 August, but it had suffered huge casualties. Some 952,000 men were listed as killed, wounded, sick, taken prisoner or missing since January and Britain's allies fared no better. French losses totalled a little over one million, those of the American Expeditionary Force around 280,000, the Belgians some 30,000, the Italians 14,600 and the Portuguese, who had entered the war in 1916, at least 6,000. Germany had suffered equally, recording some 1.5 million casualties – even before the final battles of October and November are included.

THE ST QUENTIN CANAL

This battle, against the most heavily defended part of the Hindenburg Line, was the most important engagement of the last weeks of the war. The attack was spearheaded by an Australian corps and opened on 29 September 1918. The target was a narrow strip of ground, where the canal ran through a tunnel, but the advance soon stalled with heavy casualties. However, other British units crossed the canal at Bellenglise and punched through the line, making the remainder untenable.

Right: Men of the British 46th Division who successfully crossed the St Quentin Canal are congratulated by their commanding officer.

Pistols

Handguns were widely issued to troops during the war but were the main weapon carried by officers, partly as an indication of rank. They were useful weapons in confined spaces, such as trenches and vehicles of various sorts.

Revolvers and automatic pistols were the personal sidearms of officers of every rank, from the youngest second lieutenant to the most senior field marshal, and as such were as much a symbol of authority as a potentially deadly close-quarters weapon. There were other soldiers, some not necessarily of the officer class, who also made use of these weapons and this was in part because they operated in confined areas where it was considered impracticable to wield anything as long as a rifle. The types of troops in this category included airmen, tunnellers and, of course, tank and armoured car crews. The military police were also usually permitted to carry sidearms as they needed their hands free to check paperwork and manhandle troublesome prisoners if necessary.

Pistol Designs

There were three types of pistol available in 1914 – the common revolver that had a rotating chamber holding something like six rounds, and two types of clip-loaded automatics – recoil-operated and "blowback" designs. There tended to be a small number of major pistol manufacturers in each of the main combatant nations and they dominated production. Webley produced a staggering 300,000 of its Mark VI revolver for the British armed forces from 1915, for example, but even with that scale of output pistols were still sometimes in short supply and some less-known types were pressed into service as a stopgap. Britain, for example, made use of US Colt automatics which were largely distributed to the Royal Navy, the Royal Naval Air Service and the Royal Flying Corps.

Other nations also had favoured manufacturers. Luger is synonymous with German pistols but Germany's armed forces also used smaller quantities of designs like the Mauser and Beholla automatics. All of these were also sold to both Bulgaria and Turkey, some 22,000 to the former alone. The armed forces of the other Central Power, Austria-Hungary, also used German designs but they also had their own 1911 Steyr automatic and other types. On the Allied side, the major

MAUSER AUTOMATIC

This weapon, probably the most powerful pistol to see service in the war, went into production in the 1890s and first found favour with the Italian Navy. During World War I it was deployed by the German armed forces but in a modified, re-calibred form from 1916.

First issued: 1894
Calibre: 7.63mm (0.3in)
Magazine: 10 rounds
Overall length: 280mm (11in)
Weight: 1.13kg (40oz)
Muzzle velocity: 440m/sec (1,444ft/sec)

STEYR M1911

The Austrian Steyr "Hahn" M1911 was a successful semi-automatic design and remained in military service until after WWII. It was renowned for its durability and ease of maintenance and was used by several countries.

First issued: 1911
Calibre: 9mm (0.354in)
Magazine: 8 rounds
Overall length: 216mm (8.5in)
Weight: 1.02kg (36oz)
Muzzle velocity: 361m/sec (1,185ft/sec)

sidearms' producers were Lebel in France, Glisenti and Beretta in Italy and Colt and Smith & Wesson in the United States. Belgium, Russia and Serbia either bought in pistols or built them under licence, although Russia did have some home-grown types available.

COMBAT USE

Pistols did have their uses, despite having a comparatively short range. They were effective in confined spaces and were of some value in trench fighting but more experienced and therefore possibly more wary officers often abandoned them as the war progressed. This was in part because they marked the wearer out as an officer, thus making it easier for the enemy to identify and neutralize him. An officer might prefer to make himself more anonymous by carrying a standard rifle.

However, the revolver or automatic pistol remained a potent signifier of authority throughout the conflict and the vast majority of officers continued to carry them into battle despite the potential risks.

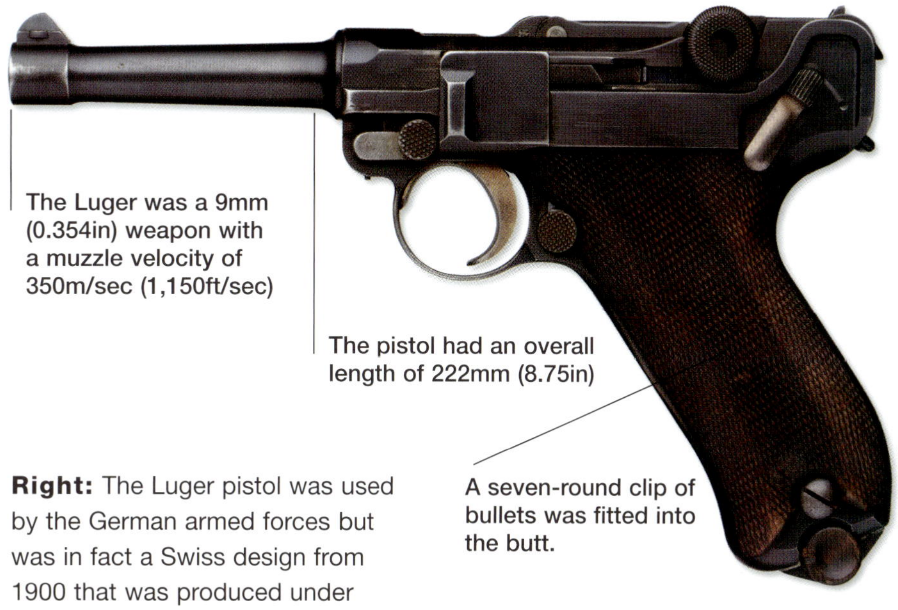

Right: The Luger pistol was used by the German armed forces but was in fact a Swiss design from 1900 that was produced under licence from 1904 onward.

There is also no doubt that one particular blowback pistol, actually a Belgian-made seven-shot 7.65mm (0.301in) Browning Model 1900, played a key, indeed pivotal, role in World War I – it was the weapon used by 19-year-old Bosnian Serb nationalist Gavrilo Princip to assassinate Archduke Franz Ferdinand and his wife, Sophie, Duchess of Hohenberg, at Sarajevo on 28 June 1914.

WEBLEY MARK V

This weapon in several slightly different marks was arguably the most ubiquitous sidearm of the entire war. It was the standard British service pistol throughout the conflict and hundreds of thousands were produced.

FIRST ISSUED: 1913
CALIBRE 0.455in (11.4mm)
MAGAZINE: 6 rounds
OVERALL LENGTH 235mm (9.25in)
WEIGHT: 1.0kg (35oz)
MUZZLE VELOCITY: 180m/sec (590ft/sec)

Left: The Glisenti was a seven-shot 9mm (0.354in) Italian pistol that had an overall length of 216mm (8.5in) and had a muzzle velocity of 275m/sec (900ft/sec).

Armoured Cars

Armoured cars offered scouts a degree of protection and firepower that could not be easily matched by cavalry patrols but they were often fitted with under-powered and unreliable engines and were therefore not really suited to off-road action.

The first viable petrol engine and the first petrol-driven vehicle appeared in 1885 and the first recognizable armoured cars began to emerge in the period after 1902. As is the case with most new technologies, there was generally little standardization at first. Many of the designs were merely experimental or made from what resources were locally available, and only a handful or so ever saw action on the battlefield. Generally, they were built on chassis derived from civilian cars or light trucks and covered in armour plate of various thicknesses that gave them a boxy rather than streamlined shape. They might be fully enclosed or open-topped, and have one or more turrets, while armament ranged from light to heavy machine-guns and up to small-calibre cannon. Most ran on four pneumatic tyres (with two driven wheels) but a small number made in Russia were half-tracked.

Armoured cars were mostly built by the car and truck manufacturers of the day, such as Minerva, Mors and SAVA (Société Anversoise pour Fabrication des Voitures Automobiles) in Belgium; Austin, Lanchester, Talbot, Wolseley and Rolls-Royce in Britain; Peugeot and Renault in France; Büssing, Daimler and Ehrhardt in Germany; and Fiat and Lancia in Italy. Some, especially British and Belgian designs, were produced in one country and exported to other Allied nations but it was not uncommon to find them being captured and used by the enemy. Germany used some British-built Austins taken from Russia, while Austria-Hungary deployed types captured from both Russia and Italy.

ROLLS-ROYCE ADMIRALTY PATTERN

This British-produced armoured car was based on the Silver Ghost civilian car and was used from late 1914 by the Royal Naval Air Service but the various squadrons were taken over by the Army in late 1915.

ENGINE: 40–50hp Rolls-Royce
TOP SPEED: 80kph (50mph)
CREW: 2–3
MAX. ARMOUR: 12mm (0.47in)
ARMAMENT: 1 x 0.303in (7.7mm) Vickers Maxim

Below: Armoured cars in Russian service – a French-built Peugeot (foreground) and a Belgian Mors.

LIMITATIONS IN ACTION

Armoured cars only truly function during mobile warfare and they are used for reconnaissance and intelligence gathering, launching ambushes, outflanking the enemy, or pursuing a defeated foe. In World War I they served on most fronts, but were more common or saw more active service in some rather than others. This was partly due to the nature of the fighting. On the Western Front, they played an active role in the first stages

Right: A Belgian Minerva armoured car fitted with a single Hotchkiss machine-gun in action during 1914.

of the fighting in 1914 before the trench lines were dug and in the latter part of 1918 when operations once again became more fluid. Terrain and going also influenced their deployment. Many were heavy, underpowered and lacked traction so they were unsuitable for crossing hills, muddy ground or soft sand. One of the main problems was that the wheels of armoured cars were exposed, thereby making them vulnerable to enemy fire. Equally, the armour plate was effective against small arms fire but only beyond certain distances and was wholly ineffective against any type of artillery fire.

British Designs

Britain led the way in wartime armoured car development in 1914 when a Royal Naval Air Service officer, Commander C. R. Samson, used cars largely sourced from around Dunkirk to rescue downed pilots and report on the movement of enemy troops and airships. Samson began by using poor-quality locally produced armour plate but then started requesting better materials from his superiors who in turn asked a number of British manufacturers to design purpose-built armoured cars. Austin eventually produced the most, many of which were earmarked for Russia, but Rolls-Royce undoubtedly made the best. The first three Rolls-Royce (Admiralty Pattern) types made their debut in December 1914 and both they and later models were sent to the fronts where the fighting was more mobile. They were especially active in the Middle East, serving with considerable success in both Palestine and Mesopotamia (Iraq).

PANZERKRAFTWAGEN EHRHARDT

The Ehrhardt was one of three types of armoured car in service with Germany from 1915 and was arguably the best. An updated version (pictured here), which appeared two years later, was little different except for the addition of armour plate over the headlamps and rear wheels.

Engine: 85hp Ehrhardt
Top speed: 60kph (37mph)
Range: 250km (155 miles)
Crew: 8–9
Maximum armour: 7mm (0.276in)
Armament: 3 x 7.92mm (0.312in) machine-guns

Final Battles in Italy

Italy had come close to disaster in 1917 but in late 1918 its forces, supported by troops from various other Allied nations, inflicted a decisive and crippling defeat on the Austro-Hungarians at the Battle of Vittorio Veneto.

The collapse of Russia in 1917 meant that both Germany and Austria-Hungary could transfer some troops from the Eastern Front, if not quite denude it of forces, and thus bolster their efforts elsewhere. Germany also withdrew its troops from Italy in spring 1918 in preparation for a series of major offensives on the Western Front and urged Austria-Hungary to crush Italy alone. The plan was to launch two simultaneous attacks in the northern Trentino sector of the front and one in the north-east along the River Piave.

Above: Austro-Hungarian troops killed during their army's failed attempt to cross the River Piave in June 1918.

Below: Two Italian officers pose in front of a medium artillery piece sited in a camouflaged emplacement overlooking the Piave.

Austrian Aims

Field Marshal Conrad von Hötzendorf, Austria Hungary's Chief of Staff until sacked in November 1917 and now commanding in the Trentino, had targeted Verona as his objective, while recently promoted Field Marshal Svetozar Boroevic von Bojna on the Piave was looking towards Padua. Their efforts would effectively be conducted in isolation because of difficult terrain and a lack of connecting roads. To make matters worse, the reinforcements sent to the Italian Front had been split so that neither was strong enough to carry out his allotted task. The Italian Commander-in-Chief, General Armando Diaz, had also been forewarned of their forthcoming offensives.

Conrad's Eleventh Army attacked on 15 June and made some initial progress against the Italian Sixth and Fourth Armies before it was stopped in its tracks and then thrown back. Boroevic performed only a little better along the lower reaches of the Piave but his advance was halted when heavy rain turned the river into a raging torrent and Italian bombers disrupted his supply lines. Diaz then threw in his own reserves and these brought the Battle of the Piave to a halt on the 22nd. The Austro-Hungarians had suffered 190,000 casualties and their army was mostly finished. Demoralized, undermined by mutinies and split by ethnic tensions, the army was able to offer only token resistance by late summer.

Italy's Waiting Game

Diaz did not immediately launch a major counter-attack to finish off the Austro-Hungarian armies, much to the chagrin of his Allies, but spent the next months preparing his troops for action and watching for favourable events on the Western Front that would make his job easier. His offensive finally opened in late October when the Italian Fourth Army pushed forward but it soon met stiff opposition from the Austro-Hungarian Belluno Group and was thrown back at the Battle of Monte Grappo on the 24th.

Left: General Armando Diaz, the Italian Commander-in-Chief from November 1917.

The main attack involved three armies crossing the Piave on the 24th and moving on Vittorio Veneto but the Italian Eighth Army advancing in the centre was stopped almost immediately by the Austro-Hungarian Sixth Army. French units attached to the Italian Twelfth Army, itself led by French General Jean Graziani, did get across the river on the left flank. British troops of the Italian Tenth Army under a British general, the Earl of Cavan, had managed the same feat on the right by the 28th. An ever-growing gap now appeared in the Austro-Hungarian lines and their units simply fell apart, with the Allies eventually taking some 300,000 prisoners in the Battle of Vittorio Veneto. All of northern and north-east Italy had been cleared by Diaz's armies by early November and Trieste, an Italian objective since May 1915, finally fell on the 3rd. Austria-Hungary had asked to discuss armistice terms on 29 September and an agreement was finally signed the day that Trieste was occupied. It came into force at 15.00 hours on 4 November.

Below: US troops, only a few of whom served in Italy, launch grenades against Austro-Hungarian positions in September 1918.

Liberating the Balkans

The many Allied troops in the Balkans had been so inactive that they had become known as the "gardeners of Salonika" but in the last months of the war they achieved significant advances and forced Bulgaria to capitulate.

The Allied effort in the Balkans had largely been moribund since troops had first arrived in Salonika during 1915 but matters changed with the arrival of a new commander, General Marie Guillaumat, on 10 December 1917. Guillaumat was never able to make a major offensive because the Allied high commands were diverting forces and equipment to other more active fronts but the French general, nevertheless, spent his time well. He wholly reorganized and reinvigorated what had been a demoralized command, poured oil on the troubled waters of Anglo-French relations and set about planning a large-scale offensive.

KEY FACTS

Date: 15 September – 4 November 1918

Place: Across the entire Balkans

Outcome: The Allies knocked Bulgaria out of the war and advanced to the Danube.

New Commander

Guillaumat was transferred back to France in June 1918. His replacement was another able French officer, General Louis Franchet d'Espérey, and he finalized Guillaumat's plan of operations, which involved an offensive all along the line from the Aegean Sea in the east to the Albanian border in the west. German troops had been withdrawn from the Balkans and transferred to the Western Front in early 1918 and the Allies, who had recently been reinforced by various Greek units, faced a roughly equal number of Bulgarians but enjoyed a significant advantage in artillery and air support.

The final Allied offensive began with the Battle of the River Vardar, which opened on

THE BALKANS CAMPAIGN

The Allies struck out north and east from Salonika to clear the Balkans.

15 September when French and Serbian troops pushed forward on a 24km (15 mile) front. The Bulgarians fell back rapidly and Anglo-Greek forces made similarly good progress when they attacked around Lake Doiran on the 18th. Bulgaria was now so weak that it soon offered a ceasefire but the proposal was rejected by Franchet d'Espérey on the 25th and he ordered his command to press on. British units crossed into Bulgaria the same day, while the French took Uskub (Skopje) in southern Serbia on the 29th.

As pressure mounted elsewhere, especially on the Italian Front, Austria-Hungary began to withdraw its troops from the Balkans, chiefly from Albania, Montenegro and Serbia, and this further isolated Bulgaria. The Bulgarians sought an armistice on 26 September; the talks began in Salonika two days later and Bulgaria officially ceased fighting at 12.00 hours on the 30th.

This did not end the Allied push through the Balkans as Franchet d'Espérey's troops now fanned out in all directions. Serbian units on the western flank liberated their homeland as they advanced while to their right French troops moved into eastern Serbia and overran western Bulgaria. British troops pushed deeper into eastern and coastal Bulgaria and also began driving through European Turkey in the direction of Constantinople. Italian forces stationed in southern Albania joined in the general Allied advance, taking the north of the country from the collapsing Austro-Hungarian Army while Serbian forces liberated neighbouring Montenegro.

Above: Serbian troops on the march. They had the honour of liberating their own capital, Belgrade, on 1 November.

Last Acts

The crowning moment came on 1 November, when the Serbians liberated Belgrade, their capital which had been occupied since late 1915. An armistice with Austria-Hungary came into effect on the 4th at which point the various Allied forces were lined up along the River Danube, the Serb border with Austria-Hungary and Romania. Romania had been largely overrun by the Central Powers in 1917 and had signed the Treaty of Bucharest with Germany in May 1918 but in the last act of the war in the Balkans its government actually declared war on Germany for the second time on 10 November – just one day before the Armistice ended the conflict.

Right: Lightly wounded casualties are evacuated from a British first-aid dressing station by truck somewhere on the Salonika front, late 1918.

The Battle of Megiddo

Many British troops were withdrawn from Palestine in the early part of 1918, but the whole campaign was reinvigorated in September when a short, cleverly planned campaign shattered the opposing Turkish forces.

The British war effort in Palestine was virtually closed down for much of 1918 as their commander, General Edmund Allenby, saw a sizeable part of his forces, some 60,000 men in all, transferred to the Western Front to help deal with Germany's offensives there. Aside from a few minor operations by his own troops, Allenby had to rely on the Arab irregulars under Lawrence of Arabia on his right flank, who were harrying various Turkish positions and the Hejaz railway between Amman and Medina. Allenby was reinforced in late summer, especially by Indian troops, and he laid plans for what would be the final and most spectacular offensive of the campaign.

Three Turkish armies, some 35,000 men and 350 guns under the German General Otto Liman von Sanders, were holding a substantial defensive line running inland from the Mediterranean coast from a point a little north of Jaffa to the valley of the River Jordan. Allenby commanded some 55,000 infantry, 12,000 cavalry and 540 guns and planned to launch the bulk of them, 35,000 infantry and 400 guns, against the Mediterranean flank of the Turkish positions. This was defended by just 8,000 Turkish troops with 130 guns. Once a hole had been punched through the line, Allenby's cavalry would flood through and then the whole of the British line would swing north and east, pivoting on the Jordan Valley.

KEY FACTS

Date: 19–21 September 1918

Place: Palestine between Jericho and Jaffa

Outcome: The Turkish defenders were overwhelmed and forced into a headlong retreat.

Left: Senior British officers are shown around the Mosque of Omar, Jerusalem, in May 1918.

Deception Plans

Allenby used several ruses to mislead the Turks as to his true intentions. British fighters swept the few German aircraft from the skies preventing aerial

Below: A British supply column crossing a river in central Palestine on the eve of the Battle of Megiddo.

Above: Australians of the British-led Imperial Camel Corps in a camp near Jaffa.

reconnaissance; dummy camps and cavalry lines were built in the east near Jerusalem; a false date for the attack was leaked; and fake plans for horse races on the actual day were publicized. The offensive, known as the Battle of Megiddo, opened on 19 September and was spectacularly successful. The infantry on the coast quickly punched through the Turkish lines and the cavalry poured through, fanning out as they did so. Bombers and ground-attack aircraft struck at communications choke-points and Turkish headquarters all the while, making any cohesive response virtually impossible. The Turks were overwhelmed by the 21st and what began as a retreat soon turned into a wholesale rout.

Into Syria

Allenby drove his forces forward at lightning speed. Damascus was captured by Australian and Arab forces on 1 October and Beirut fell to an Indian division the next day. British mounted units continued to spearhead the advance and took Aleppo on the 26th in what was one of the last major actions of the war in the Middle East. By this stage of the conflict Turkey was crumbling fast and its envoys signed an armistice on the 30th after four days of discussions in Mudros harbour. Hostilities throughout the Middle East ended at noon the next day. Allenby had conducted a brilliant campaign – in 38 days he had advanced around 560km (350 miles) and effectively destroyed three Turkish armies, taking 76,000 prisoners in the process. His own losses were comparatively minor with some 850 men killed, 4,500 wounded and 380 missing.

The campaign in Palestine had effectively lasted from January 1915 to October 1918 and the British Empire forces suffered a total of 51,500 battle casualties, a figure that included some 5,300 ANZACs and 11,000 Indians. In all some 10,000 men were killed. Turkish losses are unknown but probably reached over 135,000, including more than 100,000 prisoners.

GENERAL EDMUND ALLENBY

Allenby (1861–1936) was a cavalryman by training but took over the British Third Army in October 1915. He had frequent clashes with his superior, General, later Field Marshal, Douglas Haig, and was effectively demoted by transfer to Palestine in June 1917. The move transformed Allenby's faltering career and he proved a most imaginative commander, one who used aircraft, artillery, cavalry and infantry in a manner that has been likened to an early form of *Blitzkrieg*. His crowning moment came with the superbly managed Battle of Megiddo in September 1918.

Right: Turkish prisoners, just some of the tens of thousands captured in the final weeks of the war.

Cruisers

Cruisers were a key component of all of the world's major navies during World War I and they were capable of operating both independently, often far from home waters, or as part of the main battlefleet in large-scale actions.

Cruisers were originally developed by the British Royal Navy in the latter part of the 19th century. They were smaller than existing battleships but faster and still able to undertake long-range, ocean missions. There were originally two types of cruisers. Armoured cruisers were deployed as scout warships with the main battle-fleet and had large-calibre armaments and significant side armour. Protected cruisers dispensed with the thick side armour but did have some deck armour. These types mainly operated in defence of trade routes or foreign naval stations, or formed the core of the squadrons deployed to defend imperial possessions. All of the combatant nations had cruisers of one type or another by the outbreak of war – for the Allies France had 37 and Russia 15, while for the Central Powers, Germany had 52 and Austria-Hungary 9.

Above: HMS *Warrior* was the lead vessel in a class of four armoured cruisers but was lost at Jutland.

Below: Germany's *Goeben*, a battle-cruiser, leads *Breslau*, one of a class of four light cruisers completed in 1912, out to sea.

Cruiser Roles

Britain had a large force of armoured cruisers in 1914, around 40, but they had in fact been made largely redundant in the scouting role with the main fleet thanks to the development of the dreadnought battle-cruiser, the first of which was launched in 1908. Britain also had some 100 protected cruisers on the eve of war but these increasingly gave way to lighter, faster types. Germany's heavier cruisers were largely relegated to secondary duties by the outbreak of war and its main High Seas Fleet relied mostly on light cruisers. The distinction between armoured and protected cruisers and light cruisers was quite stark. The last were roughly half the displacement, had a high speed and carried guns of much smaller calibre.

Nevertheless, both of the original types continued to see action. The British deployed them to hunt down Germany's surface raiders and sent them overseas where they formed the heart of the local squadrons, often along with older pre-dreadnought battleships. From 1917 onward they were also used nearer home as convoy escorts. Germany, in contrast, used many of its light cruisers to harry Allied shipping lanes and merchant ships in the first few months of the war before they were largely hunted down, although light cruisers also saw action with the country's main battlefleet.

Losses in Combat

Cruisers were therefore present at many major naval battles during the war. There were 13 British and German warships present at the Battle of the Falklands in late 1914, for example, and all but three, all British, were either armoured or light cruisers. Similarly, there were numerous cruisers at the biggest naval engagement of the war, the Battle of Jutland in 1916. The various parts of Britain's Grand Fleet mustered 8 armoured and 26 light cruisers while Germany's High Seas Fleet had 11 light cruisers.

Cruisers were potentially highly vulnerable in battles involving larger warships and this certainly proved to be the case at Jutland. Germany lost four light cruisers, including the *Rostock*, which had to be scuttled after suffering heavy damage from a torpedo fired by a British destroyer, and *Wiesbaden*, which went to the bottom after receiving multiple shell hits. *Elbing* and *Frauenlob* were also sunk by torpedoes. The Grand Fleet lost three of its armoured cruisers, *Black Prince*, *Defence* and *Warrior*, to gunfire from larger warships.

The Allies lost a total of 39 cruisers of all types during the war, while the Central Powers lost 28 to various causes.

Léon Gambetta

The French armoured cruiser *Léon Gambetta* was largely designed for coastal defence and the protection of trade routes and was unfit to serve with the main fleet in large-scale actions, as even by contemporary standards it was slow and poorly armed. The *Léon Gambetta* was sunk in the Gulf of Otranto on the night of 24 April 1915, victim of a torpedo fired by the Austro-Hungarian submarine *U-5* (captained by top Austrian U-boat ace Georg Trapp, later made famous by the musical *The Sound of Music*).

Laid down: 1901
Displacement: 12,250 tons
Crew: 734
Speed: 22 knots
Main armament: 4 x 194mm (7.6in) and 16 x 164.7mm (6.4in) guns

HMS *Black Prince*

This British armoured cruiser was launched in 1907 and was stationed in the Mediterranean in 1914. It then served with the Grand Fleet's 1st Cruiser Squadron. During the Battle of Jutland in 1916 *Black Prince* was hit by 21 German shells, 15 of them from heavy guns, and sank with all hands.

Laid down: 1903
Displacement: 13,550 tons
Crew: 857
Speed: 23 knots
Main armament: 6 x 9.2in (234mm) and 10 x 6in (152mm) guns

Germany's Naval Mutiny

By late 1918 Germany had effectively lost World War I and both the armed forces and the home front were rocked by political unrest that became manifest in mutinies among the troops and street violence in many towns and cities.

In August 1914, Germany's decision-makers, effectively Emperor Wilhelm II, the men he appointed to his cabinet and the military, promulgated the idea that they were fighting a defensive war to counter French and Russian aggression. This was accepted by the German people and opposition politicians, including the left-leaning Social Democratic Party (SDP). They and their supporters agreed what was termed *Burgfrieden*, a political truce. This lasted until July 1917, when the main centre and left-wing parties united in the Reichstag (German parliament) to force through the "Peace Resolution", a demand for an end to hostilities without annexations or indemnities. It so enraged the military and right-wing parties that its publication effectively ended *Burgfrieden*.

Above: Armed naval mutineers photographed in central Berlin during November 1918.

Strikes and Hunger

Thanks to the ongoing British naval blockade, conditions for ordinary Germans worsened rapidly in 1918 and provoked increased civil unrest. One million workers went on strike in January, leading to a wave of repression and even the temporary arrest of the SDP's leader, Friedrich Ebert.

Matters deteriorated over the following months and in September Field Marshal Paul von Hindenburg and General Erich Ludendorff, who had effectively been running the country's political affairs since the collapse of the *Burgfrieden*, returned power to the Reichstag. They hoped to quell further unrest, preserve their own reputations and shift the blame for Germany's collapse on to the country's politicians. Prince Max of Baden was named as chancellor on 3 October and a coalition government dominated by moderate members of the SDP came to power. Ludendorff was fired on 26 October and Hindenburg retired.

Mutiny and Rebellion

Yet events were spiralling out of control as more radical elements demanded more substantial changes. This was especially so among groups like the Spartacus League, which had been invigorated by the previous year's Bolshevik takeover in Russia. The Imperial German Navy was not immune to such revolutionary zeal and Bolshevik-inspired agitators made use of a rumour that the fleet was to be deployed in a suicide sortie.

Left: Further signs of the collapse – rebel soldiers join forces with civilians to defy the government.

Above: Socialist activist Rosa Luxemburg was killed by right-wing paramilitaries in 1919.

SCUTTLING THE GERMAN FLEET

The Imperial German Navy was handed over to the Allies, chiefly the British, as part of the Armistice terms of November 1918. The various warships, including nine battleships and five battle-cruisers, sailed from Germany on the 21st and went into internment at the British base at Scapa Flow in the Orkneys the next day. Some of the ships' crews and captains remained on board and these resolved to scuttle their vessels if it looked like they would be handed over to the British as part of the Treaty of Versailles. The order to scuttle was given on 21 June 1919.

Below: The battle-cruiser *Hindenburg* after being scuttled by its crew.

Disgruntled sailors in Kiel, already fed up with poor conditions, mutinied on 3 November, allied themselves with strikers and issued demands for peace and reform. The unrest spread to other naval bases and then broke out in towns and cities across the country.

The government's response was too little, too late. Prince Max resigned on 9 November after announcing – without authority – that Wilhelm II had abdicated. Power was passed to Ebert, although the prince had no legal right to do this, and the Prince's vice-chancellor, Philipp Scheidemann, then announced – without Ebert's agreement – that Germany was to be a republic. Even this was not sufficient to stop the growing unrest. Ebert's provisional government became more and more convinced that the calls for peace and food were being used by the extremists to engineer revolution and the creation of a Bolshevik state.

Ebert turned to the new head of the German Army, the right-wing General Wilhelm Gröner. Gröner and a cabinet member, Gustav Noske, worked on a strategy to put down the unrest. Army units and *ad hoc* groups of ex-soldiers with right-wing sympathies, known as *Freikorps*, used great brutality to quell the revolutionaries. A rising by the Spartacists was dealt with very swiftly in January 1919 and their two leaders, Karl Liebknecht and Rosa Luxemburg, were murdered. The last pockets of resistance had been rooted out by April 1919.

Right: General Wilhelm Gröner, who acted to put down unrest in Germany during 1918–19.

The Peace Treaties British, Italian, French and US leaders at the Paris Peace Conference.

The League of Nations The Assembly of the League during one of its early sessions.

War and Remembrance Germany's grandiose memorial to the victorious Battle of Tannenberg.

THE AFTERMATH OF WAR

World War I has long been portrayed as an unnecessary war but this view has only a passing relationship with the truth. The various Allies fought for a variety of motives, some not always laudable, and some were to a degree culpable in its outbreak because of their pre-war actions, but they were right to go to war. The popularly accepted misreading of events in part occurred because the "Great War" was soon overshadowed by World War II, a conflict in which the issues were – and are – seen as being absolutely clear-cut. Yet many of the factors that make World War II a just and necessary war were present in 1914–18: the need to oppose dictatorships, naked military aggression, atrocities against civilians, the use of "uncivilized" weapons and genocide, for example, were all unfortunately present in World War I.

World War I was therefore a necessary war but it did not get the peace settlement it deserved. Some of the victors' aims were highly commendable but Britain and France largely wanted a return to a sort of pre-war status quo minus the Central Powers, while Germany was hit by draconian penalties. The treaties were largely if not entirely driven by self-interest and they undoubtedly played their part in the process that would lead to a new world war in just two decades.

The Armistice Joyful Londoners take to the streets to celebrate the end to the fighting in 1918.

The Peace Treaties A French guard of honour greets delegates at the Paris Peace Conference.

War and Remembrance The dedication of France's Tomb of the Unknown Soldier, Paris.

The Armistice

Germany was no longer able to maintain its war effort by October 1918 and in November sought an armistice. There was little in the way of discussion and the terms were wholly dictated by the Allies during a very brief meeting.

The last year of fighting saw Germany's fortunes transformed. In June 1918 its armies controlled more territory than at any other time in the war, yet a few months later the country had been roundly defeated by the Allies and was rent by revolutionary turmoil. There was no one reason why Germany lost the war but its position became untenable for several reasons – not least the British naval blockade, the ongoing arrival of huge numbers of US troops, the failure of its offensives in France between March and July and the succession of Allied attacks from mid-July onwards. The once superb German Army was increasingly undermined by falling morale and political agitation. Morale on the German home front was also collapsing, largely due to shortages of virtually every basic necessity; the political and industrial unrest that this was generating could not be contained.

Above: A joyous victory parade in New York. US troops return home to a thunderous reception.

Below: The other side of the coin. Dispirited German troops return home to little fanfare.

The ultimate cause of Germany's defeat was that the army chiefs who effectively ran the country, Field Marshal Hindenburg and General Ludendorff, finally realized that they had lost the war and, with that realization, they lost their nerve. The two generals effectively relinquished power in late September. They persuaded Emperor Wilhelm II to agree to ask for an armistice and accept that a new government, one not tainted by a close relationship to the crown or military, was needed. Prince Max of Baden became the new chancellor on 3 October and he sent pleas for an armistice to US President Woodrow Wilson on the basis of the latter's Fourteen Points peace proposal of January 1918. There was a flurry of diplomatic notes between the Allies and with Germany before the latter finally agreed to the last of the various Allied pre-conditions, including the abdication of the emperor, on the 20th.

Armistice Talks

Prince Max finally decided to begin substantive talks on 6 November and a delegation was put together, made up of middle-ranking politicians and comparatively junior military officers. Discussions on the details of the

Armistice began at Compiègne, the headquarters of the *de facto* Allied Commander-in-Chief, Marshal Ferdinand Foch, on 8 November. Foch headed a purely Anglo-French delegation and it soon became apparent to the German delegation, headed by Matthias Erzberger, that there was to be no discussion on the basis of Wilson's Fourteen Points but merely a list of draconian demands.

Above: Emperor Wilhelm (third from left) waits at the Dutch–German border as a refugee. He spent the remainder of his life in exile.

Punishing Germany

There were 34 clauses in all and they were essentially designed to cripple Germany militarily and economically. Among other things they required German troops to evacuate all occupied territories in 14 days, including Alsace and Lorraine, and within 28 days Allied troops would take over Germany west of the Rhine and establish bridgeheads to the east up to a depth of some 32km (20 miles). Huge quantities of weapons, 5,000 locomotives, 150,000 pieces of rolling stock, 10,000 trucks, and all submarines and warships were to be given up. All monies taken from foreign banks were to be handed over, there were to be reparations, and the naval blockade was to remain in force.

These clauses stunned the German delegates but, after seeking higher approval, they signed the Armistice at 05.05 hours on the morning of 11 November and it came into force at 11.00 hours. The war was finally over but the peace treaties had yet to be signed.

President Wilson's Fourteen Points

US President Woodrow Wilson made several attempts to broker a peace deal culminating in this set of proposals that were put before Congress on 8 January 1918. The first five points covered general principles for a new world, including freedom of the seas, an end to secret treaties and arms limitation. Points 6 to 13 addressed specific territorial issues, such as the Franco-German dispute over Alsace and Lorraine. Point 14 called for the establishment of an international body to settle disputes between member nations.

Right: Londoners celebrate the peace in November 1918, a scene of rejoicing common in towns and cities across Europe.

The Peace Treaties

Although President Wilson wanted to ensure that Germany was not humiliated by Britain and France, he was out-manoeuvred and the Treaty of Versailles imposed harsh reparations on the defeated country that left a legacy of bitterness.

World War I did not end in November 1918, only the fighting stopped. The war was formally concluded by a series of peace treaties, each named after a Paris suburb where the talks were conducted. The discussions, together known as the Paris Peace Conference, lasted from 12 January 1919 until 20 January 1920. The conference was attended by the leaders of 32 Allied countries and Associated Powers and 23 other states that were classified as "powers with special interests", including the Arabs of the Hejaz. Controlling affairs were the major victorious powers – Britain, France, Italy, Japan and the United States – who were collectively known as "powers with general interests". None of the former Central Powers was invited to attend and Russia's Bolshevik government simply refused to travel to Paris.

Above: Allied war leaders meet for the Paris Peace Conference. From left: David Lloyd George, Vittorio Orlando, Georges Clemenceau and Woodrow Wilson.

Below: The signing of the Treaty of Versailles in the Palace's Hall of Mirrors, 28 June 1919.

Aims of the Powers

Two representatives from each power with general interests formed the Council of Ten, a body that was originally established to look into questions of humanitarian aid but soon took on a wider brief and began considering territorial questions. From March 1919 the Council of Four, the leaders of the powers with general interests minus Japan, dominated the ever more fractious discussions.

Left: British troops move into Germany after the Armistice. Allied forces occupied German territory up to the left bank of the River Rhine.

US President Woodrow Wilson looked for conciliation with the Central Powers, especially Germany, while France's Prime Minister Georges Clemenceau wanted to impose severe terms on the defeated. His British counterpart, David Lloyd George, took something of a middle course, while Vittorio Orlando, the Italian Premier, was only concerned with making territorial gains in and around the Mediterranean. He left the conference in April after the other Allies had agreed to give part of the eastern Adriatic to the new state of Yugoslavia.

Treaties Agreed

Five treaties were eventually agreed – Trianon with Hungary (4 June 1919), Versailles with Germany (28 June 1919), St Germain with Austria (10 September 1919), Neuilly with Bulgaria (27 November 1919), and Sèvres with Turkey (10 August 1920). The treaties were in some respects not dissimilar in that they imposed on the Central Powers, especially Germany, various territorial losses, financial reparations and military restrictions. These terms were severe enough to cause lasting resentment among the defeated, particularly in Germany, which was hit hardest and also had to accept a war guilt clause that made it alone wholly responsible for the outbreak of World War I.

Although he secured agreement to establish the League of Nations, a prototype for today's United Nations, Wilson was thwarted in several ambitions, largely due to Britain and France's self-interests. He did manage to create a number of new nation states out of the old Austro-Hungarian Empire but Britain and France stepped in when it came to the Turkish Empire and took over several territories, including Syria, Lebanon and Palestine, as neo-colonial mandates. Japan was permitted to take Chinese territory that had been seized from Germany in 1914, a decision that led China, a power with special interests, to reject the conference's decisions. The Paris Peace Conference actually left many issues unresolved and satisfied few of those who attended. Indeed, the various peace treaties were never fully adopted and the US Congress refused to ratify the Treaty of Versailles when it was put to the vote in November 1919. Wilson's League of Nations project did go ahead but in a much-weakened form.

Right: A French honour guard stands to attention as delegates arrive to discuss the final terms of the Treaty of Trianon with Hungary.

The League of Nations

US President Woodrow Wilson successfully argued for an international body to settle issues between its member states but, although it was a laudable ambition, the League of Nations never really functioned and it faced a succession of major crises.

President Woodrow Wilson went to the Paris Peace Conference of 1919–20 wanting the negotiations to progress along the lines suggested in his Fourteen Points peace proposal of January 1918. This was a document of intent for a safer, more democratic post-war world and one of its key clauses called for the creation of a League of Nations, an international body to arbitrate on differences between states and maintain peace. To some extent his idea captured the mood of the time as many had come to reject the tenets of pre-war diplomacy with its emphasis on maintaining the balance of power and secret treaties.

The League established its headquarters in the city of Geneva in Switzerland, a traditionally neutral country, in 1920 and it had three main bodies. The Secretariat, under a secretary-general, was a permanent body of officials from all of the member states. The Assembly also included representatives of all the member states and each country had one vote. It oversaw the greater part of the League's activities, including its budget, and met annually, although much of its work was undertaken by committees. The Council was originally made up of the five permanent members – Britain, France, Italy, Japan and the United States – and four members elected by the Assembly. The Council met at least every three months, or more often whenever there was an international crisis, and each member had a single vote. The number of permanent members rose to six in 1922 and to nine in 1926.

Above: The League of Nations Assembly in session.

Below: The rise of Italian fascism – Benito Mussolini (in suit) marches on Rome in a successful bid to win dictatorial powers, late 1922.

Above: Troops muster during the Russo-Polish War of 1920. Poland, once part of Russia, was a creation of the peace settlements.

Above: French troops march into the Ruhr in January 1923 after Germany had defaulted on its reparations payments.

TASKS FOR THE LEAGUE

The League also established a number of other bodies to look at various problems. The Permanent Court of Justice was established at The Hague in the Netherlands in 1921 and consisted of 15 judges of various nationalities who settled legal disputes brought before them. The Mandates Commission oversaw Germany's former colonies and some parts of the former Turkish Empire, while the Disarmament Commission was to control the sale of arms and limit their manufacture. The International Labour Organization was entrusted with improving workers' pay and conditions and monitored trade unions also. The Health Organization coordinated international responses to outbreaks of cholera and typhus in post-war Europe and also had a broader remit to investigate world health.

SUCCESS AT FIRST

The League of Nations had many laudable aims and it did have some early successes, dealing peacefully with disputes between Finland and Sweden (1921), Germany and Poland (1921), Italy and Greece (1923) and Turkey and Iraq (1924). Yet in truth it was a weak organization that to some seemed too Euro-centric and dominated by the victors of World War I. The United States, which was retreating into isolationism, never actually became a full member; the USSR was a late addition to its membership; and Germany only joined in 1926. The League also lacked financial resources and could only use economic sanctions to enforce its rulings as there were no clear rules for using military force against an erring state.

These weaknesses became clear in the 1930s, when right-wing, militaristic states openly challenged the League. Among these were Benito Mussolini's Fascist Italy and Adolf Hitler's Nazi Germany; Japan simply walked out of the League when its aggression in Manchuria was criticized. The outbreak of World War II in 1939 consigned the League to the dustbin of history but it was not formally dissolved until 18 April 1946.

Right: The Nazi Beer Hall Putsch of November 1923 failed but saw the emergence of Adolf Hitler on to the wider German political scene.

War and Remembrance

There was no single response to the outbreak of peace in November 1918 except relief that the bloodletting was over, and our current attitudes to the conflict have been largely moulded by a series of mythologies rather than hard historical fact.

There is no doubt that many of the world's leading nations paid a high price for taking part in World War I. In broad terms some 65 million men were mobilized between 1914 and 1918 and of these some 42 million served with the various Allies and 22 million with the four Central Powers. The Allies recorded around 4.8 million dead and 12 million wounded, while the Central Powers' figures are roughly 3.1 million and 8.4 million. Civilian deaths, excluding those from influenza, totalled some 6.6 million.

The initial public response to the end of this immense carnage varied considerably. Many people were certainly left grieving or nursing both physical and psychological wounds, while some, probably the majority, were simply glad the slaughter was over. Others, chiefly those on the victors' side, felt the war had been just and one worth fighting, while many of their counterparts on the defeated side were left confused and feeling betrayed by their leaders. Other people, especially in the former territories of the Austro-Hungarian and Russian Empires in eastern and central Europe, were soon able to celebrate their freedom from oppression and new statehood, while others, particularly, the Arabs of the Hejaz, felt their dreams of independence had been betrayed by the Allies.

Above: The memorial at Thiepval on the Somme to 72,000 British troops with no known grave.

Below: The main French cemetery at Verdun, including the vast ossuary housing bones of the unidentified.

A Futile War?

World War I has in many ways become mythologized down the decades and no more so than in Britain, where it is largely associated with waste and futility. This is probably in part due to the fact that Britain, almost alone among the combatants, suffered more casualties in World War I than in World War II. But it is also down to bad history. People on the Allied side did believe the war had a just purpose – the British Victory Medal of 1918, for example, carried the words: "The Great War For Civilisation" and the earliest Armistice Days were more about celebrating comradeship than commemorating the dead. Similarly, Germany's biggest memorial to the war was not to its own dead but a massive monument celebrating the victory over the Russians at the Battle of Tannenberg in 1914.

The still widely held view of a pointless war actually began to emerge in the late 1920s, largely due to a plethora of semi-fictionalized personal accounts that highlighted the undoubtedly horrible realities of trench warfare, books like Erich Maria Remarque's *All Quiet on the Western Front* and Robert Graves's *Goodbye to All That*, and the work of poets like Wilfred Owen and Siegfried Sassoon. But these had their counterpoints – Ernst Jünger's *Storm of Steel* positively revels in the war. Yet it was the former that were ultimately more persuasive and helped to engender the myth that the lives of brave men had been wasted by incompetent and unfeeling commanders.

ALL QUIET ON THE WESTERN FRONT

This fictionalized study of German troops on the Western Front, published in 1929 by the pacifist German author Erich Maria Remarque, was one of a slew of mostly anti-war books written in the 1920s and has greatly coloured perception of the conflict. It tells the story of a group of German soldiers, some young, some older, and the somewhat ironic title refers to the "official" German Army communiqué issued on the day that the central character is killed. The book has been filmed on a number of occasions but the US version released in 1930 is widely regarded as the most successful adaptation.

Above: A poster for the first film based on Remarque's book.

JUDGING THE GENERALS

The reality was that most, if not all, generals were both competent and caring and that trench warfare, which was by no means universal, was a product of a temporary technological imbalance that favoured defensive over offensive weapons and tactics. The generals of the time recognized this and tried many ways to overcome the stagnation of trench warfare – different types of artillery barrage, the use of gas and tanks, for example – but the reality was that they were only just able to succeed by 1918. Perhaps the saddest myth concerning World War I was that held by those who had lived through it and, like the author H. G. Wells, believed they had survived "The War to End All Wars".

Below: The dedication ceremony of the grave of France's unknown soldier underneath the Arc de Triomphe in Paris.

Below: Germany's memorial to the Battle of Tannenberg. Hitler ordered the site to be levelled as advancing Soviet forces neared in World War II.

A

B

C

DE

JK

L

M

N

OP

R

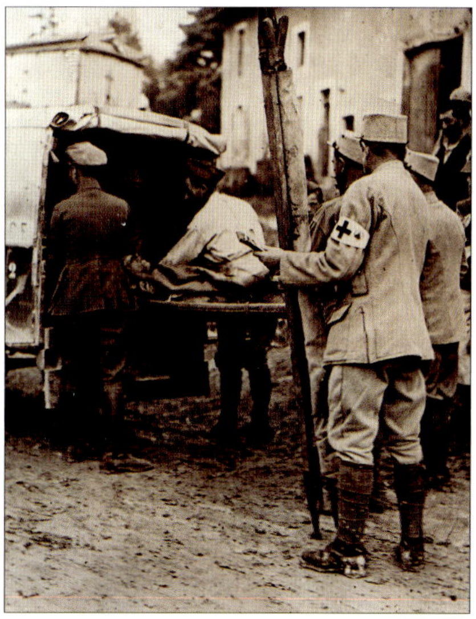

This is a special edition produced for
66 Books Ltd,
Unit 2, Eastman Way, Hemel Hempstead,
HP2 7DU, United Kingdom

A CIP catalogue record for this book is available from the British Library.

Publisher: Joanna Lorenz
Editorial Director: Helen Sudell
Packaged by Toucan Books
Managing Director: Ellen Dupont
Editor: Donald Sommerville
Project Manager: Hannah Bowen
Designer: Elizabeth Healey
Picture Researcher: Debra Weatherley
Maps: Julian Baker
Proofreader: Marion Dent
Indexer: Michael Dent
Production Controller: Ben Worley

PUBLISHER'S NOTE
Although the information in this book is believed to be accurate and true at the time of going to press, neither the authors nor the publisher can accept any legal responsibility or liability for any errors or omissions that may have been made.

akg-images spine, back cover t l to r:1 and 4, 2, 10l and m, 11l and r, 12t, 14b, 15b, 16b, 19t, 21m, 27r, 36, 37t, 38l, 39t, 46, 47b, 50b, 51t, 54b, 56, 57bl and br, 62b, 65tl, 65b, 67t, ml and br, 68tm, 72b, 78b, 80r, 81b, 86t, 90t, 91t, 92t, 103b, 107b, 112, 113bl, 115l, 120tr, 121tm, 124, 125b, 126l, 130b, 151b, 182, 185t, 187br, 188t, 189b, 217t, 241b, 242tr, 243m, 244b, 245t, 247b, 248b, 249tl, 249b, 251br, Bildarkiv Pisarek 243r, 251bl, Jean Pierre Verney 37b, 43t, ullstein bild 17t, 31b, 35b, 39b, 43b, 44t, 51b, 71m, 73t, 74b, 102t, 103t, 111t, 114t, 118bl, 120tm, 123b, 129l, 136, 137t, 168b, 173t, 183b, 203bl, 206bl, 211t and b, 219r, 225b, 231b, 233t, Erich Lessing 198b, RIA Novosti 101t, **Aviation Images** 207t, P. Jarret 215b, **Corbis** front cover t l to r: 2 and b, back cover t l to r:3 and b l to r:2, back flap, 14t, 27bm, 44b, 53t, 60t, 110b, 142, 148l, 171bl, 184l, 195t, 198t, 200t, 202tl, 203bm, 209b, 218r, 222, 223t, 225t, 226t and b, 227t, 233b, 242tl, 246t, Hulton-Deutsch Collection 3m and r, 20r, 21l, 26r, 29t, 33t, 45t and b, 47t, 58t and b, 69bl, 76, 78t, 80l, 86b, 91b, 92b, 109t, 110t, 113t, 120tl, 125t, 128t, 135b, 138t, 139t, 145t, 146b, 165bl and bm, 177t, 188b, 190, 191b, 204t, 223bl and br, 227b, 230b, 236t, 242tm, 248t, Bettmann 3l, 7b, 10r, 12b, 13t, 15t, 16t, 18t, 19b, 23t, 47mr, 49t, 55t, 60br, 69bm, 87b, 90b, 93t, 95b, 106b, 107t, 108t and b, 114b, 119t, 121tr, 123t, 128t, 129r, 135t, 164tm, 180t, 187bl, 194b, 202tm, 206t and br, 224r, 240b, 246b, 255 Museum of Flight 216b, Alinari Archives 232b, Scheufler Collection 24t, Underwood & Underwood 23b, National Aviation Museum 31tr, 98t and b, 99t, Sean Sexton Collection 55b, Richard Klune 250t, **Getty-Images** front flap, 4 l to r1, 5 t l to r:3 and b l to r:3, 146t, Roger Viollet 1l, 30r, 31l, 48b, 121bl, 160t, 161b, 239r, 250b, Hulton Archive 1m, 5l, 12b, 20l, 21r, 22, 23m, 35t, 48t, 49b, 50t, 52t, 54t, 59b, 62t, 63t, 68tl, 70, 81mr, 89r, 100b, 102b, 126r, 127, 128b, 130t, 131b, 134, 139b, 140b, 142b, 143t & b, 147b, 148r, 149b, 151t, 152b, 154, 155m and b, 158t, 159l and r, 160b, 162t and b, 163b, 164tr, 167b, 169t, 171t and br, 172b, 177b, 179t, 185b, 193t, 194t, 195b, 201t and b, 202tr, 203br, 204b, 207b, 208b, 209t, 210t and b, 214, 216t, 217b, 219l, 221b, 231t, 232t, 235t, 237b, 240t, 241t, 243l, 244t, 245b, 247t, 249tr, 251t, Time & Life Pictures 36ml, 64, 178, AFP 186, 187t, 189t, **Photographs reproduced by permission of the Trustees of The Imperial War Museum, London** front cover t l to r:1(Q 065882) 3(PD CRO 30) and 4(LC 32), back cover m and t l to r: 1(Q 65882) 3(PD CRO 30) and 4(LC 32), 3 COL 224, 11m Q 51128, 17b Q 51128, 26l Q 5004, 28t Q 53509, 30l Q 58653, 32b Q 60706, 33b Q 79792, 38r COL 224, 40bl Q 48445, 43mr Q 6157, 57t SP 438, 60bl Q 64301, 63b SP 1053, 65tr Q 18062, 66 SP 374, 71t Q 114867 and b E AVS 862, 72t PD CRO 30, 73tr Toucan Books, 73b Q 34105, 77b CO 3392, 79b Q 29001, 81t Q 65882, 84l Q 1375 and r Q 4092, 85l Q 23816 and r E(AUS) 2677, 88t Q 20640 and b SP 365, 89l Q 61156, 93b Q 13806, 95t Q 38891, 96 Q 13427, 99b SP 1141, 100t Q 23732, 104t Q 24781 and b Q 24440, 105t Q 107237, 106t Q 79823, 109b Q 13667, 111b Q 20220, 113m Q 56276, 115r Q 68200, 116 LC 32, 117t Q 58470, bl Q 110343 and br HO 122 A, 119b Q 12033, 131t Q 43463, 132t CO 991 and b CO 811, 133t Q1490 and b Q 4057, 137b Q 54534, 140t Q 9248, 141t E(AUS) 694 and b SP 1892, 144t Q 20627 and b SP 413, 145b SP 114, 147t Q 32159, 149t Q 15597, 150t Q 20794 and b Q 64302, 152b Q 38705 and b Q 13239, 155t Q 39007, 156 SP 748, 157t SP 1501 and b SP 2501, 158b SP 771, 161t Q 20636, 164tl Q 24739, 165br Q 24869, 166 CO 1178, 167t Q 5171 and m Q 6434, 168t Q 80861, 169b Q 67910, 176b Q 3999, 179b E(AUS) 939, 180b Q 1371, 181b Q 7134, 183t Q 6282, 184r CO 1751, 191t Q 86175, 192l Q 24891 and b Q 24926, 193b Q 24869, 196l Q 24191 and b Q 24739, 197t SP 560 and b Q 24294, 199t Q 18887 and b Q 19954, 200b SP 2270, 208t E(AUS) 757, 215t Q 67228, 220t Q 3245 and b Q 50845, 221t Q 5829, 224l Q 50649, 235b Q 31801, 236b Q 12971, 237t HU 75737, 238t Q 21940, 239l Q 38292, 241m SP 1635, 253 Q 24891, 254 Q 1375, 256 Q 11586, **Photo12.com** 75t and b, **Royal Armouries Museum, Leeds** 5r, 228l and r, 229t, bl and br, **Royal Navy Submarine Museum** 163, **Popperfoto.com** 6, 40br, **TopFoto** 7t, 27t, 32t, 52b, 53b, 61t, 68tr, 69br, 82br, 83t and b, 87t, 94b, 101b, 105b, 118r, 153b, 174 t and b, 175b, 176t, 181t, Roger-Viollet 20m, 24b, 25t and b, 34, 172t, 173b, Heritage-Images 29b, 74t, 79t, 175t, 230t, Ullstein Bild 238b, Alinari 40t.